Alaskan Travels

BOOKS BY EDWARD HOAGLAND

—Essays—
The Courage of Turtles
Walking the Dead Diamond River
Red Wolves and Black Bears
The Edward Hoagland Reader
The Tugman's Passage
Heart's Desire
Balancing Acts
Tigers and Ice
Hoagland on Nature
Sex and the River Styx

—Travel—
Notes from the Century Before
African Calliope
Early in the Season
Alaskan Travels: Far-Flung Tales of Love and Adventure

—Fiction—
Cat Man
The Circle Home
The Peacock's Tail
Seven Rivers West
The Final Fate of the Alligators

—Memoir—
Compass Points

Alaskan Travels

Far-Flung Tales of Love and Adventure

EDWARD HOAGLAND

Foreword by Howard Frank Mosher

Arcade Publishing • New York

For the wild places I have loved,
from Alaska to Mount Kinyeti in Equatoria,
to Arunachal Pradesh in the Himalayan foothills,
and all the rest.

• • •

Copyright © 2012 by Edward Hoagland

All Rights Reserved. No part of this book may be reproduced in any manner without the express written consent of the publisher, except in the case of brief excerpts in critical reviews or articles. All inquiries should be addressed to Arcade Publishing, 307 West 36th Street, 11th Floor, New York, NY 10018.

Arcade Publishing books may be purchased in bulk at special discounts for sales promotion, corporate gifts, fund-raising, or educational purposes. Special editions can also be created to specifications. For details, contact the Special Sales Department, Arcade Publishing, 307 West 36th Street, 11th Floor, New York, NY 10018 or info@skyhorsepublishing.com.

Arcade Publishing® is a registered trademark of Skyhorse Publishing, Inc.®, a Delaware corporation.

Visit our website at www.arcadepub.com.

10 9 8 7 6 5 4 3 2 1

Library of Congress Cataloging-in-Publication Data is available on file.
ISBN: 978-1-61145-503-8

Printed in the United States of America

Contents

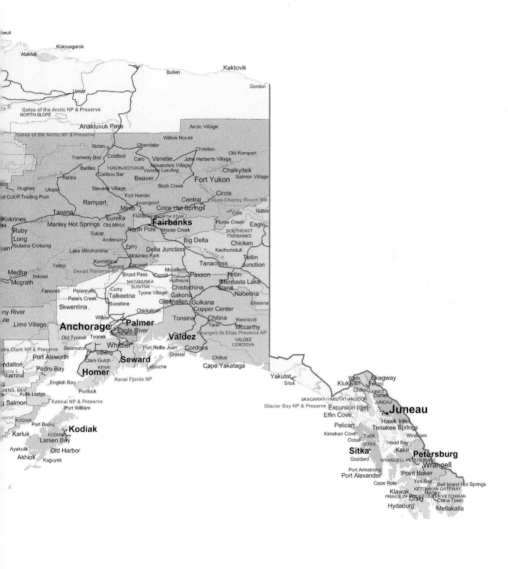

Foreword

A few millennia have slipped by since the first Alaskans speared great woolly mammoths on the banks of the Yukon River. The Indian and Eskimo subsistence hunters are mostly gone now, as well. Likewise the Russian sealers and missionaries, though you'll still find their Orthodox churches scattered here and there in Alaska's "ragamuffin hamlets." No more steamboats loaded with bearded gold miners chugging up the brawling coastal rivers, and most of the dog team drivers are "white hobbyists." High on a tributary of the Yukon, the "roadhouse" where trappers and rivermen once stopped for "caribou and homebrew" has long since collapsed into an overgrown clearing.

In 1983 Edward Hoagland, at fifty and already the author of a dozen acclaimed novels and non-fiction books, struck out from New York City for Alaska, to explore and write about what remained of America's "last best place." Over the next several months, pencil and notebook at the ready, he traveled from the Arctic Ocean to the Kenai Peninsula and from the backstreet bars of Anchorage to the Yukon River. The book that emerged from his journey, *Alaskan Travels*, is an American masterwork in the tradition of Twain's *Life on the Mississippi*.

Hoagland plunges right into his story with a walk through the wild side of Anchorage. Then he's off to the bush in a four-seat Cessna ski plane, with a remarkably kind and capable young traveling nurse named Linda. What wondrous sights they see: leviathan jawbones marking the graves of whaling captains; the "Ferris–wheel–like" salmon-catchers, known as fish wheels, studding Alaska's rivers;

bowhead whales with their "handsomely white-napkined chins," and "gleaming carmine" stacks of salmon fillets drying along the riverbanks. Not to mention the "veritable piñata" of Alaskan wildlife—beavers, ducks, walruses, eagles, seals, salmon, trout, pike, sandhill cranes, and "beachcombing" bears.

At the same time, Edward Hoagland never lets us forget that "Alaska plays for keeps." It's not just the primeval wilderness that can swallow you up without a trace, and the killing cold that we know about from Jack London. Sure, early on in *Alaskan Travels,* Hoagland evokes the boreal climate with such sentences as "My breath coated my glasses with ice if I covered my face with my parka hood, even briefly, and the very snow emitted strange, pained, squeaky sounds underfoot, as if suffering too." But the darker horrors of Alaska have to do with "the collateral damage of a culture's collapse." Don't look for Sarah Palin, or even for world-class journalists like John McPhee, to tell us much about our forty-ninth state's astronomical divorce rate, alcohol- and drug-driven suicides—four times the national average in native villages—or routine child abuse. Much less the woman Hoagland heard about who "shot herself in the foot to get shipped out of town by the authorities, away from her husband who had beaten her so bad she hid all night in a sweathouse to save her life."

Like his great literary forbear, Thoreau, however, Hoagland (who's been called "the last American transcendentalist") is a born celebrator. He's especially fascinated by the stories of Alaska's last frontiersmen and frontierswomen and will trek absolutely anywhere to meet them. My favorites? The Eskimo whale-hunter, Joe Towksjhea, "an older, worldly guy who late last April, in a skin boat manned by seven paddlers and a rudderman, had harpooned a twenty-seven-foot bowhead." And, of course, Hubert Koonuk, "born in 1911 but still an ace polar bear hunter" who had "totted up a reported thirty-six in his life, including the fresh one draped dripping underneath his skin boat on its rack at the side of the house."

Hoagland's equally good on the parade of "back-to-the-landers, self-dramatists, and counter-culturists" drawn to this "ultimate place." Yet, if you have the requisite "robust energy," if you're ruthless and hard-driving enough, Alaska's still a place where self-made realtors and TV moguls, "emirs of the north," can amass fortunes. We meet them in *Alaskan Travels* as well.

What makes *Alaskan Travels* the most personal and powerful of Edward Hoagland's more than twenty books is the beautiful and stately love story at its heart. His new book, with the courageous frontier nurse, Linda, as its most memorable character, has both a strong narrative arc and a deeply personal theme. As she and the author travel together to isolated communities like Red Devil and Hoonah, where she tests residents for TB and, on an impromptu basis, treats them for everything from gunshot wounds to depression, their affection for one another deepens into that best of all amalgams of passion and genuine companionship. Their gentle love story makes me proud, in this frighteningly dehumanizing era, to be human.

For the frontier novel he was working on at the time, Ted Hoagland "needed to see a string of rivers." Not surprisingly, he chose the "wide, deep, potent, silty-yellow multiplicity of the Yukon," and one of its major tributaries, the Tanana. "Tanana" also happens to be the name of the big "pushboat," designed for shoving heavily-loaded barges, which carried Hoagland and Linda five hundred miles downriver.

Off they go on an unforgettable expedition. I've never set foot in Alaska, but I was with them for every mile as the "Tanana," with its "gold-painted moose horns affixed to the pilothouse," zigs and zags across the river, seeking the deep-water channels, from Twenty-mile Slough to Swede Boys Camp to Johnny Frog's Cabin to Purgatory.

Then, right in a bend where it could, and did, cause the most possible havoc, the unluckily named *Bingo* sank from an encounter with a sandbar. The wrecked *Bingo* was the handiwork of two more amateur "hobbyists" from the Lower 48, who "must have supposed the wild, lock-less Yukon was like the harnessed and leveed Mississippi." Hoagland's account of its salvaging is hilarious and sobering in equal portions—a splendid wind-down to the best book to date by a writer I regard as one of America's very best, and quite possibly its most original, since Thoreau himself.

Howard Frank Mosher is the author of ten novels and two travel memoirs.

CHAPTER 1

• • •

Arrivals: In Anchorage

A S A NATIVE NEW YORKER, thirty years ago, it was my pleasure and my passion to embark for Alaska periodically—that top hat of the continent—on magazine assignments but really because I had fallen in love with a nurse whom I had met in Fairbanks, though she was based first in Juneau and then in Anchorage. I was early fiftyish, mired in a deteriorating marriage; she seventeen years younger and divorced from a psychiatrist in her home state of Massachusetts— her father an alcoholic ex-CIA operative, her brother a golf pro. She herself was superb at what she did, however, and perhaps the kindest person I've ever known. She was in charge of the nursing care of all the tuberculosis patients in the state.

At Minneapolis I'd switch from my New York flight to North-west Orient's Anchorage-bound airplane, which landed briefly in Se-attle on the way so that the bourgeoisie in suits could scoot up the ramp fastidiously, to be replaced by checked-shirt construction guys headed for Prudhoe Bay, or salmon-boatmen, or middle-aged riff-raff who had fouled their nests in the Lower 48 and hoped that high wages plus desperate circumstances could swallow their bile and pull them out of bankruptcy once again. Furious-looking young oil-rig employees with lopsided hands, pugnacious moustaches, and misfit beards jostled brush-cut military noncoms dragging duffel bags, and the occasional sidelong glare indicated that certain passengers weren't used to being stuffed next to other people like this at all and were go-ing to Alaska precisely to prevent it. Several miles of leeway between cabins suited them. The bristle of mistrust, or suspicion of outrageous behavior from others, telegraphed that they expected it of themselves, at least if they didn't swig a couple of soporific drinks quickly enough. The stewardesses, appearing to understand this, helped. Alaska flights gather a provisional cast anyway. Will the weather even permit you to land? Will somebody be there to meet you, as promised, or the commercial opportunities still be extant? On one return trip, a young lady seated next to me sobbed uncontrollably the whole four hours back to Seattle.

On my first visit to Linda's, when she lived in Juneau and following our meeting in Fairbanks—after the plane had dived between the famously hairy mountains fronting Juneau's airstrip—she hid from me in the arrivals lounge in order to get another gander before revealing her presence. So I had to wander like a homeless bunny rabbit through the terminal, until her pity was aroused and she came forward to hug and lead me to sleep on the floor of her sublet, up a steep boardwalked hillside. It was a splendid means for a feminist seventeen years younger to cut a lover down a size before permitting him to take her clothing off. Juneau is in Alaska's banana belt, but at colder climes, if your girlfriend kicks you out in the middle of the night, the air might be thirty below outside and any "male chauvinist pig" (to use the argot of the era) would soon be oinking for mercy at her door. Though I wasn't that, at forty below at Point Hope on the Chukchi Sea my eyelids froze together when we stepped off the ski plane, and she needed to lead me about for a while, besides protecting me from a few Eskimo toughs who liked to beat white men in retaliation for a century of exploitation (since the one white tourist you don't beat the shit out of would be the nurse's boyfriend). But Alaska is a rough spot to be out of your element. The hobo jungle along the railroad tracks in Anchorage is hair-raisingly cold in the winter, and the court system for indigents, when I sat in on a few sessions, harshly brusque. Since the gold rush, or whaling days, it's been a gambler's destination, and they don't coddle losers. *Don't get stranded here* is an important message that must be conveyed. It's a long trek home, and the Canadians don't want you broke on their territory either, begging your way two thousand miles down the Alcan Highway to the safety net of relatives or whatever. Besides identification, they demanded evidence of cash from down-at-heels travelers at the border.

In Anchorage, "the closest city to Alaska," as locals like to put it, once we passengers had debarked past the polar bear, Dall sheep, and caribou situated in glass cases to welcome us to the 49th State, the baggage carousel presented a headlong tumult of wooden crates, steamer trunks, huge taped cardboard boxes, tarpaulin sacks, and backpacks, snow gear, tents, stoves, and climbing equipment for "assaults" on Mount McKinley or the like that some had flown in for, as if life were not adventure enough already. The military contingent retrieved their troop-ship stuff, and civilian berserkers or trophy hunters and gun nuts had rifles in canvas cases to collect, and air mattresses, sleeping bags, helicopter parts in cartons. Some of us were here to try solving our problems, others probably to complicate them.

My Linda, sweet-smiled, creamy-skinned, sable-haired, and solidly light on her feet, had been waiting at the entry with a coyote-ruffed, state-supplied Eddie Bauer winter coat, so I could accompany her to far-flung Indian and Eskimo villages on her monitoring rounds. Her two basement rooms on "L" Street were within walking distance of her office and the oil company skyscrapers and high-rise hotels, yet cozy for our menagerie of love games, like "Buzzing Bee," "Bitey Fox," "Tommy Turtle," "Snoring Leopard," and a block or so from a splendid crenellated view of the Chugach Range, mountains wilder than any others neighboring a significant American city, or across Cook Inlet, off the Pacific Ocean—Anchorage is a seaport—others appeared as miniature volcanic peaks. Alaska, twice as big as Texas, had only 420,000 people living in it in 1983, half of them around Anchorage, which the rest of the state considered "Los Anchorage," with its wide streets, shopping malls, and negotiable climate—drier than Juneau's, warmer than Fairbanks. Even so, nineteen hours of summer sunlight becomes only six hours at the December solstice—when the arctic villages Linda visited just offered sunrise colorations on the horizon at high noon. I loved the midnight sun in June in those same places, when the sun instead simply flirts with setting, and chained teams of sled dogs may holler at each other in nonstop elation; but was plenty content with starlight round-the-clock for our winter interludes, sleeping catch-as-catch-can on a clinic or schoolroom floor with my friend, while she tested the populace of the hamlet for tuberculosis. Oddly enough, during a stint in the army a quarter-century before, I'd worked in a TB hospital myself, and so was comfortable in the vicinity of sputum collection cups. Her own nursing career stretched back to catheterizing old men's penises in a New York City hospital (and once saving the life of a stranger in a restaurant in Greenwich Village by the Heimlich maneuver). Out of rainy Juneau, she had been responsible for the itinerant care of five Tlingit island villages, visiting each by boat or plane in rotation: front-line medicine, indeed. These frontier nurses, apart from pre-natal exams and well-baby immunizations, sometimes possessed im-mense powers of advocacy in determining who got flown out to see a doctor after the onset of heart murmurs or was recommended for reconstructive surgery after falling drunk into a campfire. A hernia's bulge, a cleft palate, were easy; but not the knife fight after dark that led to pounding on the clinic door when the nurse had gone to bed. Was it only a Romeo, or a man mortally bleeding? There was no state trooper within a hundred miles—and fog might negate flying. Next day, in a torso on the table, what *was* a tumor? You certainly couldn't cry wolf a lot, bringing in a plane.

So Linda had spent part of her weekends in a neighborhood sauna in Juneau with a can of beer, fitfully weeping. In the beginning, my helpfulness may have been to bolster her confidence to accept a pro-motion from the field to this supervisory job in Anchorage; and we had driven the seven hundred miles there together from a ferry dock in Haines, sleeping in the bush beside the road until her rattly heap gave up the ghost when we finally reached pavement. We'd then hitchhiked from about Glennallen, giggling at the adventure—the boulevards of the new city, with a live caribou penned into one front yard, facing the British Petroleum office tower. The Captain Cook Hotel was finest, but wages were good and there were other hostelries and restaurants about with seafood chefs. At The Monkey Wharf, capuchins cow-ered inside a glass case behind the bar, while a band played rock. The Great Alaskan Bush Company featured bottomless-topless stuff, and Chilkoot Charlie's was the toughest of several bars where people went to get into fights and pass out afterward in the parking lot. At the Pines you could leave your table, handing your glasses to your girlfriend, strip to borrowed trunks, and box another tyro in a regulation ring for a purse of fifty bucks. The immense, extravagant skies seemed to promise melodrama, with two million sockeye salmon being harvested every day from Bristol Bay during their spawning season.

Linda had taken me by ferryboat from Juneau to her former postings at Hoonah, Angoon, and Tenakee Springs on Chichagof and Admiralty Islands, where eagles abounded and ravens posted themselves on every rooftop, both embodying a creation myth and as though enjoying a sort of natural adjunct citizenship. Besides giving hefty sums of money to fund collective native corporations, the Alaska Native Claims Act of 1971 had turned over forty-four million acres to the state's seventy thousand Indians, Aleuts, and Eskimos to manage, making the local Tlingits' sense of self-governance muscular. But as we walked Hoonah's paths, I'd seen how fond the women and the elders were of Linda. The tides, fog, sea mammals, and sea wrack were exhilarating to us, and fresh netted fish delicious, but her responsibilities had been heavy. Without colleagues or equipment, when was a pregnancy problematic, or a stomachache a stomachache and not appendicitis? Later, on tours north by chartered ski plane, landing on a frozen river to check that an Athabascan child with TB, wintering with her parents at a trapping camp, was receiving her daily medication and not feverish or coughing (separately, a teacher flew in, too), we'd stop at downstream villages to look at other patients, as well as perhaps help the district nurse keep track of an individual injured in a snow machine flip-over, and monitor an epidemic of hepatitis B that was germinating in native communities. The most poignant interviews I witnessed were with older people whose hepatitis had transmogrified into liver cancer and who, dying in a cabin with a view of sunlight glistening on the tundra out the window, might never see another medical professional after Linda left. Her brief job was to delicately ascertain that they were where they ought to be: that a son would keep the stove going, that there were no alcohol problems in the home, and that the hamlet's health aid, sketchily trained in morphine administration, could be counted on to mitigate the pain. But most important was what the person wanted, because Linda could fly them out to a hospital for terminal care where their comfort would be assured. Yet a hospital offered no grandchildren traipsing in and out, no arctic shimmer in the sky or Brooks Range through the windowpane, or bowhead whale skin cut morsel-sized and berries-in-blubber to suck on. It was discussed sidewise, softly. Did they want clean sheets every day, an R.N. to manage the morphine drip, and tomato soup on a tray, but never to see the northern lights? Usually, with ten thousand years on a rim of the world, they shook their heads, no.

On an Anchorage barstool you'll meet a thirty-something fellow who has flown in from Bangkok with a money belt full of gemstones—"much safer than drugs"—to sell in the gold, gun, fur, ivory, or *oosik* stores (an *oosik* is the long bone in a walrus's penis) on Fourth Avenue. Another guy has burned out as a social worker in Fort Yukon, he tells us, because he was in charge of child welfare and family relations and when children were beaten up by drunken parents he got accused of racism if he tried to intercede. Proposing to remove an abused child to foster care brought the old charge of deracination—cultural imperialism, when kids were shipped to distant boarding schools to remove "the Indian" from them—and threats by the father to shoot him in the middle of the night. Although the rest of the town was stumped as to how to protect the child, protecting *him* seemed not so high on the agenda

Thirtyish souls are typical, because they've had a decade to knock around in the Lower 48, butting their heads against limitations, mostly their own, that they hope won't operate here. On the other hand, a gas station owner from Arizona, decked out in a Confederate general's campaign jacket and cap, told us he'd bought a garage on the Denali Highway, where he could let his hair down, wear verboten costumes with a bear-claw necklace, get as drunk as a skunk, joke about "necktie parties," enjoy some red-skinned poontang, and fire off his Kalashnikovs behind the station whenever he wanted. "What you do stays in the permafrost."

In Anchorage, Linda and I re-explored our bodily rituals (which were such that I was impotent with anybody else for a year after we broke up), and drove into the rugged Chugach Mountains, set so closely above the breezy city, to scramble to the tree line and gaze down. "Our least educated marry their most educated," another social worker had explained about the dynamics of white-native matrimony. And you could see it as you rambled, or on planes, where a seatmate said the escape provided by marrying a motor pool corporal had proven a disappointment when he took her home to the Bronx or the Ozarks. "I like Alaska better. I don't ever want to go back there again," she said, her face going bleak and gelid with the loner's stare of somebody soon to shed the Motor Pool boy.

CHAPTER 2

• • •

To Red Devil

A T THE AIRPORT AGAIN, WAITING for a Wien Air Lines 737 converted mostly for freight to fly us to the Kuskokwim, we watched
an L.A. flight come in—the men starting beards already and, boots on
the ground, acting a trifle rude and proprietary because they wouldn't
be penned in by their neighbors any more. Over the shining sea ice of
Cook Inlet at noon, and Chakachamna Lake alongside Mount Spur
and a jumble of other Alaska Range ridges and peaks, the webwork of
quirky-looking creeks and lakes of the Stony, the Stink, the Holitna,
and the Hoholitna rivers, the Lime Hills, and Hungry Village, Cotton
Village, Itulilik, and Chuathbaluk, for an hour or so, with the lower-
ing sun brightening the snow surplice-white, to the Yupik Eskimo
district town of Aniak, on the big Kuskokwim River. In Anchorage,
we'd been eating at Our Guy From Italy Pizzeria and Simon and Sea-
fort's fine seafood restaurant, but now in our abbreviated passenger
compartment, we saw people's faces settling closer to survival mode
from the city's sociability—the immediacies of obtaining warmth,
meals, comfort for one's children in the exertion of hip-high snow-
drifts, piss or spit that froze before it hit the ground, sparse wildlife,
unwieldy clothes. It was after Christmas but midwinter, and without
trundling into the little town, we geared down, loading our duffels,
straight into a single-engine, four-seat, Harold's Air Service Cessna
207 for an hour's chartered flight up the Kuskokwim. This meant
past the Holokuk River, and Horn Mountain, old settlements called
Napaimiut and Oskawalik, the loaf-shaped or moundy Chvilnuk

Hills, and severe cut banks at the bends of the main river itself—all glimpsed below the incongruously small, still ski of the plane below my window—to the ghostly village of Red Devil, which was named for the vermilion cinnabar ore that miners formerly had a helluva time extracting for mercury.

The Kuskokwim, eight hundred-fifty miles long, heads on the northern slopes of the Mount McKinley massif in Denali National Park and flows into Kuskokwim Bay on the Bering Sea, but during that shorter span than the Yukon's eighteen-hundred-mile-plus course, roughly parallels a good deal of the Yukon. And both rivers had friction points where the coastal Eskimos were prevented by the interior Indians from penetrating further inland. The salmon runs were glorious most of the way up and elders could negotiate a balance of interests, but hothead battles did occur. Red Devil—although a white town with a youngish population of gold prospectors and the like—lay across the river from Crooked Creek and Sleetmute, two native settlements where historically the two cultures, upriver Athabascan and downriver Yupik, had rubbed shoulders and either traded or clashed. The Yupik, a separate linguistic group of Eskimos from the Inupiat or Inuit of arctic Alaska and Canada, were sometimes called "Asiatic Eskimos" by early anthropologists because their real stronghold was over across the Bering Sea in Siberia; but the Yukon Indians on occasion battled with the Inupiat, too, north, across the Brooks Range, about salmon streams or caribou plateaus, as well. The sun was going to set at three fifteen, so our pilot, a youngster like so many in the bush, took off again for Aniak matter-of-factly as soon as we stepped off his skis. It was thirty-three below. Frost tweaked our nostrils instantly and the footing on the plowed airstrip was slippery but soon laboriously knee-deep. Parched small spruce trees had been seared black, and Linda's hair began to frost at the ends, turning as gray as mine. Her assignment was to skin test the populace of all three road-less hamlets after a rash of positive diagnoses from the river's communities down at the regional hospital in Bethel, a bigger town, pop. thirty six hundred, but almost as isolated, near the Kuskokwim's mouth.

We were met and whisked to the Red Devil school building, where she set up her testing station at a table in the front hallway since the town had no health clinic or other public building. A short, nervously chatty line formed, with snowmobile headlights roaring up outside when the sun went down. Though only thirteen kids were enrolled in this two-million-dollar, two-classroom school, more were hopping around because this was the special "Slavic" Christmas and New Year's holiday, proudly celebrated instead of the Western calendar on the Kuskokwim, since Russian Orthodox missionaries had reached the river's peoples first. So we had home-schoolers in from cabins in the bush getting their forearms scratched. Homesteaders, gold miners, old folk—it was a white town, where European spouses of adventurers sometimes found themselves biting off more than they had expected to chew, such as this TB scare, or the gunfire heard lately across the river in Sleetmute. Sleetmute's schoolteachers and social worker had decided to commute from here. Prospectors secretively working on placer claims along the George River, nearby, and its tributaries, when the ice broke up, were relaxing in the sociability provided by the school's electric generator, washing machine and lights, the oil furnace, and the gym to shoot baskets in where Linda and I had unrolled our sleeping bags on the wrestling mats.

"The willows, the river, and the spruce. That's about it," a woman explained, when I asked her what she had. The sputum jars to hawk into unnerved her a bit, and they hadn't cleared enough gold dust to winter in Hawaii or in Cancun. Her family "Outside" had mailed her a mouton overcoat, but instead of wearing it she'd scissored it up to sew elbow-length mitts for her husband and kids. She was also disassembling a mink hat they had sent, to fashion cap bills for the marten hats people preferred here for warmth, although . they caught some mink as well as marten on their traplines. Marten fur was the breadwinner in these forests during the winter. George Willis, born in 1904 and in Alaska since the Second World War, had taught her husband everything. When I asked if she and her husband cleared a profit sluicing the gravel on their creek, she laughed cautiously, sizing me up to be sure the gossip was correct: that I was "only the nurse's boyfriend," not a mining inspector who happened to arrive on the same airplane.

"Have you ever met a miner who made a profit?" her husband said—his beard as bushy as a muffler around his throat and graying at the ends and roots. Like her, he'd aged quite fast around the eyes, but their skin looked young, as if preserved by the cold. Addressing my innocence, he added that certainly prospectors sold their dust to a bank, to be reported as income and set against deductible expenses, but any pretty nuggets they found by energetically exhuming a side hill streambed, they peddled privately to a savvy jeweler. "And then you sell out and move to New Zealand!"

Linda, after an informal presentation to assure everybody, including absentees, that the bad old days of quarantine were over (I'd met Indians who'd been shipped to Arizona in their youth), set up further appointments, told the laggards not to procrastinate because after tomorrow she'd be moving to Sleetmute and Crooked Creek, and explained that although the spike in hospitalizations had raised concern in Anchorage, probably the disruption to your life if you turned up positive would be limited to a course of pills. Her mini-audience, jittery about this first field test in a decade, joshed one another and practiced looking askance, then shunning each other. With no store or active church, the school, equipped with showers, fluorescent lighting, washer-dryers, a kitchen, a basketball court, and a movie screen, was everybody's hangout in Red Devil; and in their high-top, insulated boots, wolf-ruffed, down-fluffed parkas, strapping on headlamps for the dark, and kicking their snowmobiles to life, they left reluctantly for kerosene-lit log cabins all over.

When alone at last, we examined the schoolroom charts of presidents past and dinosaurs and ferns, the crayonings of faces, continents, and stars. The gym was multi-purpose, featuring fold-out luncheon tables converted from bleachers that faced the basketball court and scoreboard, a stage for assemblies and play-acting, and the film screen. I swished a hoop while Linda caught up with her paperwork. Supper was boiled freeze-dried stuff we'd brought, garnished with condiments we found by raiding the industrial fridge, plus a brick of government-issue jack cheese. The pantry shelves were stacked with bins of dried pudding, instant potatoes, powdered eggs, spaghetti, macaroni, and jumbo cans of USDA clingstone peaches or Bartlett pears. All of these staples, along with larger freight and drums of furnace oil, were barged upriver from Bethel every summer.

Linda often slept in schools when surveying the health of villages that had no clinic, and we'd choose the kiddie classroom for its prismatic posters, zany artwork, flags-of-the-world wall displays, and Dr. Seuss or Walt Disney characters gazing down at us as we lay on the floor. The little desks didn't block our view of the shimmering starscape or white moon, or even aurora borealis, tremulous out the window, like sleeping in a planetarium. Zipping our sleeping bags together, we were decorous in deference to our surroundings. Tonight, though, the wrestling mats in the gym offered food for thought or athleticism—Hippetty Frog, Tony Tiger, Squiggly Spider—and by three a.m. I was so relaxed I felt like a deadeye at shooting baskets.

Cross-country skis were stacked in the vestibule—each child was provided with a free pair—and in the upper-school classroom a plastic human skeleton kept a pair of gerbils company. These surveys were much less stressful for Linda than some of her former front-line nursing days, when she grew to be a familiar figure in her regular round of villages and a drunk might wait for her to visit to claim he had testicular cancer and demand a crotch exam. The woman who knocked timidly on the door after-hours, hemorrhaging from her fourth miscarriage, might also be lugging a child who was crying with an unbearable earache. The middle-aged man with chest pains wanted a lengthy talk as well, and another with a bleeding ulcer—*was* it an ulcer or an incipient tumor in the colon? No roads, no doctor, no hospital. No policeman, either, when the woman with the miscarriage looked battered but wouldn't admit it. Could she stay safe until the social worker's next fly-in in a month or two? Even the husband, who was avowedly suicidal? The suicide rate among Alaska's natives was four times the national average, and Linda knew him because he came to office hours to discuss his hemorrhoids and constipation or contusions from falls. Another man who had circled the clinic the night before, trying windows, might apologize in the morning. But was his solemnity a sham while he stared at her to fuel his fantasies or plans for her next scheduled cycle through?

The so-called Molly Hooch Act, as it was informally known, from the original plaintiff's name, mandated that the State provide far-flung high-schooling so that native children could receive it close to home: not be split off from their culture, as the promising ones had been under the old system of boarding them in academies in places such as Sitka, a Tlingit island near Juneau but far away from here. Oil riches had enabled a statewide follow-through, even chartering planes for basketball games between schools a mountain range apart. Our arrival was less cheery, however, foretelling fewer spontaneous sleepovers this winter and more quarrels between couples, only one of whom had actually wanted a year of bush adventure in mid-Alaska. Yet the classroom decorations seemed so lively at breakfast time, as to prove that temporary teachers shuttling in for yearlong contracts, perhaps to pay a mortgage off down south in Oklahoma, didn't burn out like the lifers did. The crayonings thumb-tacked to the wallboard were so endearing, I wondered whether Linda mightn't regret her feminist decision not to have children. Not that feminist ideology had to involve that, but at the time hers, later reversed, did. Since I was already blessed with a teenage daughter, it caused us no arguments. Abused, she believed, by her father, she had experienced a difficult adolescence, then married and divorced, with no close male friends except for baffling topsy-turvy boyfriends. The bad stutter I was afflicted with appealed to her extraordinary well of kindness, but also possibly because my handicap prevented me from behaving as bewilderingly fickle and macho as other men. What I was good at didn't involve shooting things or flashing money, and with her taste for underdogs, she wound up marrying a Guatemalan revolutionary. Our problems related to our differing stages of life. I had published nine or ten books, was in the midst of my career, and while I could have married a nurse and stayed in Alaska for a period of years, I needed stability, whereas she was headed for a dozen years of graduate school, first in public health, then in anthropology, at Johns Hopkins and Berkeley, out of sync with the steady focus of place and purpose I needed. I did eventually leave my quarter-century marriage, but for a couple of quiet decades in a college town in Vermont, while Linda successfully pursued her further dreams elsewhere.

She'd booted me back to New York, in a brittle mood, once before. But now we weren't shaky at all, just bulking up on calories from that industrial refrigerator and running the oil furnace to keep warm, while the remainder of Red Devil's motley citizenry showed up to have their status checked and hear the good or bad news.

CHAPTER 3

Crooked Creek

WHITE TOWNS ON THESE CROSSWISE rivers in Alaska, like the Yukon and Kuskokwim, tend to be on the south bank with a northern exposure, like Red Devil was, whereas the ancient Indian settlements like Crooked Creek—where Harold's Air Service's Cessna lifted us on a following day—were located facing south for maximum winter sunshine, as well as on a bend where the king and chum salmon runs could be netted more efficiently. Crooked Creek's hundred-and-ten reserved and tetchy Yupik citizenry lived in chinked log cabins (not barged-in, white man's prefabs and trailers) in spread-out fashion on a bench at the Great Bend of the Kuskokwim where its namesake tributary flowed in, with gold-bearing mountains in relief on the northern skyline. Fish traps at the river's elbow had fed innumerable dog teams during the successive minor rushes auxiliary to those occurring more famously on the Yukon around the same period.

This school had a bigger basketball court and four imported teachers dressed in ripstop, windowpane-weave nylon wind pants, with Saskatchewan coyote ruffs on their parka collars drawn tightly around their faces, and Gore-Tex breathable over mitts with pile on the back to wipe your runny nose on, plus Quebec Sorel boots and Norwegian polypropylene long johns on underneath, they said, at thirty-five below in the noon sunshine. The locals wore the sort of nondescript windbreakers you might see on somebody in interior Maine and were complaining about broken Ski-Doos or a chainsaw chain. But "any house that's throwin' smoke, there's sure to be kids in there," the health aid said. Otherwise, why would people bother? Her own warm cabin had a cradle strung from the ceiling, and a loche (burbot) fish weighing ten or a dozen pounds that her husband had caught from under the river ice lay in a basin on the floor for supper. Health aids were usually pillars of the community and their husbands good providers.

The tiny Russian church was chair-less and painted green inside, but hung with tinsel and religious pictures. No priest officiated any more, but a choir had mustered to sing Yupik and English carols, the church also functioning as an anti-"Gussuck" (or Caucasian, originally from "Cossack") bastion. Alexei, Mishka, Wassily, Olga, Natasha, and Stasha were some of the names I heard, though half the population was still Indian, not Yupik Eskimo, as much of the Kuskokwim's humanity had been. Stony River, a settlement at a tributary we wouldn't get to, a bit upstream, was the first all-Athabascan village. Generally, Anglicans or other Protestants from Canada or the south had reached the interior Indians before Orthodox missionaries paddling east from the coast, so nowadays if they wanted to thumb a nose at the conquering Americans, Indians needed subtler means than celebrating Russian calendar holidays instead of American ones as the Eskimos did.

This in fact was the fourth day of "Slavic Christmas," so although Linda had set up shop in the tiny clinic, she had to make several house calls to test men lying passed out on their couches or unconscious in bed. The Swiss wife of the hardware store clerk and the Danish wife of the special ed teacher were dismayed to discover they had become "converters," positive for TB on their skin scratches now—and doubly sorry their husbands hadn't taken them to Hawaii with the other teachers. Three white gold hunters working twenty miles up Crooked Creek and twenty-five trappers, mostly native families situated fifty to a hundred miles up the Holitna River, were also unavailable. The plane hassles, a painful head cold, the catch-as-catch-can appointments, and living arrangements were taking a toll on Linda, and bunking on more gym mats in a classroom with anatomy charts, lab-type sinks, and rows of lockers held less allure than in Red Devil. But our Swiss (petite and brunette) and Danish (rangy and blonde) new friends took us under their wings to drop in on a marathon beer party that was winding down. It seemed to be a fidgety affair, where tension by ten o'clock was flaring inscrutably, yet not directed at us, the handful of whites. An old Eskimo fellow holding court in one corner of the log room shouted boastfully, "I am an Eskimo!"—only to be answered in seesaw rhythm by another old guy, surrounded by young men in the opposite corner, yelling, "I am an Indian!"

Hoping there would be no sewing-up for Linda to help the health aid do that night—she'd seen broken-bottle havoc before, and then the wounded guy asking for plastic surgery—we returned to our schoolroom library of *National Geographics* and diagrams of the human digestive system, the sacks of kidney beans in the kitchen, boxed Kool-Aid, bins of powdered sugar, gallon cans of label-less (we opened one) peas, and ate. I woke before Linda as dawn lit the tall windows. Then, in order not to wake her, I went out to walk, uphill, toward the wee church and old cemetery, gripped by the temperature like an adversary you lean hard into. Improved hydraulic technology and the free-floating price of gold had whetted white prospectors' interest in combing through the ass-ends of supposedly played-out goldfields in the immensity of this Yukon-Kuskokwim terrain, but for the Eskimos and Indians it was still a basket of fish and fur cycled through the year, with moose meat and salmon the staples of life.

You couldn't stroll, even in long johns, the cold was so bitter. Scattered, one-story log huts sat silent on the steep icy slope, with cordwood and a snow machine parked in front of each, so there weren't the chorusing dog teams staked at individual hovels in the snow. Running dogsleds had become primarily a sport for white hobbyists now, but caribou and moose haunches were laid for storage on many of the roofs, as in the old days, along with a beaver that hadn't been skinned. Nobody was awake, no battery radios, no barking from inside. Yet I noticed a yellow, rag-sized, rag-shaped scrap of something lying on the white crust of yard-deep snow in front of one particular, substantial cabin. Expecting a scrap of cloth, I found instead a dappled white and yellow mutt-sized, pet-sized dog with its front legs chopped off—no doubt frozen dead after having been tossed out the door in the midst of last night's holiday festivities. Staring flabbergasted at the wretched pathos, I could imagine how the children inside must have wailed and shrieked as their father grabbed and swung the kindling axe, holding the puppy by its hind legs, and their mother, primarily thankful that it wasn't one of *them*, hustled them to bed. The frigid cold had been a blessing—stifling the whimpers soon. The legs awaited the morning's recriminations, too.

Linda, after coffee, zipped on her snow pants for the day of explaining to a patient with emphysema that TB was different, and not to worry because she would radio Bethel to send more oxygen canisters when the pulmonary technician made his semi-annual rounds. She dandled any edgy child while chatting up the mum. Our school-shelf tapioca and cocoa didn't quite replenish the energy drained in breasting the face-slapping wind.

We were offered $150 hand-sewn marten hats, and met George Willis, seventy-eight, who built his barrel-stove-warmed cabin in 1945 after his discharge from the Second World War. "Georgetown," a miners' homesite at the mouth of the George River, was named for him. His Uncle Oswald had been prospecting on the upper Kuskokwim since migrating into the country from the Nome gold rush, as that flagged out in 1906, and had discovered some of the first cinnabar here. Already in Nome at fourteen, Oswald had been digging at a likely placer bench but stopped a few feet higher in the sand than the strike was—the next guy got the gold. Also, he was shot there by an "outlaw," but once he was well, he "got his man." With a pistol in his hand, old Oswald could throw a tin can in the air "and keep her a-bouncin.'" George himself had first arrived in Alaska in 1941 on board the S.S. Yukon, docking at Seward. Trapping in the bush all that winter, he never heard about Pearl Harbor until he emerged with his furs the next April. In retirement now, he kept eleven chickens to watch and had collected seven eggs the day I visited with him. The three thirty sunset streamed through the window, lighting his jutting nose and jaw and the white whiskers he was trimming with an electric shaver, using a small mirror and a generator that he cranked with his free hand, opening or closing the damper on the stove meanwhile with his foot. His desk of fancy oak had been salvaged from a saloon that closed with the mining. Said last spring's breakup occurred on May 10th, and barges could run until October. At the end of the airstrip he'd caught a lynx recently, near the unmarked grave of an old-timer he knew, and last fall he chased a black bear up the beach with his headlamp after it broke into his smokehouse and sprang a trap that he'd set there. The trap didn't catch it, but in its panic it got tangled in the chain, whose toggle snagged. So the bear went into the smokehouse again to cure, along with the fish.

Julian Creek—"the Julian Strike"—along with Spruce Creek, upstream from us on Crooked Creek (as was the famous hamlet, Iditarod), is where the gold was, but he found "color" just digging in his garden. Mostly he kept busy, though, working on his uncle's mercury claims and marrying a Stony River Indian woman; had three boys and five girls. A happy family, some in Anchorage or on the Yukon now. The daughter cooking for him wore a brown T-shirt under plastic bib overalls and a stocking cap. The Indians on the Stony, he said, "used to rustle pretty good for themselves" with their trapping and fish camps, before the welfare checks began.

Every bit of sun could count. We saw mean red frost burns on the cheeks of an Indian boy whose father Linda gave pills to. At thirty years old, he'd never swallowed one before: needed to be shown how. My breath coated my glasses with ice if I covered my face with my parka hood, even briefly, and the very snow emitted strange, pained, squeaky sounds underfoot, as if suffering too. Gloved fingers or muffed ears still hurt, and the moisture in my nostrils froze. Ice crinkled on my scarf after it had touched my mouth. My extremities felt as though they were starting to die, and Linda's pants had stiffened like a cowboy's chaps, but smoke plumed from little stovepipes, marking pockets of human life roundabout.

The level of the Kuskokwim had dropped below its lid of ice, and below where people had set their tubular fish traps in the eddies. But the mail plane landed with a blaring ring you wouldn't hear in ordinary temperatures and dropped off an X-ray technician, trained in Des Moines, he said, with a portable machine to snap pictures, to help Linda, which he began promptly to do, reading a Ranger Rick comic book in between shots. One patient passed out before the procedure—a drunk who'd come in from "a trapline two bends down"—but was propped up by the shoulders between his cousin and his wife for the camera. Most, however, displayed a soft sobriety in the swing of their stride, a humility, as they coughed their greenest phlegm into the sputum cups. Besides the Gussuck, George Willis, other old fellows lived in town: Alexei Peter, a Stony River Indian, and Johnnie John, a Yupik. Because Alexei Peter was a widower, you'd see him peeling potatoes and onions for himself, though his son brought him stove wood and the occasional spruce grouse. His nose had lengthened and bent with age so much that he called it his "poke," or bag. He told me Indians were blamed for killing game, but it was really wolves that killed the game. "Wooliff kill birds, lotsa beaver, young bears, anything. Clean it out!" Another man, his friend Belasha, bearishly middle-aged, said I should have come for Christmas Day—"Eats lots. And nicer then. Not supposed to drink that day."

Johnnie John, a short, stocky, good-humored man with a peaceable face, led me home to a square-cut, warm log cabin full of grandkids. "Julie, Pac Man!" called a girl, running from the bedroom to tell Julie what was on. Johnnie said his dad bought the first muzzleloader in the village "from the Americans." They'd had a few steel traps, used deadfalls for wolves, wolverines, and lynx, and made their own shells for that first "hammer-gun." Fished all winter through the ice for "lush" (loche) for the dogs, because lots of people were going up and down the thoroughfare of the river on sleds. Skin boats in the summer, sewn of moose, caribou, or bear hides. "And nobody packum priest. He come self. He travel all time. Live over on the Yukon at Russian Mission. Now priest got to have money all the time to travel by plane."

Belasha's father had also come from Russian Mission. The shortest trail from the Yukon to the Kuskokwim ran more or less from Russian Mission across marshland and squiggly lakes to Aniak, via Dogfish Village or Kalskag; then, leaving the Kuskokwim on a short cut to Crooked Creek, you'd go up Ohwat Creek from Crow Village, behind Russian Mountain, and next to DeCourcy Mountain, south again. He said there were more grizzlies on the mountains now because the old-timers used to kill them with a .30–30 or spears and bows and arrows. "The mountains were your living room. You didn't want a grizzly hanging about. And people were strong. Had to be, from dragging the bear out on a coaster." He gestured to show how the tumpline went around your forehead, with which you pulled the sledge. Or strong from rowing on the river or lining the freight boats up current against the worst of the rapids. Used to feed the dogs on wolf kills in a hard winter—"Every day, teams traveling all over, or boats in the summer. Goodness sake! People don't know nothing about the country now, or how to set a trap." Belasha's father "used only wood," only deadfalls for catching "link." Lynx pelts were his livelihood and he'd chop a month's supply of firewood for his wife and children before he left to run his lines.

There used to be fish traps, too, everywhere along the river for the loche "lush." Link and lush were the staff of life in the winter, or people ate sheefish, a large whitefish, or pike, when the ice went off in May, before the king salmon started their momentous run; whereupon at its height, Johnnie John's three daughters, working on a raft moored next to his fish wheel, might cut and clean five hundred salmon in a single day, to dry on racks built on the bank. He said his twenty-seven-year-old youngest son had shot four black bears drawn to the smell last summer. But then he'd drowned.

"Still miss him. He helped us," mourned Johnnie John. "Could shoot a spruce chicken (grouse) just in the head, not to touch the meat," when chicken in the store cans "is sometimes bum." Said one family in town had four sons, but they actually bought their firewood, the sons were too lazy to chop it. A good boy, his had been; and needless to say, I didn't venture to confirm whether his death was one of the recent epidemics of suicides.

"Good berries this fall," Johnnie said. "Even salmonberries. Last year's salmonberries was bum." You boil the berries and put them in the ground, then in the winter take them out and they taste good; no smell. "Eat Eskimo food. Don't eat store jam. I talk to my girls, tell them don't be lazy, and don't sell no berries, don't sell no fish. Let the others pick their own, catch their own. I like country, get lonesome for being out in the woods. But that pretty bum when a bear come and eat your whole day's berries and you don't have your gun! When a bear grabs my fish and runs uphill, I shoot him and he rolls down again. At the fish wheel bear comes to smokehouse smell. He don't like the smoke so he back out, but want the fish so go back in. Shoot him then."

Johnnie had cut a moose hide into a harness for his dogs. "So now they are going to have to haul me some wood." Said his dad was one-fourth Indian and thus much bigger than most Eskimos. But *he* was rather small, maybe because his father kept him out in the cold so much to toughen him—though he never felt mistreated at the time. His dad could pack half a moose on his back after sawing it in two. Yes, he conceded, when I asked, there was fighting to the north and east between the Indians and the Eskimos in the old days, but not on the Kuskokwim and lower Yukon. "Didn't like to fight. Didn't like to. Would send troublemakers back. Would kill all but one of them and send that one back." He waved his arm dismissively—a small, dexterous, gentle-looking wife backing him up.

On the great kitchen range at the school, we fried hamburgers, heated tea and soup, the generator running the lights and fridge round-the-clock. For January 13th, the Russian New Year's Eve, we stayed up till midnight, hosted with smoked salmon strips, moonshine, coffee, and *Akutaq*, known as "Eskimo ice cream," which was a salmon-flavored frozen concoction of dried berries and wild roots shredded into sweetened Crisco, as a substitute for the seal or bear blubber that previously had been used. Blubber consumption, because of the cold, was quite central to these winter celebrations. And I found, from my limited experience, these Yupiks in below-the-Arctic regions friendlier to transient whites like me than either the arctic Inupiats, above the Brooks Range, or interior Athabascans I had met in Yukon towns like Tanana and Fort Yukon. Both these groups had been mauled a good deal in earlier eras by whites—whaling crews butchering in the Arctic Ocean, or gold-rushers scrambling for another Klondike, abusing any hapless Indians who were indigenous. Here, the early Russian missionaries had had the advantage of not being accompanied by a swarm of brutal freebooters as the later Americans often were. And it was an in-and-out coastal trading culture, cumulatively bridging seafaring and mountainous understandings.

Nevertheless, I did find, with particular reference to my handicap of a stutter, a more flexible stripe of sympathy in Indian towns. This may have been a cultural twist, if the original Athabascan religion left wiggle room for aberrant weaknesses that were perhaps thought to mask strengths—blind or stuttering shamans with clairvoyance, for instance. The climate on the middle-Yukon, with a hundred-plus degree temperature fluctuation, cascading fish runs, bird life, and mammal migrations, allowed for subtle natural mysteries, laddered prosperity or poverty, and division of labor, a variety of talents. Over the centuries the vise-like Arctic, by contrast, allowed less leeway for individuals whose stumbling could endanger the community. Grandpa with the broken hip was left behind on the ice. So my stutter in the Inupiat village of Point Hope, above the 68th parallel, might provoke laughter—certainly no curiosity—whereas in protein-rich Fort Yukon, variegations in weather, biodiversity, the very presence of trees, allowed more margin for error, for limber judgments or an attitude of wait-and-see. Garbled speech might flow from or engender intuition. The relationship of Athabascan Indians to grizzly bears seemed more complex than the regard Inupiat Eskimos had for polar bears as well, which were better eating and mainly food.

At the New Year's party at the school, I talked with Paul Genne, a Gussuck vocational teacher of welding, woodwork, and small-engine repair (as for a chainsaw, outboard, or Ski-Doo), who plowed the Crooked Creek airstrip as a sideline, and scrimshawed fossil walrus or mammoth ivory and fashioned gold nuggets into jewelry. When classes let out for the summer, he told me he earned $75 a day plus his keep for magnetometer survey work for a mining outfit. Had no girlfriend at the moment, but his last one had "charged me a year of my life for sewing me a pair of sealskin mukluks, a marten hat, and a moose skin vest." Migrating caribou you'll spot on a mountainside in bands of twenty to seventy, with a wolf following you can "outlaw" (shoot) with your .270. "These Eskimos ought to shine it on" (walk away from), he said, their Welfare, Energy Assistance, and Aid to Families with Dependent Children checks or food stamps and just go trapping, fishing. When bear-hunting, he said, a black will run and shy away, but a grizzly comes around on you. You trail him and he'll swing right onto your back track.

CHAPTER 4

• • •

Sleetmute

WHEN THE SUN ROSE AT nine thirty, we promptly hopped by Super Cub a tad upriver to Sleetmute, the ragamuffin hamlet set where the Holitna River joins the Kuskokwim. At this site Russians established a trading station in 1832, so contact was early. Our seatbelts felt very short because folks are wiry here; and climbing out again, I blinked repeatedly to keep my eyelids from freezing shut; my nose and ears and mouth began to die. But the Indians in this sketchy, defunct traders' hub wore their earflaps and the cap bills on their three-tailed marten hats tied up, as if the temperature seemed pretty mild to them. Axe in hand, dragging a child's sled for his firewood, one gentleman nodded peaceably to us at the steps of the boxy, cramped health clinic, where, with our duffels, backpacks, and sleeping bags, we were going to spend the night. Not the school, because if the gunfire resumed, the clinic should be a neutral spot. Nobody was likely to want to shoot up the same shack where they might need to be carried in on a blanket litter later on.

Linda groaned, remembering panicky studs lugging a gutshot Lothario into her clinic on a Tlingit island such as Chichagof, late, with blood smeared all over them, when she was in town for wellbaby exams, and no state trooper or doctor any closer than Juneau or the clear daylight hours. No cops or medics were even that close to Sleetmute and we did indeed hear gunshots exchanged between two feuding cabins, the logs absorbing the bullets, after a long, terse day of forearm TB-scratching and sputum collection. The food shelf boasted cans of peanuts, peanut butter, peanut granules, and peaches and peas. A beaver hung on a meat pole next door, waiting to be skinned. Also a fluffy, five-foot lynx and a plush, thick-furred otter longer than that, if you counted the tail. While she worked, I climbed above the half-abandoned village to the Russian churchyard with double-barred crosses and, on the ridge, a private homestead graveyard for Sinka Gregory. A stumpy old man below employed a crooked walking stick bent in the opposite direction from the zig-zag of his back and thus serving him well.

Only one resident refused to spit into a cup, telling Linda that he had "spit enough for one lifetime—you have to die someday anyhow." Said if government people kept bothering him he'd stay out on his trapline until he did.

In the early native hospitals, and as late as the 1950s, it was true, the X-ray technician said, that considerable hare-brained surgery was performed. Lungs were purposely collapsed, using paraffin that might then have been accidentally left in the pleural cavity afterward and now showed up as a lump on the X-ray, or, worse, could melt and leak during a siege of high fever and gradually be coughed up and partially enter the stomach, to be vomited up in small quantities. In the X-rays of older persons he could sometimes identify the traces of botched operations attempted by young resident surgeons practicing their novice skills, or bored civil servants relegated to what they regarded as an asshole of the world: tinkering as a consequence.

When Linda completed her testing, a couple of snowmobiles crossed the river to fetch us to the Vanderpools' Trading Post on the other side. The Vanderpools bought furs from the Indians and sold them liquor. They had four planes parked on a spindly runway outdoors and walrus and narwhal ivory, worked-bead collections, and scrimshawed whalebone displayed inside, together with about thirty assorted guns hanging on the wall. Reddish to sable-dark marten skins, dried to a papery crackle, were piled on a table to be sewn into hats lined with poplin, which are worn fur-side-out in town for show, but fur-side-in for insulation during winter weather.

Three guys called Golgo, Moxie, and Wassily dropped in for coffee, as we got acquainted with Joe and Gail Vanderpool. But Joe's middle-aged sister, Mary, was unsociably complaining that she had been "seeing blood on the trail long before the health aid or that

German nurse reported anything was wrong to Anchorage. Why did they wait so long to do anything about it—till now we have to rush around?" By blood on the snow she meant, of course, from coughing, and Linda sympathized with anyone fearful they might have been exposed unnecessarily. But she realized too that there might be a political angle to this squabble. The health aid in Sleetmute named Hope Starr and, like Linda, also an outsider, not local, but whom Linda had befriended immediately, had been involved in a recent campaign for Sleetmute to vote itself dry—as Crooked Creek supposedly was. This would have sharply impacted Joe Vanderpool's business because the rationale for his liquor sales to the natives—who showed up with their government checks or crafts or furs by snow machine once the river iced over and by skiffs otherwise—was that since Sleetmute, the closest village, was legally wet by community ordinance, whoever they were, or wherever from, people could claim they were heading with it across a couple of the river's curves just to there.

Because of the appalling suicide rate in native towns statewide and a rash of tragic incidents along this river—eleven souls drowned between May 28th and July 22nd during the past summer, nine of whom were found to have been drinking prior to their deaths—Hope had regarded the liquor vote as a health issue appropriate to fight for. But the Vanderpools and the Mellicks, another trading family nearby, and other pro-wetters, brought in all of their outlying relatives who could claim Sleetmute residency for the vote, and won; then for good measure, ousted Hope from her health aid's job by council vote, so that the district authorities in Bethel had had to appoint her to a supervisory post to keep her voice on the Kuskokwim at all. Drunks drowned in the winter also, when a Polaris might founder in a hole in the ice, but these emergencies seemed more ambiguous than when an experienced boatman simply tipped himself over in the summer current. "You know how it is," an Eskimo woman confided to me on the Vanderpools' front porch. "Being a woman, they'll beat us when they drink. But they beat us if we say not to, or if we don't drink, too." She said she'd left her husband to live with a white man in Bethel for a time, yet came back so as "not to shame the children." And back in Crooked Creek, Alexei Peter, the Athabascan, had told me sarcastically how "these Eskimos" would yell at a party, "I am an Eskimo!" but then do nothing about it—"don't fish or hunt." And thereafter, if one of them punctured somebody's chest with a skinning knife or smashed his head with a tire iron, he might get off because white society would say, "Oh, he was only drunk and he's just an Eskimo."

Joe and Bob, the Vanderpool brothers, had grown up during the 1920s on a homestead in McGrath, a notable town near the head of the Kuskokwim, a hundred air miles upriver from where we were and a collecting point for numerous forks off the western facings of the Denali massif of the Alaska Range. Their father had been drawn up the river during a brief gold rush here in 1910, then stayed to trap and farm. It had been several kids out berrying who first stumbled upon the cinnabar find at Red Devil—a seam of red marking the ground. The mine didn't close until 1971, after operating for about thirty years and employing fifty or sixty men in a shaft that sank six hundred feet, with side chambers halfway down; the company earning $700 for a seventy-pound flask of mercury. Both brothers, after toiling there a while, obtained pilots' licenses, which, along with buying furs and selling whiskey—he charged $26 for a half-gallon of rye—was still Joe's livelihood. Wolverine pelts brought the trapper from $125 to $450; lynx, $150 to $350; otter, $60 to $125; marten, $15 to $60, a spread determined by both color and size. Lighter marten were worth less, or if spruce pitch had gotten stuck in them. The Holitna River marten were orange like a fox and averaged $35 apiece, while on the main stem of the Kuskokwim below Sleetmute, the darker gene pool could fetch $50 for the same length of skin.

Bob was a charter pilot, too, and still resented what he blamed Joe a good deal for—the DC-3 lying askew at the end of their airstrip with its right wing sheered off. Merely glancing at it was a financial pain and—like their dad—Bob preferred homesteading. He had a fish wheel—a Ferris wheel-like device turned by the current's force that automatically catches in its upswinging baskets spawning salmon swimming against the same current—plus a dog team, a garden for potatoes, onions, cabbages, carrots, turnips, and a hothouse of plastic sheeting for tomatoes and cucumbers, all set on a bench alongside the George River at about where the mini-gold rush on the George hadn't panned out. Bob had married a Sleetmute girl, Natasha Ann, much as his Dad also had, and, now sixty-seven, remembered when riverboats steamed up and down the Kuskokwim, not just the annual tugboat pushing oil barges, and families mushed their dogsleds all winter on the river ice to sundry trapline camps—not driving noisy snow machines from town to town for a binge. He said ice travel can certainly be risky in the flux of spring and fall, but seldom otherwise unless you're either drunk, or on a moonless night when the currents' holes in the thick cap on the river may not show. You must drive slow, aware beforehand of where each tributary creek comes in, turbulent underneath your treads. He added that Indians appeared to be rendered drunk remarkably quickly, yet could hold a large amount of booze without throwing up or passing out, as if considering it too precious a cargo to lose: a propensity that might contribute to the drownings. And even when you're married to one of their relatives, like him, he said it's important never to drink along with them or allow them to get sloshed in your house. But Indians don't fight well, if you do. Somehow they never learned how, or aren't aggressive and intense enough, and don't fight one another hard either, he said, as often as they'll hit a woman or a child. As for himself, with his boat and drift net and buoys, he can catch twenty or thirty chinook in half an hour at the height of their run, so it's a decent life, even at subsistence level. And how nice and warm, this time of year, zero degrees could feel!

I joked that if you believed Thomas Mann's great tuberculosis novel, *The Magic Mountain*, which I'd scared myself by devouring while at work at my army hospital specializing in tuberculosis, then cold, Swiss-like days should be good sanatorium weather. Alaskans are packaged so diversely that you may meet committed readers anywhere, and I encountered both long-haired Vietnam veterans and peace demonstrators who had helped stifle that particular war, rubbing shoulders and chafing at what had driven them up here, "out of America," though their diagnoses might not have coincided. But now we were hearing from Joe a sad tale about a romantic white couple who had been living together for four years, the last one trapping eighty miles or more up the Holitna River, until they angrily split up, with the guy appropriating the third of the string of three lakes in their trapline territory for himself, leaving her the first for herself, and the second as a buffer between them. The house they'd built on the first lake together he granted to her as a home, but then when she went out to visit her parents, he dismantled that and, utilizing the logs to construct a new cabin for himself, left only the roofing material for her in a heap on the ground. Anchorage trailed just Reno and Las Vegas among U.S. cities in its divorce rate. In exaggerated fashion, Alaska had all the elements of the American West—Baptist and Hippie, Developer and Tree Hugger. Anchorage was growing five to fifteen percent per year, and a young woman named Connie Yoshimura, for example, could arrive from Iowa with no previous real estate or selling experience, "except waitressing," and within six years at her own agency be moving ten or fifteen houses a month.

Coyote hairs from my parka ruff stuck in my eyes from snuggling it close, but the temperature had eased by eighteen degrees in two hours as snow clouds clogged the mountain passes. Sleetmute's health clinic, the night before, had felt like a furnace because the oil heater, if you turned it on, as of course you had to, only burned full-blast. Besides Linda's emergency visit, a venereal disease nursing consultant occasionally dropped in, and the regular Public Health Service nurse came three times a year. Also an alcohol and abuse counselor, a public assistance social worker, an environmental sanitation specialist, and the regional Public Health Service physician. Not neglect, but insufficient bandaging for all the difficulties.

Rob Fredericks, a teacher we'd met during the testing procedures, said living in Crooked Creek for a year had disheartened him because "it was just watching a people die." The younger ones could speed the process by drowning on a boat trip to Red Devil to buy drink, or get home with the load, but then, at least in the winter, freeze their feet, black by morning because they'd passed out, dead to the world, with their extremities poking out from under the blankets and no fire. For Rob and his girlfriend, Alaska was a wonderful departure from St. Louis or Bakersfield, raising sled dogs, feeding them lox you caught yourself, and credentialed with a contract from Fairbanks, ultimately to receive oilfield money, till you decided you should get serious and let the Wild West adventure end. But nothing was an interim for them. And with satellite TVs, they knew the score.

By dogsled Rob carried us along the Kuskokwim to a side slough on the other side where the Sleetmute health aid Hope Starr and her partner, Paul Reisman, had a cozy cabin we could stay in, caring for their dogs and chickens while they went to Bethel, the administrative center from which this and fifty-two other native villages on the lower Yukon and Kuskokwim were managed. Linda and

Hope, as impatient idealists, had bonded immediately and Hope was beloved by the headquarters social-services crew, who couldn't save her from the Vanderpools' machinations but had promoted her as an alternative. Her snug downstairs came with a tight iron wood stove, two kerosene lamps, two white-gas Coleman lanterns, and an extra little Blazo stove under the laddered sleeping loft, which was heaped with homey mattresses and quilts. In a root cellar underneath the floor another kerosene lamp was constantly kept burning so that the cured or pickled salmon, canned meats and vegetables, and bins of root vegetables wouldn't freeze. The chicken coop featured another, burning all the time to keep the water pan from freezing and the temperature from descending to brutal levels. In the smokehouse a caribou leg and hide hung over a pile of chum salmon, dried for the four sled dogs, one of which had month-old puppies, as well as a lithe Irish wolfhound. After Hope's defeat in the wet/dry fracas, all but the wolfhound were going to be shed in the spring, along with this leased patch of land. But Hope and her friend, a carpenter by trade, weren't fleeing back to the Lower 48, as do-gooders generally did when foiled by Alaska's entrenched savageries (there, as the cliché had it, to enlist for service with an aid group in Africa). Their plan was to homestead—a six-year process leading to ownership—in a geodesic dome on a stretch upriver near the Stony River Indians, who themselves had been relocated from a headwaters redoubt called Lime Village, in the Lime Hills, not long before. These were an Athapascan subset called the Tanaina, whereas the upriver Indians on the mainstem Kuskokwim had been bands of Ingalik or Kolchan.

So, after a minimal tour, Linda and I were left in delicious solitude to play with the dogs, collect fresh brown eggs from the bustling hens, crack them into a pan, and the luxuries of the loft. She sat on my knees facing away from me, on an easy chair, while I tugged a brush through her foxy hair a dozen times, then gave the brush to her again to let her finish the job, while I stroked her ribs and breasts—the curve of her back like a lyre and her waist like the bends of a cello. Love overwhelmed me, and her breasts amazed me by withstanding my endless handling, being so softly round yet just as firm and resilient as my bony hands. Her thick hair, like a fat fox tail, perpetually fascinated me, too—and the unexpectedness, the frequency of her laughter, her imperiousness and possessiveness yet comradeship and good cheer. "You must adore me," she said and I did. On ferry floors we'd slept together with glaciers passing in the moonlight and other deck passengers all around, and the illicit climax all the more titillating for that. And alongside the famous Haul Road, between Fairbanks and Prudhoe Bay, seven hundred miles or more of the most macho driving in America, we'd made sure to make love with me on my back and Linda in total charge.

The slough was navigable from the river, so Hope had a jonboat, with its motor wrapped in tarps for the winter, and a freighting barge beached nearby. She'd told us she had learned to walk down to the landing with a shotgun whenever drunks showed up by water in the summer. Nevertheless, as the new couple, we had visitors within an hour. Her snowmobile had roared off to catch the mail plane, but soon her friend, the rangy Danish "converter" named Ling, with a son, Eric, piggyback on the back of Ling's husband, Greg's, Polaris, arrived for tea. Greg, twenty-seven, originally from upstate New York, flew out from Crooked Creek to tutor home-schooled kids with learning disabilities. He'd been "toilet-training" greatly retarded children at a state school outside New Orleans, when they up and decided to drive the Alaska Highway in an International Scout, with $500 in cash and an Exxon card. By Fairbanks they were living in the back on rice and powdered milk, whereupon a kindly couple adopted them until Greg's résumé could be authenticated for hiring purposes. Now, his disadvantaged pupils called him "the Gussuck with raisins," because of his black eyes, and sometimes he might hold their classes in a boat outside the house, if the mother was lying comatose from homebrew inside. Although "Gussuck" can be pronounced matter-of-factly or with contempt, as people wish, living in Sleetmute for a year, hauling firewood on a derelict dogsled that progressively fell apart, and never mastering the craft of properly sharpening a chainsaw, Ling and he were surprised not to find anyone in this underemployed populace interested in selling them firewood. At the school, the teachers, who were Oklahoma transplants here, Greg said, to bail out mortgages on a family farm, took out their fear and frustration on poor Eric, not daring to hassle the native kids instead. "The best-loved teachers are the incoming ones or the outgoing ones," Ling suggested. The villagers were losing their Yupik or Ingalik languages to the steamroller of TV English, but spoke English themselves mostly in telegraph style.

Greg recounted jagged yarns obsessively: like several stories of a frightening white man called "Wolf" who was finally hustled away to the asylum at Eagle River after trying to drown his own children, and once ripped a puppy in half at a party to prove his strength for the crowd. "In any village somebody wants to be King of the Hill," but another guy, a local, murdered two of his sisters and after attempting to rape the third, drowned himself in the river's swirl in front of everybody who'd turned out to watch him. The Stony River Indians, near where Hope and her boyfriend were fixing to homestead, maintained an outwardly reticent settlement, but subject to an undertow of rancor after nightfall, harsher than the Eskimo villages. "Alaska exacts a high price," he said, and missed his shotgun flat in New Orleans, working with more severely handicapped children in that residential institution, where at least parents were not a constant problem. He liked the surprises, bizarre challenges; loved getting down on the floor with his charges, rolling, laughing—kids drawn from an entire region whom other teachers had given up on. "Maybe my vocation was working with vegetables. I don't know," he said. People his and Ling's and Hope's age came to Alaska impetuously for a couple of tryout years to clean the slate. But after twice that or more, you'd have your warmly chinked cabin with hanging utensils and herbs, cassette tapes to play when the generator was on, *CoEvolution Quarterly, National Lampoon,* and *Mother Jones* on the hand-hacked table, your trusty center post swollen with polished burls and garlanded with caribou tines, your crowded greenhouse and yard-bred malamutes, and riffle-worthy skiff, plenty of beans in your cellar, and perhaps even a ski plane parked on the river ice. "So where do you go from there?" Perhaps Bethel for groceries and a movie—but not Costa Rica, like the free spirit you once aspired to be, or "you'll get cleaned out in no time while you're gone."

Mellick's General Store, across a tributary but within sight of the Vanderpools' Mercury Inn and Liquor Store, competed but cooperated politically with them while gathering in the welfare checks. This proprietor was likewise descended from a turn-of-the-century gold-rush prospector who had married a river girl and stuck around, though instead of rifles arrayed on the wall, he had a photo of the last old-time Indian who had kept weaving fish traps out of willow withes, refusing to buy the commercial wire kind.

"But it's a pressure cooker on these rivers for the young men now," Mr. Mellick told me, "with the TVs continually broadcasting that everything they're doing is a dead end. The bad apples are squeezed until they burst." As newborns, they might have been laid ceremoniously on a grizzly bear skin by their grandfathers in order to germinate in them the qualities of a great hunter. But that doesn't help them in school. They drop out at sixteen, but not to tramp through the snow on a hundred-mile trapline. The bright lights of Anchorage suck them in, and soon the lockup, Mellick said, more sympathetically, on the whole, I thought, than Joe Vanderpool's attitude, whose piloting might have turned his head.

Moseying about as Linda worked, I ogled the slumbering moose heads, legs, and dismembered hunks of meat hung on Joe Morgan's outdoor rack, though the brains, as a delicacy, had already been spooned out and consumed. Several stillborn puppies lay in a pail as future food for his dogs, next to the sled that Joe, at sixty-two, and his second Eskimo wife, along with a grandson by his first, dragged out every day after firewood, breaking through the crust of snow covering the flooded ice lid on their side creek. For income, his wife sewed boots with sealskin soles, moose-calfskin uppers, and wolf or wolverine strips of fur as a trim on top. Also moose hide caps with marten fur on the bills.

Larry Bass and his native wife, living nearby, cleaned the Sleetmute school for wages, but had just sold Joe Vanderpool $2,800 worth of marten skins and furnished him with two crucial swing votes in the wet/dry battle. Yet whereas Gail Vanderpool immersed herself in pounding bread dough for the oven when visitors showed up, so as to participate in any conversations, I found Larry Bass's wife kneeling mousily in front of him in their living room, skinning and scraping his day's catch of pelts, while we talked and he lounged in a cushioned chair in his boot socks, like the squaw men of yore. His brother, though, was married to the petite Swiss woman, friend of Ling, the Dane, who had been so upset to learn in Red Devil that she was testing positive for TB; native women like Gail and Larry's wife had rather expected to. Ordinarily Larry's brother and his family would have been wintering on their good gold claim on the George River seventy-eight miles away. When you had workings worth protecting, it was advisable to stay on-site, except that the wife had a twelve-year-old daughter from a previous marriage for whom she wanted the socializing benefits of regular schooling, not endless correspondence courses. Now, naturally, she had doubts or regrets, Larry said, plus their eleven sled dogs had been exposed to a sudden parvovirus epidemic here in Sleetmute that had already killed four of the Vanderpools' team.

The daughter in question sat watching Kermit the Frog, when free, which she couldn't have done way up in the wilds on the George River, but had been disappointed after much eager anticipation of her first day of school when some of the other students didn't ramble in till noon. And the school cook complained to me too, because, the salary aside, it was no fun preparing lunches for only a dwindling roster of ten, counting the Basses' children and her own—"and government cheese running out of our ears"—fretting additionally because she had also become a TB "converter."

To cheer up a bit, I returned to Joe Morgan's cabin again, with its slumbering moose heads outside and him sprawled in a chair because of his emphysema, he said, but looking decidedly "Irish," or perky, nonetheless, although his voice sounded more fluent in Yupik than English now, after all of these years. Direct, humorous, quick, he joked with me that after seventeen years of blowing up cinnabar seams with nitroglycerin at the Red Devil mine, he kept some of it in an envelope in a drawer to jump-start his heart when it gave out. He'd gone out to visit a son who had married an Eskimo girl down in the Kuskokwim delta, even below Bethel, toward Napaskiak and Eek, with the notion of possibly staying there "for the duration." But the terrain depressed him. "Not a hill. Not a willow!" Moose eat willows and he could still drag home a moose.

· · ·

Back in Crooked Creek, another white man, "Trader Thomas," sold staples and sat on the town council, along with his Eskimo wife. His white father had built famous riverboats during the gold rush and supposedly had slept with a notorious number of squaws. Thomas eschewed the harem model but cherished the idea that he resembled some jungle trader near the headwaters of the Amazon, his wife "the Queen of the Silver Dollar," as, jolly-bearded, he told us.

Trader Thomas was having fun, but our most poignant conversation was with the circuit nurse who'd helped call Linda in. Her
job as itinerant in charge of several settlements corresponded to what
Linda had done on the Tlingit islands in the southeastern belt of the
state, but instead of flying out of the administrative center at Bethel,
she'd rented a cabin right here in Crooked Creek to participate in
the life of the community—chainsaw, woodstove, dogsled and all.
Although from the Lower 48, she appeared to be thriving in the
manner of many vigorous folk who venture north at thirty or so to
explore their fancies and resources. Like Hope, the Sleetmute health
aid, she should have been an absolute prize for the community but
instead was being driven out: in her case not by a clique of liquor
dealers or vote of the council. Her mistake had been romantic. As
part of entering the life of the Kuskokwim, she'd fallen into an affair
with a young man who had helped her train her huskies into a pulling team and learn to hunt caribou, trap salmon, camp in the snow
with a birch fire, and other skills. But when the relationship soured
and he socked her, drunk, he refused to relinquish the connection.
Didn't simply beat on the door but climbed the spruce ridge behind
her house with his rifle every evening and shot, not her, but one of
her beloved dogs when she let them out to pee. Other people disap-
proved, yet not enough to risk their necks by confronting him. Nor
could you summon law enforcement a hundred-sixty miles by air
from Bethel to try to sort things out. He was a wild card, but claimed
the dogs were his and men commonly shot dogs in spates in these
towns. "Had a gunfight at the O.K. Corral last night," you'd hear
somebody in a white town say who had grown sick of dog racing and
the kibble bill. She'd bought 'em but he'd trained 'em. The police
had suicides to investigate, or the occasional "bush justice" murder,
where somebody was bushwhacked by an unknown enemy. Kung Fu
was the rage among Crooked Creek's young blades at the moment,
and they would have told her to pick her boyfriends better next time.
The killing of the dogs, one by one, one a day, broke her heart, but
nobody except her thought she might be next, and trying to put him
in jail would scarcely enable her to stay on the river and function in
her job. She needed to transfer, she informed us sadly by firelight in
a friend's cabin where she was sleeping for safety's sake. A bear's liver
was soaking in a pan of milk to mellow its taste before we cooked it,

and a pair of trophy caribou antlers lofted in prayerful uplift among the shadows dancing on the wall, an eloquence doubled by the candles' and kerosene lanterns' fickle flames.

Rob Fredericks, the disillusioned teacher who'd carried us by dogsled to Hope's cabin, also had ferried us to hear her out in her sanctuary, temporary as it was, with a dog or two left that she'd fly out with—her pretty face wizened with worry, amber locks chopped. As a boy, Rob had watched *Nanook of the North* and first aspired to go and live among the Eskimos. He arrived in Crooked Creek as a Bureau of Indian Affairs contractor to build four prefab houses, until he noticed that children might break into them as soon as they were half-finished in order to try to keep warm when their parents were partying; and heard of a woman who shot herself in the foot to get shipped out of town by the authorities, away from her husband who had beaten her so bad she hid all night in a sweathouse to save her life. His girlfriend, who'd moved to Alaska six years ago, now drove an ambulance in Bethel and fought forest fires for the Feds during the summer. It was lucrative for both of them, and—berserk and chewed though he sometimes looked—maybe better than the flat-planed, simplified rounds of other white guys who slept twelve of the twenty-four January hours and cut and hauled stove fuel during the rest.

CHAPTER 5

• • •

Trapping Camps

O N JANUARY 17TH, JOE VANDERPOOL, "Air Vanderpool," flew us
in his Super Cub up the Holitna River, sitting in tandem on
the floor dogsled-style behind him, past Kiokluk Mountain, to three
trapping camps near abandoned Tanaina settlements called Nogamut
and Kashegelok, landing successively at each so Linda could check
the separate families' children's medications, listen with a stethoscope,
and collect sputum. The fathers acted alarmed when I also stepped
off the plane, until Joe assured them I wasn't a game warden, whereupon they'd relax, usually grin, and show me their lovely red fox and
marten skins, beaver, otter, and wolves on stretchers. Much of the
winter's meat was cached on each sloping snow roof, wedged under
canvas to keep the gray jays, woodpeckers, and ravens from peck-
ing at it. A Yamaha Excel III snow machine was parked at the door,
ready to cover the various outflung lines up creeks and watersheds, a
hundred traps at beaver houses or in trees, with scent lures concocted
from fermented fish, dissected glands, or sexual pheromones, and a
dead bird thrown cunningly under a snare. We met Sammy Parent,
Randy Nook, and their families, who would remain self-contained
until they moved in the spring to fish camps down on the big river.

Very low in our "summertime plane," as Joe described it, we
flew directly across the hills, gazing down at snow patterns sculpted
by the compass and topography, steep or wet, sparsely marked by
spruce trees on any north slope, swooping to a swamp or slough. Or
a knoll might show a cabin where we were expected, with willow

branches delineating a strip where the skis could set down. The cabin would have a radio antenna sticking out among the bark slabs laid across the log rafters, peaking at about six-and-a-half feet along the ridgepole, over a floor ten by fifteen feet. One patient was an old man Linda wanted to confirm was swallowing his pills, and collect a spit sample from.

"Who's here?" she asked, as soon as her feet touched the ground.

"Just me, him, and the housekeeper," said a middle-aged son. Almost any trapper had a housekeeper, if he wanted one.

Inside, three wooden bunks were placed against the three walls, plus a barrel mounted on a metal base for a stove, nails in the logs to hang clothes on, and a table with chairs for amenities. Four fleecy dogs were staked outside, next to their sled, and a beaver carcass and skinned ermine and marten had been laid aside on corner house logs to feed them. Also grouse and snowshoe hares for the trio of humans, and an eviscerated porcupine, a moose's head and legs, and several sheefish from traps set in the Holitna's eddies. The beaver's tail had been severed, as a special delicacy for the stove, like the moose's nose. But a regular meat rack outside had loads of butchered cuts—even a quartered mountain sheep—that a cluster of fluffed-out chickadees were nourishing their bodies from. Snowshoes, skis, and skates for grandkids were stacked beside the door, because old guys visited with their families from another couple of camps every two weeks when a correspondence-school teacher flew out for three-hour, hands-on sessions with them (four, during the longer hours of the spring). I met the teacher later—a pale, huge, Scandinavian-type who looked like a trapper himself and was responsible for educating the children of eight families running traplines cumulatively amounting to above a thousand miles on this web of rivers. The most ambitious kids would be eligible for Mount Edgecumbe boarding school in Sitka on Baranof Island in a few years.

We landed at another campsite whose clump of men seeing me accompany Linda were restive until Joe promised them I was irrelevant. "Wow," I said flatteringly, focusing on the lynx, wolf, and wolverine skins fitted on a row of stretchers in front of their huts.

"Moses Little Fish weighs twelve-and-a-half pounds," Linda was reporting by radio to a Bethel hospital administrator: which was excellent news, since his mother did have active TB. Hard to stymie, she examined the recalcitrant men as well, taking temperatures, re-filling medicine bottles. The mothers seemed grateful, but their husbands, after offering us pilot biscuits and jack cheese to nibble on, were glad to wave us off—"We'll be seeing you guys!"—allowing the valley's wildlife to settle into infinite and primordial silence again.

Our skidding descent into the slough at Red Devil, overcrowded with Vanderpool's other planes, was complicated by the placement of both the side hill and the junked DC-3 with one wing off, lying askew. The low cold sun, as round and white as the moon, soon disappeared behind the windy clouds, and my nose, ears, chin, and cheeks began to die. Yet when we returned to Hope's cabin by snowmobile, the chickens' kerosene lamp was still burning in their hutch to keep the water liquid in their pan and they'd laid eggs for us during the day. Only the dogs' water had frozen, but they could eat snow. When we whistled at the northern lights to test the legend that whistling brings them closer, indeed our warm breath refracted the air so as to do so. I dreamt of living animals strung painfully on a wall within their pelts, and Linda burped a lot, as she did when tense—her stomach acting as a seat of her vulnerabilities. The pressures on her had been accentuated by time constraints when jumping about and the wilderness ethos, where outsiders could be considered nosey, negligible, arrogant, or fly-by-night. On the other hand, despite her bouts of broken sleep, we had never felt closer than while clasping each other, hunching in tandem on the floor of these vibrating airplanes.

Next day, for $629 billed to the State, a sulky Joe Vanderpool (because we'd stayed at his political foe Hope's house) flew us by Cessna downriver to Lower Kalskag, past Horn and Russian Mountains, on the right, and Chvilnuk, on the left, with caves or mine holes staring out in some places like eye sockets. First, though, he dropped down for a hasty stop at Crooked Creek, keeping the engine running, while Linda obtained sputum from a suddenly frightened Yupik gentleman in a snowmobile suit whom the hospital had radioed to meet her at the airstrip because his skin test had turned positive and he was coughing. We asked how Eva, a second-grader from a honey-bucket, dip-water household who had been coming alone and early to school to be fed, was doing. Two teachers were waiting for a social worker to fly in and find out what else was wrong. There was also a nineteen-year-old unmarried Eskimo girl, pregnant with her third child, who had been making no pre-natal preparations for the event, to ask about.

From the plane we noticed a moose dodging through a marsh that had dropped one of his antlers but not the other one yet. Beyond the Holokuk River we flew over the ancient site of Kvygympaynag-myut, a Yupik village across from which the Russians in the 1830s established the Kolmakovskiy Redoubt for bartering, like the post near Sleetmute, at the Holitna. The Kalskag area had experienced a spike in TB cases too, so the school superintendent himself picked us up. A Sky Van was unloading a ton of bagged dog food for the three-hundred-mile race that was scheduled for this week. He, like his counterpart in Aniak who supervised the upriver schools, hailed from southern Oklahoma where he'd coached football for a quarter of a century and married an attractive English teacher, who had accompanied him here four years before. But, owning two places, he could fly home from Anchorage in twenty-four hours. I'd met many Midwestern teachers across Alaska who were laying up a nest egg with Prudhoe Bay oil money.

At the school where we would sleep, the students' snow machines were parked. But we watched unhappily as an autistic boy was taught how to sweep the gym, then shake the broom precisely three, not four, times, while naming the "push" or "whisk" implements and the dustpan—who covered his humiliated head with his poor arms at every mistake he made. The Orthodox priest also dropped by to meet Linda at the clinic, a plump, comfortable, reflective Yupik man, who served churches up and down the Kuskokwim and its delta and along the coast. Fresh and pink from his steam bath, sixtyish, a leaderly type with a companionable wife, he admitted to being regarded as neglectful by parishes such as Sleetmute and Crooked Creek that rarely got to see him, but had officiated as far south as Wrangell and Juneau. The health aid, meanwhile, was helping Linda prepare for the queue of people who were going to be tested, struggling to remember her Yupik to translate for the old-timers. She was a comely, hesitant woman getting married the next week, although we heard her boyfriend shouting at her that evening for a couple of hours. A month ago, she told us, she'd been called out of a basketball game to try to revive the town's policeman, who had shot himself in the head with his service pistol while having a drink with friends. Then she'd had to fly with the bouncing body in the back of a Cessna to Bethel for the closest doctor to do an autopsy.

"It was bum," she said. "*Moother!*" Still suffered nightmares.

Next morning I walked to the church, which was decorated with pictures of the Holy Family, a candle lit in front of each, and a chandelier and sacristy, a handsome pulpit and altar, and communicants' pews tinseled with silver, red, and gold. In the priest's one-room parsonage a similarly celebrative air prevailed, though he was wearing black vestments, but with a four-skin marten hat and all the tails dangling. A frozen moose haunch lay atop the wood stove, thawing for a Twelfth Night Feast of the Epiphany. The twelve grades in Lower Kalskag's school comprised a hundred-ten pupils, so it didn't convey a threadbare air. But we'd chosen the primary classroom for our sleeping bags because of its trapezoidal tables, building-block castle, posters enumerating reptiles and birds of prey, color charts, and alphabet in cursive. Since the gray log clinic boasted a bullet hole in a window and axe cuts in the door memorializing an attack by the town's Wild West contingent, no one objected to our bunking in the school. And the pantry's USDA provisions seemed ducal—sacks of Whole Wheat Flour, Short Grain Brown Rice, cans of Hood River Apple Sauce, French Fried Potatoes Crinkle Cut Oven Type, Dry Yellow Split Peas, Diced Green Bell Peppers, Fresh Veg-All. So multiplex an assortment of government-surplus food indicated how much closer we were to a superintendent's office than previously. Sleetmute's super flew in from Aniak only once a year, and their collectively shared school principal three times, except for emergencies. A doctor also visited only once a year: which explained the added tension to some of Linda's survey trips. Were various diabetics or asthmatics being cared for? Had temporary symptoms other people had complained of—blood in the stool, a spreading mole, a dragging leg—become chronic? When should you stop the ulcer pills and operate for cancer? Suppose you lanced a cyst that wasn't a cyst? Were bed rest and pills helping that mental patient? Who, of the angry voices on the radio from that town, was reliable?

Kalskag was close enough to Bethel for Linda to be spared the lymph node and swallowing-obstruction stuff, but the teachers, villagers, even the dogs, looked a bit benighted even so. Here was this clean, bright, oil-moneyed school with new desks, sunny windows, hot showers, track trophies, maps of the oceans, placards of the Coliseum and the Parthenon, Bunsen burners, a movie library—a mecca for those age six to eighteen. And then, presumably, you sliced and dried salmon, picked salmonberries, mossberries, cranberries, blueberries, bunchberries, raspberries, winter-berries, caught grayling and blackfish, jackfish, and steelhead, snared rabbits and ground squirrels, shot ptarmigan, collected duck eggs, and shot your moose, so you could sit and eat jerky, feeding a fire all winter, for the rest of your life? The robust, intricate, old-style trapping expertise was mostly the province of geezers or else white newcomers ambitious to prove they could pioneer in every craft and respect.

At the Anchorage fur auction, people had worn bearskin hats or wolf hats with a mink sewn crosswise on the top. On the last day total sales had reached 6,000 skins, and $15 raw coyotes went for $50 if tanned; $20 beavers for $150, in bales of ten. I'd remarked on how many of the trappers were white—though bearded and bristly as hedgehogs—and lean and pained-looking, with glistening, solitary eyes, yet how many individual bidders, who wanted a bundle of top-grade white foxes to take home and work on in their raw state for the next half year, were elderly Indian, or Eskimo women with no man of the clan sufficiently involved anymore to catch furs for them. For young folk the trapline's lore and hardship, reading the snow, knowing the territory of each quarry, were eclipsed. They wanted to try Bethel, then Fairbanks, but if their attributes turned out to be not marketable, generally drifted back. So after the ice melted on the Kuskokwim this past spring, eleven people had drowned by midsummer. In the winter, a drunk could stumble home, forget to light the fire in his hovel before passing out, and be found in the morning but not classed as a suicide. However, the drownings, often in plain sight, had been extraordinary.

At the clinic, a child with an earache was brought in, although the health aid appeared to be tipsy. We heard mutterings that a one-year-old suffering fits and breathing problems had gone untreated for four months since the district nurse's last visit and a heart patient similarly. And a cancer patient in town: how secure was *his* pain management? The axe scars in the front door had had circles drawn around them. I wandered out, dismayed at that and also because Linda's sputum collection was unappetizing to observe and bruised some patients' sense of privacy. Although for a year in the army I'd read war brides' TB slides as a hospital technician, I hadn't watched the sputum itself hacked up. (I say "war brides" because it was mostly the Korean and Japanese girls American soldiers married who contracted the disease, just as the native population here possessed less resistance.) From grown people's cabins, I heard the voice of *Sesame Street*'s Cookie Monster broadcast, because that was the channel they got. Even the CB radios villagers chatted on as a substitute for telephones altered their voices to Donald Duck's timbre. A shopkeeper's widow ordered me to stop stuttering when I entered her store, because stuttering brought on windstorms. Her cruel smirk drove me to revisit Archpriest Vassily Epchock's modest house. Promoted last year, at fifty-eight, he said he'd been a priest for eighteen years before that, traveling lots, living in borrowed B.I.A.-built prefabs with linoleum floors and maybe a cross taped to the window. Even this hospitable church had fake-tile linoleum. Clothing, plastic greeting cards, Slavic and Gussuck calendars, and a toy seaplane hung on his walls, and he wore an arctic-fox hat with the white tail plumed like a fine scalp lock on top.

His family was preparing the Epiphany feast, in memory of the congregation's dead, so a rug had been spread across the floor with three ten-gallon pots on it. One contained moose stew; another a grouse, goose, and ptarmigan mélange; and the third spaghetti. There was also a plate of pilot biscuits with homemade jam, a pitcher of Kool-Aid, a bowl of so-called Alaska Jell-O, which consisted of low bush cranberries boiled with flour, sugar, and water, and some regular store Jell-O, Oreos, and a large bowl of *Akutaq*, or "Eskimo ice cream," compiled famously of Crisco as a substitute for blubber, with berries and sugar stirred in. In the wilds, nutritious roots were included that had been gathered and hoarded for winter by arctic mice in their chambered burrows, then raided by knowing people, and, Vassily told me, tasted like sweet starchy rice. Another family helping in the preparations had adopted the Gussuck name "Crisco" for themselves, in fact, but had a member dying of military TB. They'd contributed loche fish, and a platter of macaroni and cheese cooked in seal oil. The Littlefish family, also there, had a patriarch, named Golga, who was dying of liver cancer after hepatitis, and who told us, when we checked on him, that he felt "dizzy like a drunk."

As a stranger in these roadless towns, you trust people more, knowing they probably came by dogsled or snow machine from a similar settlement, such as Holy Cross or Dogfish Village on the Yukon, whose course swings closest to the Kuskokwim's here. If not invested in the place, they were recognizable to folks who were. "You guys gonna keep an all-night vigil?" a woman asked Vassily via CB radio. Each family had its own frequency and would ask him to turn from #twenty-three, the general one, to theirs, for private chats. Linda, at the clinic, was also talking on these to individual patients as well as the government receivers at Bethel's hospital or social agencies, or a colleague in Aniak.

Toothbrushing and contraceptive illustrations adorned the clinic wall, along with vitamin charts and man-in-the-water instructions tacked up. But, except for Linda's venture and a VD nurse and respiratory therapist who separately dropped in three times a year, the Public Health Service's emphasis was on infant and child care. "*I guess we're real dumb, us natives!*—is what we thought when the Gussucks walked on the moon while we were staring at it and worshiping it!" explained a new friend, a grandfather waiting to hear from Linda whether he might have TB. Kasigluk was the Yupik name for Kalskag and the mountain behind it (denoted as "Hamilton" on the map). It's a clicky language, heavy on the K's. The sun rose and set at nearly the same point on the horizon in January and the runway needed to be roughened with a scraper after plowing; the ice underneath got so slick planes skidded while landing, as ours had. His generation did the most drinking, he added, because, at fifty, they couldn't either try cutting the mustard at the University of Alaska in Fairbanks, or still draw much satisfaction from knowing where the bears and beavers were holed up: ancestral knowledge among a people, as well as the bears and beavers, enabled a judicious harvest, like the bottlenecks that caribou were sometimes driven into, if there were hunters enough.

"Yes," a retired couple in the vestibule agreed: a storekeeper and his wife, a former health aid, who had arrived from Minnesota in the 1960s (she still used the term "thrush" for sore throats). A young purist in hand-sewn parka and mukluks hiking thirty miles to drag back antlered meat instead of going to the grocery store was not likely to win the heart of the modern Yupik girl, with typing and bookkeeping skills, who wanted to work in Bethel's offices, not sew mukluks. "But it was like the Fourth of July around here for a while," the man said. "And not just the gunshots. People were beating on their wives with gaff hooks and shotgun stocks." It had been a siege of frustration detonated by the whites' moonwalk, but didn't subside until a brave schoolteacher started photographing the women's contusions and tape-recording their accounts.

The granddad nodded affirmatively that it was awful, before sliding into stories about trekking from his trapline on Whitefish Lake after his snow machine broke down. Dogs were better than a Ski-Doo—you learned that in the end—even small dogs. "Look like scrub dogs but can pull on top of a crust of snow" that big dogs punched through. Dogs were dependable, as a carburetor wasn't, and his sharpest regrets, as we talked, were of "disposing of" dogs that, in his inexperience, he shouldn't have: once, a wonderfully spunky smart short-hair he was too ignorant to realize could survive the climate here, although, on other men's dog teams, he later saw its littermates did. And worse, once his whole dog team—he was sick for weeks after shooting them. "Lots of fish to catch if you have dogs. A fish a day each dog eats, even if you've decided not to use them—use the three-wheeler or the Ski-Doo instead. And in a high-water summer you maybe got no fish. Too much rain sent them around your nets." Or if there's *no* rain, the river soon becomes so clear the fish can see the nets sufficiently to avoid them. He said somebody had invented a boat with sled runners on the bottom, so you could motor upriver to your trapping camp with your heavy supplies before freeze-up, and come back with your furs under dog power on the ice. During a blizzard, he said, you can either cover up and suffocate or open your hood to breathe, and freeze. Then dogs are good as blankets.

CHAPTER 6

• • •

The Kusko 300

L INDA'S ASSIGNMENT HAPPENED TO COINCIDE with the annual "Kusko 300" dog mushers race. Three hundred miles, forty-four teams this year, many with over a thousand miles of training runs behind them. They started Wednesday, January 19th, at noon from Bethel, and eleven hours later, the pacesetters could be expected to reach Kalskag, en route to Aniak, the halfway point, where they would turn around. We'd already watched the televised, tails-up launch of the teams, yodeling out of a double-barreled chute, jostling, jockeying with one another, sometimes hauling a tire behind the sled, or with an extra man riding on it for a mile or two to slow them down until the driver got them, not snapping at a rival bunch but pulling seriously, under control. A shortage of snow diverted the race at first from the Kuskokwim's bare ice to some adjoining tundra for a dozen miles. Getting to Aniak ahead of everybody else would win the leader a thousand dollars, plus a thousand pounds of kibble. First prize for returning to Bethel was five thousand dollars; second, four thousand; third, three; down to two hundred for the twentieth; half the entry fee of a hundred would be refunded to anyone who managed to finish at all. Seven dogs constituted the minimum, although some teams had twice that many yanking the sled, and at least five must manage to finish.

The TV commentary, in both English and Yupik, was soon displaced by *Sesame Street* again, but like the rest of Kalskag, we stayed up until the wee hours, whiling away the evening with Bingo, to watch the silent files of dogs begin to appear about one a.m., escorted by hefty, quiet men wearing miners' headlamps on ear-flapped hats and bunny boots, who blundered around under the quarter-moon to figure out where they were supposed to tie their dogs, aligning their sleds for a quick departure, and report to the referees. Kalskag's own pinioned dogs announced all of this hullabaloo raucously, but not the tired newcomers, who flopped down in place to cool their mouths with snow. Many mushers had prepositioned dog food and supplementary gear at this waypoint as a hundred-mile rest stop, meeting friends perhaps. But the very first driver had materialized inconspicuously, registered the feat at the officials' tent with a minimum of time-wasting fuss, obtained warm drinking water, and moved out as soon as the vet had inspected the condition of his dogs, intending to feed and water them and catnap more privately somewhere up the trail, motivating them not with a whip but by just jingling a food pan. One of the few natives competing, he was a Koyukon from the village of Huslia on the Koyukuk River named George Attla, who was used on several health department posters as a hero to his people, the subject of a documentary, "Spirit of the Wind," and therefore a target of resentment among the racist whites.

Other front-runners brewed up individual menus of cooked chicken, moose meat, salmon, with kibble and water for each dog in their string of eight or nine. They could drop off any one of them that might have developed "strawberry foot" and wasn't pulling, to be airlifted back to Bethel. But since Linda was the only health-care professional for human beings who chanced to be in town, she was thankful not to be called upon. Apparently these men had conditioned themselves for jogging three hundred miles in three days behind a sled, because when anybody rode, his team pulled slower. The gliding headlamps, steaming breath, bulging parkas shifting among the fagged-out teams, too tired to wag a tail or bark at other packs, included men swaddled in their bedrolls beside a sled, or guys telling friends who had flown in for moral support about an inopportune encounter with a moose on the trail that had riled the dogs, or an icy overflow where the Tuluksak River came in that got everybody who wasn't paying attention wet. In people's kits were Coleman stoves for warming the team's water, or individual booties for dogs that had a history of cutting their paws—all tended like a high school coach helping his players.

The school building, with central heating and public toilets, was a popular resort, like the red-painted log hut that functioned as town hall. Officials feeding the beacon fires on the riverbank or register-ing and assisting racers warmed up there, distributing Purina Hi-Pro from the treasury of the stuff stacked in the jail. On Main Street and the outdoor basketball court, tethered teams were recouping: and not in a Jack London scene. No fights, and the best pulled from fine spirits like racehorses or dogs hunting and herding, not fear. A group of six friends had arrived in a span of twenty minutes around four a.m. and puttered together in the warmth of the check-in tent, then hand-fed tidbits to their lead dogs as if this were a high point of the year for them, and, as in a big-city marathon, just finishing would be okay. A tempestuous wind had bowled over sleds and dogs on several naked stretches of the Kuskokwim beyond Lwethiuk and, marshaling their collective wits, they were "glad to get here!" One had "lost a dog" on this first leg, however, and would be penalized if she didn't turn up. She had gone lame; he'd "put her in the basket" on his sledge but the sled hit a rock later on and flipped over, throwing her out, which so terrified her that she darted off.

Twin-hitched, the dogs weren't especially furry or husky: more parti-colored, with reliable moxie, and included a few Labrador and Chesapeake retrievers. They weren't weight-haulers. After all, the Iditarod race, almost four times as long but the template for these contests, commemorated a 1925 dogsled dash to Nome from the An-chorage area, delivering diphtheria medication, when speed and not bulk was the point; a hundred miles a day had become the norm for those racers, too. Another guy had lost his team for two hours when he was thrown off the sled and the dogs ran away. When he finally caught up by following their tracks, a swing dog had been killed in a fight. He was exhausted already from breaking trail a good ways for a new lead bitch. They looked less chastened; stood curiously sniffing Kalskag's carnival of activity or rolled on their backs because of the harness's chafing. Each sled was standardized, three feet high at the handlebars, with a canvas sling full of dog food, sleeping bag, axe, and emergency pack in between. The vet examined the dead dog, as well as a live one with a mitt on a scabbed foot, but decided to let him continue along the four-hour rush to Aniak. In a few years, women would be entering and winning these races, including the Iditarod, by employing a gentler rapport with the dogs. But now the creatures curled their tails between their legs when handled and stared into their masters' headlamps as into the eyes of god.

Linda and I had been invited to sleep in a retired schoolteacher's cottage in order to free up the school. Since I was a little sick from my helpings of Eskimo ice cream at Vassily's party, I wasn't an ideal guest, but the lady, a widow, seemed willing to overlook that for the fun of talking about books; had even read my last. She owned a small, select library of classics, a woodpile abundantly replenished for a pittance, and the drama of arctic skies—auroras, the sun's daily flirtation from the south, the matchless stars. Via polar routes, it was a budget hop to Kyoto or Covent Garden. I didn't know her circumstances, but her retirement on-site beside this major river where she had worked, instead of to a climate like California's, did not seem forced. No grizzly skins hung on her wall, or other baggage from hackneyed scripts that send people to Alaska for a spell, hugging themselves to keep warm and on the phone during their off-time, then home with chuckling anecdotes that everybody can perceive are uneasy. She was completing a life choice.

At the town hall, coffee and sandwiches were on offer, and a radio room for the racers. *Tundra Drum*, the river's newspaper, was on sale, and in the general store more cans of Crisco, for further celebration. "Don't blame me if you get sick," the archpriest had told me; and I didn't. The second night was louder because the dogs' owners hadn't pushed them so strenuously perhaps, or something had gone wrong. The man might have pulled a muscle or somehow gotten their heads turned around. Yipping, yapping, lonely single dogs were being dropped from their teams on doctor's orders. The Anchorage vet's stethoscope had diagnosed a pulmonary edema at this point; or for a frozen teat, a shoulder strain, "no more feet," "burnt out." They howled forlornly in their crates for the team to come back for them, but most drivers had started with a surplus so they could officially abandon one or two. To do it unsanctioned on the trail meant being penalized by an hour.

"Are you keeping a vigil?" an Eskimo woman teased me, who was watching a diet program on TV instead. The principal from Oklahoma was telling muleback, squirrel-hunting yarns to a Norwegian couple who were in town adventuring. We suppered with them, laughing because white dogs were also called "Gussucks." The first day, the winds had blown at fifty miles an hour on the treeless fifty-mile stretch of tundra out of Bethel. Some of the lead dogs had just wanted to quit, dive underneath the snow. But now, January 21st began warming so fast, certain creeks unfroze and overflowed, with blockages soon soaking the snow covering the river ice, to complicate the route by forcing a detour. Although the one famous Indian, George Attla, was entered, these hectic stopwatch rallies, purposeless except as competition, were unrelated to the real rhythm of the season—the stop-start of winter traplines, with sets checked and re-baited, and then the yearly balance of moving to Spring Camp, when subsistence people left their winter huts for the marshlands, as the first migrating waves of ducks and geese were flying in from the south and muskrats emerging from under the thawing ice. After all the sawing and boiling scraps off a rooftop moose—more fresh duck than you could eat! And succulent black bears came out of hidden hibernation to gorge on wetland greens, on which moose also descended from the higher pitches where they wintered to feed. Fresh too, salads, needless to say. Fish Camp followed, on the rivers, for the monumental salmon run; and Berry Camp in the fall, where the women, from tents or shanties, filled baskets with the winter's sweeteners, while their husbands stalked any wildlife fattening on the same bushy slopes. This kind of cyclical packing or sledding which the natives' dogs did in moving camp—hauling necessities or hunks of game around—was different from the racers' concentration. A future Iditarod champion I knew on the Yukon was feeding his team on other dogs he'd chainsawed up, after shooting them because they weren't pulling hard enough on practice runs, or dead dogs he bought from the Indians for a dollar apiece—the Indians ran teams of their own but considered what he was doing "bad medicine," a value system to leave alone.

Before the clang and clash of mining equipment, the donkey engines, and steamboats on the arteries, people who were skimming silently downstream in a bark canoe, a skin boat, or a dugout saw much more wildlife, including sometimes the "Hairy Men" or "Wild People," who had kinky hair four to six inches long and left tracks in the snow or tundra moss seventeen inches long by four inches across (thus "Bigfoot")—remarkably narrow, but blunt-toed, not with the claws marked out in front, like a grizzly bear's. And if they stole from your fish camp, they did so neatly, almost "politely," lifting the latch and taking a row or two of filets from the smokehouse without smashing and slathering everything else with claw rips and bite scars, like a bear. The ancestors of the interior Yupik Eskimos living here when the Russians arrived reportedly had been ousted from the Kobuk River area, to the north, and driven south by Inupiat Eskimos raiding down from the North Slope coast and themselves pushing out, in turn, the local Tuluksak bands. While crossing the Yukon to reach this less desirable haven of the Kuskokwim, they'd had to fight as well, of course, the natives living there—arrows flying between flotillas of canoes—after concealing all their children in meat caches near the bank so they wouldn't be kidnapped or killed. A recent battle almost started again when a boy from the Kuskokwim, in throwing a stone, put out the eye of a Yukon boy. The second boy's clan wanted him turned over to them so they could gouge out *his* eye. Eskimos mad enough at a white man may call him "Spitface," because he's so pale, and an estimated half of the Yupiks on the Kuskokwim died in an epidemic that swept through in 1838–39 as a result of their early contact with the Russians.

It took forty-eight hours for a bump on people's arms to indicate exposure to TB, so that's why we hung around the towns so long, or else needed to drop in again. Except for the Oklahoman, who chewed tobacco, folks here sucked at a lump of snuff held under the lower lip, and carried a coffee can around to spit into. The Norwegian couple had gone fishing with a schoolteacher for pike and blackfish in Kukaklek Lake and Hooking Creek, about fifteen miles toward the Yukon's complexities. We went instead to look at Kalskag's cemetery, attractively planted with paper birches and a handsome spruce. But a raw brown mound of dirt covered the coffin of a recent suicide, who would be properly buried after the ground thawed in the spring. In the meantime his poor mom had laid a ladder of hothouse flowers on him, and a Russian cross had been planted by the archpriest.

We watched the tails of the returning teams, like flags, and listened to their claws clack on the street's icy crust. Having run at least a hundred-ninety of the three hundred miles by now, looping around Whitefish Lake after the town of Aniak in order to add some extra distance before starting downstream, they had braved a whiteout windstorm on that side trail without getting lost. The best drivers groomed alternative leaders for a team, sometimes paired together in the front, or else vying to be permitted a turn. For instance, he might have a "Go Home" dog, older, smarter, though slower, for the most puzzling, dark-hour stretches; a "Chasing Leader," for catching up with rival dog teams ahead; or a "Trail Leader," for breaking passages through deep-drift slogs and divining where the route should wind during a blizzard. In what could start as a fourteen-dog hitch, they wanted power dogs and speed critters, which would be whittled down at checkpoints as conditions changed. Heavy-coated northern dogs layered with fat were not so suited to the milder turn the temperature was taking now.

The leader was expected to counter with all his strength any break in discipline if the team crossed paths with a rabbit or a moose, and right behind him or her in the gangline were the "swing" dogs, younger, tireless, dependably enthusiastic, and perhaps potential lead dogs themselves or leaders who had been rotated back for a spell. Harnessed just ahead of the sled were two "wheel dogs," muscular pullers expected to brace and brake with their weight the tendency of a sled to skid sideways on a turn, and between the swing dogs and wheel dogs, the "team dogs" were hitched, the most expendable. "Hike," "Gee," "Haw," and "Whoa" were the basic commands ("Hike" being "Left"), and since we had about seven hours of serviceable daylight, most of the contest was waged by headlamp for the humans.

What the dogs scented throughout I don't know, but, after sixty-five hours—six less than the previous year—the affair ended bitterly in Bethel when the Indian entrant, George Attla, hero of the documentary, appeared to have been gypped out of victory by a cabal of white businessmen. Once again, Attla had slipped through Kalskag as efficiently as possible, not lingering in the hubbub where he might be subjected to subtle subversion or the racism of whites sniggering about sled runners broken by "niggerheads" (tussocks) in the swamps. Several mushers had got lost in the blowing snow, and now thirty-five dogs were dropped for evacuation in Kalskag. One man was rumored to have died of blood in his lungs in Aniak. Because Alaska is a place for jacks-of-all-trades, quick studies and fixes, other racers, too, skipped the *Qasgiq*, or bathhouse, and camped unseen to keep the opposition guessing, or judged the breaks their dogs needed idiosyncratically and how much food and water to put into each.

Jingling a bell, Attla had roused his team—he had a limp now, but a chief's asceticism, and stood in front of them clapping his hands to sharpen their attention, make sure they knew it was *them* that were starting next—and left town munching a pick-me-up, as on his first pass-through, then stole some shut-eye down the trail. But on his return leg, a hustling lawyer from Bethel—the best of that bunch—was on his heels, wielding a four-foot whip, having closed an hour's gap. The passage of the Alaska Native Claims act, which was perceived as a giant Washington giveaway by numerous local whites, had exacerbated resentments, much as the civil rights laws of the sixties had activated biases in the South, it seemed to me, although the history being ameliorated was shorter here and less scabrous, the bigotries looser, and the emollient such a flow of money that masses of it reached white hands, too. Attla, chunky and self-contained, with no entourage or changes of dogs, departing under the radar by jingling a bell or a food pan, without beatings or bonhomie, was uppity enough to need stopping.

And that became the nub of the controversy. After covering the three hundred miles in sixty-five hours, George Attla entered the town of Bethel a little in the lead. But the hometown lawyer, after dogging him closely for the last fifty-three miles from Tuluksak, suddenly broke their long joint silence by yelling wildly and cracking his whip—itself the length of a dog—with a popper on the end, eight or a dozen times. He hadn't let Attla see or hear the whip before or smell the fear aroused by it in Attla's team, so they shied, lost their stride, cowered, thought the race must be over and this banshee stranger about to punish them. In the dark, at six a.m., he crossed the finish line ahead of Attla by fifteen seconds; and all appeals to fairness afterward failed.

Hail the conquering attorney—in the white bars of this spraddled-out "Hub of the Delta," paper-pushing, prefab town of four thousand, still a hundred miles in from the actual sea, with its hospital the largest building. The temperature had risen above freezing, so thawing creeks entering the river had flooded its ice with water a foot deep for the last twenty miles, washing away the trail markers that had been set out. Many drivers got lost. Clarence Towarak told us his headlamp battery had burned out, and we watched Gus Chocknock trudge into Brown's Slough, registered as twelfth, with his nine dogs pulling like Cinderella's mice hitched to the fabled pumpkin, at seventy hours and fifty minutes. Snogos crisscrossed the river and slough, cheering on the fagged-out files of dogs as they appeared and flopped down, sometimes trying to hide underneath the timbers of a bridge in case there was further running to do.

We'd flown to Bethel on a workhorse Otter, over the braided river channels and vast expanse of tundra. Our Albanian taxi driver—seven months in town after a stint in Chicago—said he made two hundred dollars a day because most people arriving had no car and needed him for their appointments and then the bars. Trailer parks and erector-set housing units, known by their colors or numerals—"Red," or "3"—stood about. A subdivision was called "Subdivision," with "high-dollar" houses on pilings or stilts. Another was just named "Housing," because it was the state employees' housing, or more formally, "The Silver Corral," for the bulging, insulated interlacing of sewer, water, and steam pipes elbowed to surround the residences above ground. There was a Greek restaurant, a pizza parlor, the airstrip's hamburger joint, a health-food emporium called Ma's Place, and Swanson's department store, with a McSwanson's for lunch, and Swanson's Theatre for movies attached. Tundra Ridge and Ptarmigan Ridge were gravel roads cutting off the middle class from rowdy downtown bars or the tarpaper, plywood, and sheetmetal shacks of "Lousetown" on the riverbank, where many natives lived, next to a "retaining wall" of junked automobiles and trucks. And federal people, with Interior Department pickups to plug into the electrical hookups that kept the engines warm, lived in Quonset structures at "White Alice," an old Dew Point radar station, such as dotted the north, pointing toward Russia, each resembling a chatty-looking semi-circle of concave drive-in movie screens.

Telephone and TV disks or dishes rendered communication ubiquitous: "Did you copy? Ten-Four. Roger and out." A man called Tony and his friend told us about white girlfriends they had in Juneau, to match their Eskimo girls here. But people with the wherewithal were in Hawaii now. Five minutes of sunlight was being added every day, so eventually they'd come back to convert the ski planes we saw parked in Brown's Slough to float planes and fly up the Yukon collecting fresh salmon from fish camps for freight pilots to loft to Seattle, San Francisco, or wherever. But the "Yellow Submarine," a low maw of a prefab, ochre-and-blue, windowless-looking building whose entrance ramps were like an airline terminal's, where you came as if for intergalactic launch, was dominant, and the hospital. Several trailers nearby furnished pre-natal shelter for Indian and Eskimo mothers, due by and by. Ample Mormon and Moravian churches sat on pilings above the permafrost, whereas the Roman Catholic mission was small and ramshackle like a Third World outposting. Individual fundamentalist preachers had also thrown up preaching rooms of logs, with driftwood stoves, but St. Sophia's Russian Orthodox Church unpretentiously served most of the gray-green Eskimo huts in the slum alongside Brown's Slough.

We were going to sleep on a futon on the floor of a nurse's trailer, after she and Linda hashed over countless stories of low-level bureaucratic dysfunction, sexism, injustice, or squanderings. I'd been repeatedly impressed by the kindness of these idealistic district nurses in charmless administrative centers—their offices or cubicles diced into a hangar-like structure—whose heartstrings, however, were tied out in villages whose cultural spine related to sheefish runs, caribou or walrus migrations, ducks molting and thus unable to fly, or celestial light shows in the solstice sky. The map on the wall would be pocked with needy localities such as Quinhagak, Tuntutuliak, Akolmiut, Kongiganak, Kwigillingok, where their power, amounting to life-or-death, might be abruptly daunting. The solitude, cold—freezing a corpse as stiff as a brick—and dark left you no downtime, not even a beer joint. And would Bethel's Moravian orphanage be a better situation for a marginally abused child than the fraying social web of her home village? This was not officially a nurse's responsibility, but outside visits were so infrequent, as a practical matter it could become so. And where English was a second language, the child might not be able to answer questions privately, or even follow instructions for a hearing test. You needed to watch for physical signals, like an eyebrow's twitch. And could you stand being hated?

Nancy, the top public health nurse, plump and competent, a bridge player and conscientious community activist, was leaning toward a Third World career but in the meantime living in a trailer with a Kuskokwim guy she called Arthur Fox. She sewed mouton fur inside her wolf ruff to keep the guard hairs off her face and sometimes wore a Yupik "kuspuk," a bright-colored dress, over jeans, with kangaroo pockets in front and rick-rack trim on the sleeves, pouches, and hem. In her car with clattering chains, she drove us to race head- quarters, which smelled richly of dog food. The dropped dogs from Kalskag, Aniak, Tuluksak, etc, had been flown to the children's play yard of the Bethel Day Care Center. Her accent was "a packrat's," she said, combining the hillbilly "pitcher" with the highfalutin' "baath," and, like Linda, preferred assignments to villages such as Wainwright, pop. four hundred, on the Arctic Ocean above the seventieth parallel, where taking a half-hour break from testing for TB, she could stroll along the beach, gazing north into polar and pelagic mysteries. Walk- ing on the roof of the world for Linda was a long way from being a C.I.A. agent's daughter skipping Sunday mass with her brother for a doughnut shop, or that first nursing job, in a drug rehab clinic in New York. So intently did she peer toward the north that an Eskimo woman might emerge from a cabin to ask if she'd spotted a polar bear for her son to come out and shoot.

CHAPTER 7

• • •

Of Eagles and Millionaires

W E FLEW BACK TO ANCHORAGE and our basement nest on "L"
Street, from which to issue forth and hear visitors like Andre
Watts or Jerry Falwell or Ronald Reagan's Secretary of the Interior,
James Watt, always smiling like a Cheshire cat. I was interviewing
supple oil company executives and earnest conservation advocates. An
oil man sought to screw me, until I had him to dinner with Linda,
but nevertheless was too wary to allow me onto one of his company's
planes flying to Prudhoe Bay, sensing I wouldn't be a friendly witness.
Yet the wide avenues and glassy office buildings were sky-rich in all
directions, with seagulls and freighters in the foreground and 10,000-
foot mountains east and west. Not a climate where you would want
to sleep in your car, but in the spring, wood frogs sang in a glen a few
blocks from where we lived. Closer than that new millionaires presumably were being minted, because we smelled a scent like crabmeat
issuing from a small processing plant where factory-ship fish were being imbued with it—a scent later everywhere in "seafood salad" at deli
counters all over. The nearest movie house didn't even bother turning
on its marquee lights before its single evening showings, the owner
was so confident of his audience. Although the 1940s screen was narrow and low, the carpeting had Tiffany lampshade patterns and the
walls murals of log trucks, gold panning, trestles and sluiceways, dogsleds, and the Big Dipper winking at the North Star on the ceiling.

I was interviewing millionaires for the New York magazine *Vanity Fair*—shopping mall or television station developers—as a means

of seeing Linda and a handy avenue for inquiries, while she tabulated the hundred statewide TB cases at her office (up from eighty the previous year, negligently treated patients from the past having suffered flare-ups again). Anchorage, growing at five to fifteen percent a year, was approaching a quarter-million people, ten times the size of Juneau, the nominal capital, which is glacier-hung with steep pretty streets descending to either the Gastineau Channel or a hemlock rainforest, and plank stairs leading up to small brightly painted clapboard houses. Anchorage was, by contrast, the place with growing room for boosterism, where Connie Yoshimura, for example, could arrive from Webster City, Iowa, in her thirties "with a funny name" and no previous real estate or selling experience, "except waitressing," and in seven years be closing deals on ten or fifteen house purchases per month, even winning a national retail brokers' association award. Now she was negotiating to buy Dynamic Realty, across Northern Lights Boulevard from a Computerland, a Robo-Wash carwash, a power substation, and the Northern Lights Motor Inn, with mountains upright at the end.

I'd gotten Connie's name from Gary Holthaus, director of Alaska's Humanities programs, but because he didn't know her except through the publicity surrounding her prize, she sized me up as she might have any new customer walking through the door—money, persona, class, or type—until I told her by way of introduction that my most recent job had been teaching in the University of Iowa's Writers' Workshop, where she herself had earned an MFA a decade before—studying with the likes of Kurt Vonnegut and marrying a fellow student. Keying to me then, she said she was lately divorced for the second time and had lost a hundred-fifteen pounds with the help of hypnotherapy and a twelve-step group. Her Japanese-American face was attractively confidence-building and she said that since her waitressing tips had depended upon rapport and giving advice that panned out, her schooling had begun in restaurants, but the novel writing courses too had been a help. A constant stream of strangers appeared, asking you to put yourself in their shoes, after at most a phone call. What to show them and in which neighborhood, after calculating, on your side of the desk, what sort of financial worth they truly could call on, their honesty, the chemistry of their marriage, stability of their psyche, or what the loan officer down at the bank would think of their prospects, not to mention whether they were just angling for a free drive-around?

After appraising Linda and her relationship to me when I'd been dropped off, she now suggested that women's economic independence must precede their social independence. In leaving her Alaska husband, she'd been able to check straight into a lofty suite at the Captain Cook Hotel; no need to ask for any money from him, no delays, humiliation or immediate lawyering. And she loved to shop, as a hobby, preferring department stores for their time-efficiency, or to wing off to Hawaii for three- or four-day weekends "to get warm" in the winter, rather than indulge in a single, longer vacation that would break her stride. She'd rarely been out to "the bush" or even Fairbanks, which was too cold and provincial, and only once to Juneau, "and that was on the ferry"—yet loved Alaska for its business opportunities. People here had uprooted themselves to begin with, which created lots of turnover, like the high North Slope wages— blue-collar pipe fitters who had never made nearly so much before, yet were away from house and home, up at Prudhoe Bay, most of the time, so didn't necessarily bond with the property they'd bought, like folks "Outside." They might never have had a regular home or close family ties earlier in life, but now, rolling in all this oil-boom dough, could move in or out, trade up or down.

Connie had hired a young woman to assist her and spoke obsessively of success (although she still had a novel "on the back burner"), yet not off-puttingly because she also confessed how it was "so very isolating. True friendships take time to develop," and by definition she hadn't the time. It was awfully easy to stick in her office till seven or eight, eating ninety percent of her meals in restaurants. The goal for the future should be "to become as comfortable in my personal relationships as I am behind my desk." Anger and unhappiness had pushed her into business. "Anger motivated me; no one wanted to hire me"—fat and a woman with a funny last name, raised by her mother's parents, her father a Nisei. Everyone has tragedies, she said; most success is motivated by unhappiness, but with her ex-husband in Seattle and no present ties, she felt hers were behind her, each year was easier now, the anger over. Hotels treated her well as a businesswoman (though, characteristically, airline stewardesses in first-class did not; they still wanted to wait on men), and whereas she used to resent people with inherited wealth, now she felt problems in common with them—the having money and holding onto it—no begrudgement. "And the more successful you are, the more privacy you have; people stop calling at home at night." In a state where people drive up the Alcan Highway impromptu and penniless, anybody rich, anyway, was first-generation rich.

With her black hair cut efficiently back from her face into a pageboy bob, her expression was not habitually severe, but focused. She said she'd been a perennial student or hippie, with hangdog hair and sack dresses, attempting forays into Colorado and California post-Iowa, but "never knowing how I would make a living." Her ex-husband "thought I could sell," and when she found she could, "you might as well sell big ticket items as little ones." Her first wish was to score a fast million, then quit to write, but of course now making much more than that "necessarily changes you—it's too much fun to want to stop." Her 510 "L" Street was the best condo address in the city, she said, and she could hardly get over going home, after the summer's daily frenzy of sales, walking to the building's elevator in the soft, lingering light. As we swiveled our chairs in her functional office, she conceded, sure, there was prejudice against females in business here, as anywhere, but with such a fast pace and scarcity of serious competition you broke those barriers, including with bankers, the last male bastion. Selling individual houses had long been accepted as a feminine prerogative, but if you wanted to subdivide, build on, develop properties in this "tip of the iceberg" of what was going to happen in Anchorage, it was an edgier role and stepping on toes. Yet the harsh climate demanded the firm work ethic and orientation that Midwesterners like her had carried up with them, whereas Californians, who were also swarming north, didn't recognize work as central in the same way.

The burgeoning skyline of major-company office towers encouraged her—"I assume Bunker Hunt knows things I don't"—and she invested her own assets only locally, where she could be on the scene, and hedging her bets with rental properties that would deliver income regardless of where mortgage rates went. Salesmanship, she told me, was founded upon "product knowledge combined with a basic understanding and compassion for people." Thus, selling was "an intellectual process in which you provide knowledge to a customer," except that you needed to pick your client, not devoting the same time to a guy thinking of marrying his sweetie in six months as to newlyweds already furniture shopping. The fundamental principle she wanted to stress was that "everyone is a very lonely person inside, no matter how many friends or family they seem to have around." So treat them with consideration.

"But you must be packaged correctly," especially a woman, and especially if of equivocal ethnicity, as to your car, clothing, brief-case, and accessories, and especially on your way up. "Later, people expect you to be eccentric" and maybe wear a red dress and colored stockings instead of a quiet suit, and drive what you want, but for now "your car is your office," so she kept her Mercedes in the garage except for Sunday afternoons and drove a beige and blue Buick station wagon—good selling colors, like the beige blouse and blue skirt she wore for customers. (For our appointment, a gray open-collared dress with black stripes.) She'd read *Dress for Success* and *Live for Success*, much-ballyhooed books that "Help people from the lower socio-economic levels with their speech patterns, posture, office arrangements." And education, she said, was crucial for a woman because she couldn't work her way up from being a sheet-rock guy, plumber, or carpenter, as so many male movers and shakers had. Nor could you date your blue-collar employees, like men did their secretaries, even marrying them or a showgirl without blowing themselves out of the water. Although Alaskans prided themselves on not judging a man by his clothes, women execs were watched much more closely for faux pas; had to be chary. Connie belonged to the Tower Club, the Commonwealth North Club, and the Captain Cook Athletic Club, but preferred privacy for negotiations—was a "private person, a neutral figure" to her customers, privy to their finances, and so didn't want to meet them at dinner parties where you'd have to watch your mouth—preferred working to schmoozing at social functions, where you ran the risk of overexposure—and, learning from her own vulnerabilities and unhappy periods, wore her fur coat when chatting with a bank president, but not the junior loan officer drawing up the actual papers. In 1979 she had racked up four million dollars in total sales; in 1980 nine million; in 1981 seventeen million; in 1982 fourteen million; in 1983 twenty-two million, which won the realty prize.

• • •

"A rising tide floats all boats," Bob Penney explained to me over drinks at the Crows Nest, atop the Captain Cook, which was built on fifteen or twenty feet of Bootlegger's Cover Clay, which had turned virtually liquid when jarred by the city's 1964 8.5 magnitude earthquake, but the city fathers nevertheless rebuilt along the same grabens and faults with money from "Big Uncle" Sam. Three years later, a Tanana River flood inundated parts of Fairbanks and enabled *them* to live on the dole too, for a while; and by 1969, nine hundred million dollars was beginning to pour into Alaska for the North Slope oil leases; then by the mid-1970s the geyser of eight billion or so required to construct the oil fields and eight-hundred-mile pipeline to transport the stuff south to the refurbished, all-weather port at Valdez, flushing good wages throughout the economy and providing eighty-five percent of state revenues via oil royalties, etc, which obviated the need for income or sales taxes.

Bob had arrived in 1951 as a forklift operator, then a used-trailer salesman ("That was the housing in those days."), till he began borrowing money to lease land from the state and subdivide it into the Penland Mobile Home Park. Now he had the $35 million Northway Mall and was building a $65 million one. "Sure, I'm making a lot of money screwing up Alaska," as he admitted good-humoredly. But his son and his friends were going to make lots cleaning it up again. Like most developers, he had wilderness cabins he owned or could borrow tucked away under mountains that you could pilot a pontoon plane to for steelhead fishing. In fact, he generously invited me along for an outing, offering to provide me with a girl, too, if I wanted one. Fairbanks, in particular, boasts a Chicago-like, second-city, plunger's or miner's sort of pride in its impulsive spirit. But even taking the place as a whole, one-third of arrivals in Alaska would leave before two years were out, and another third by the end of five, so it could be wobbly to try to define who Alaskans were. Many a newbie drawn by the wage base would tell you the American Dream had already failed him elsewhere, and one young woman whose husband had left her "as soon as we bought the house" because "he liked somebody better" told me she was "going out with three guys named Bob."

The quickie beards grown like a dirty muffler to wrap around the neck and ward off mosquitoes, blurred age and identity, but on a row of bar stools could look like a gallery of nineteenth-century presidents grouped for a photo op—Rutherford B. Hayes, William Henry Harrison, James A. Garfield, and of course William McKinley, come to visit his mountain. Sly smiles or weak chins were covered up, and the beards could make friends look like strangers, or vice versa, though the sign in the window remained blunt. Instead of "No Unescorted Women," it declared *No Prostitutes*. Although a Santa Claus beard looks kind, at the George M. Sullivan Sports Arena one night the white-bearded master of ceremonies didn't announce that a lost child named Karen had turned up; he simply said, "We have a three-year-old with a broken arm." On the popcorn machine a note was scrawled: "No $100 bills changed."

While people don't wear their income on their backs in Anchorage, a C.P.A., settling in, will tell you at a party, "I want to live in a palace." Otherwise living here might constitute "a postponement." A savvily personable jeweler, thirtyish, who'd arrived eight years before with a hundred bucks in his pocket, was doing so well he had just quadrupled his office space and bought a new condominium, in spite of a spell spent in jail for a drug conviction, but when inviting us to his housewarming, fumbled reciting the directions: "I just moved, I don't know the address." Even if eschewing a side trade in drugs, an arctic jewelry business had these international polar flights refueling many times a day, carrying people with gemstones in money belts around their midriffs, not to mention the prospectors emerging by the dozen out of the bush around freeze-up with knotty nuggets squirreled into a poke that they sure didn't wish to sell through official channels. The Union Oil Company's glass office tower reflected a peculiarly dyspeptic oily glint in front of the surplice-white Chugach Range, but we joked about the family that lived in a modest frame house across from ARCO's beige skyscraper headquarters with the caribou or reindeer penned in their front yard.

Though military planes, private planes, bush planes, and commercial airliners circled the city, waiting for landing slots, a railroad engineer might wave to us as he slid through a downtown crossing. Alaska's coastline is so convoluted it constitutes half of America's, and this splendid profusion of geography—Katmai, Kenai, Ketchikan,

Kobuk, Kodiak, Koyukuk, to name a few salient "K's"—draws not only tourists but so many eagles, for instance, that I picked up a four-foot feather in front of the governor's mansion in Juneau to take back to New York and wear in my hat. Although the oilmen were rotated in and out so frequently by Sohio, British Petroleum, Exxon, Arco, Chevron, and other power players that when you talked to them their eyes were fixed on an office clock that showed Houston time, as they waited for instructions, Alaska "might get its hooks into them," as Bob Penney put it, to the point where they turned down that next posting to Jakarta, Oslo, or Angola in favor of peering under the engine housing of a Cessna on weekends for a fishing flight to Yakutat. Suppers at Elevation 92, while gazing across Knick Arm at Mounts Spur and Susitna, or down fifteen miles to the furry Bird House, on Turnagain Arm—low-roofed, much mauled by the earthquake twenty years before, but whose décor consisted entirely of female customers' panties and bras thumbtacked in festoons to the ceiling and walls, as if to emphasize how Alaskans like to boast they started from scratch, whether while nursing a muffler-less pickup up the Alaska Highway or shouldering a duffel off the ferry from Bellingham— were provisional. Governor Wally Hickel claimed he'd only thirty-seven cents to his name, and Governor Bill Sheffield, a TV repairman on arrival, were no better off than Bob Penney, now fifty-one, who was a night watchman at a lumberyard and fork-lifted in the daytime, after leaving Oregon at eighteen. Anchorage had twenty-five thousand residents and two paved roads. Then he'd inserted some stores into his fledgling Penland trailer park, which grew to become the Northway Mall, across the street from a new forty-six-acre parcel to accommodate 600,000 square feet of office space and another fifty acres for business development. He was, meanwhile, a prime mover in installing two three-billion-dollar hydroelectric dams in the gorges of the Susitna River. "People will look back and not be able to imagine how we got along without them."

Tall, slender, with sandy hair, blue, challenging eyes, and a scraggly but military-style moustache, Bob flashed a quick, aggressive, salesman-like smile, being known for scattering dollar bills from a helicopter to publicize store openings, yet also owned outlying investment properties in Seward, Fairbanks, and Valdez, a skiing chalet at Alyeska, and a fishing cabin on the Kenai for catching king salmon.

Here in the city he lived at Eighth and "O," on Bootlegger's Cove, and had an office on Blueberry Lake, where he used to shoot ducks. He'd owned eight or nine airplanes altogether by now, had had a pilot's license for a couple of decades, a second marriage nearly as long, and his kids were grown. "Bootstrappers, risk-takers" had enabled Anchorage to expand. His high-roller, late-hours, playfully hard-edged face measured me before offering to rustle me up a woman for the steelhead jaunt to the Yakutat River camp, but he also seemed proud to be employing a lady with a Harvard PhD in French to handle his building permits. From Bootlegger's Cove to Siberia "there are no roads!" he crowed. "Look out at all that space!"

Linda's driving me to these interviews afforded me a skein of respectability, even though I had no car or address at a hotel. She was the reason I'd hustled the assignment from *Vanity Fair*, but nevertheless she sometimes felt like an appendage in town, offended if she felt a rich guy glancing at her like a chauffeur-mistress or travelling-man's girlfriend. Though our politics were similarly leftist, she was more hostile to the selfish rich, seeing little good or interest in them, whereas although I now lived in a public housing project in New York, I'd grown up in an affluent suburb, gone to private schools, and was used to their gradations, incongruities, pretensions, and subtleties. When I included her in an interview, she was likely to listen to the answers to my questions suspiciously, unsympathetically, like a girl from a Roman Catholic, law enforcement background, whose empathy had then switched to the downtrodden—which was apt to stifle confidences. These were climbers, shakers, movers, grabbers, and I'd grown up going to school with the children of an Eastern version of such people.

Bob Uchitel was the next; "semi-retired" at thirty-eight, after selling his cable TV business for around sixty million dollars, who talked to me for three hours after keeping me waiting an hour, at his sumptuous home overlooking the mouth of Turnagain Arm of Cook Inlet, on West Diamond Boulevard, in the Sand Lake District. He had soft brown eyes, chest hair showing Hollywood-style through his half-buttoned shirt, a jutting graying beard, and a short-cut "Jewish Afro." He was "working at playing, auditing the course. Our time should go into investing in memories." He quoted Robert W. Service's "The Spell of the Yukon": *Yet it isn't the gold that I'm wanting*

/ *So much as just finding the gold*. He wanted, for example, to develop a 24-hour TV channel by the turn of the century, programmed by Disney, perhaps, but with the U.N.'s blessing, on which each country would have an hour, in rotation, to show how it lived. Alaskans would "keep their wealth but give away their way of life," and Anchorage become a Global Village, the most international city on earth—a Geneva of the Pacific Rim, with numbered bank accounts, etc. He liked to say with respect to business, "If you can't make it in Alaska you can't make it anywhere. But you must love Alaska, too," he added, meaning the particular conditions. And what *fun* it was to bring in strip malls, trailer courts, housing subdivisions with the basic utilities everywhere. To outfit Anchorage with the conveniences of California wasn't rocket science. As in the Gold Rush, you didn't make money out in the bush, but by supplying infrastructure, groceries, tools, entertainment, constructing an airport, laying cables and wires and a spaghetti of highways. So immediate were the necessities, how could you lose?

Yet since a fifth of Alaska's citizens were Aleuts, Yupiks, Tlingits, Inupiats, or Athabascans, he wanted to tap into that tremendous cultural fount for his concept of a global city, too. He wanted to produce a TV program called *The Earth Speaks To Us*, warning what a brief episode our existence could be, and was helping to finance a ten-hour series called *Voice of the Planet* profiling figures such as Gaia, the mother-goddess, and Pythia, the priestess of Delphi. "Earth is the Planet of Life," the prospectus he showed me began. Nostradamus, the sixteenth-century French soothsayer, also intrigued him, and hyper-logical First Officer Spock, of *Star Trek*, who Bob said spoke for us all, and the Godfather, in *The Godfather*, who, played by Marlon Brando, finally dies peacefully puttering in his garden with his grandson after a life of crime. He himself was investing in a Puerto Rican prizefighter from Spanish Harlem named Hector ("Macho") Camacho, to promote a local bout called "Harlem Bound: Whites Invited Back." (Camacho would go on to win world featherweight and lightweight championships.)

"The difference between 'I can't' and 'I tried' is what's so much fun in life," he said, and had jammed a potpourri of furniture into his grand ranch house, with an "entertainment center," Norman Rockwell commemorative plates on the wall, and a stunning seaward view.

Outdoors, he'd hired a botanist to label the trees and ferns or flowering plants so that he'd know what he owned. His interior decorator, an obliging, pretty young woman named Pam, was at the house performing secretarial duties as well. "Abodes, Castles, Bailiwicks," her card read, when she handed it to me, and she had "gutted the place" in order to redesign it, he announced happily. But when this happened to be her husband's birthday and she wanted to leave a little early, Uchitel wouldn't hear of it. His business partner's birthday was also coming up and he would need some monogrammed jockey shorts with dirty lingo imprinted on them to present to him. She must go to town, choose and fetch them and a sexy card. Job or husband: choose.

The control-freak brutality of the incident I thought might turn off the lady, as she phoned her husband to postpone their plans and left obediently; but apparently not. In Bob Uchitel's obituary in the *Anchorage Daily News* a few years later (dead on the floor, alone, as an unkempt recluse, of a wildly hemorrhaging cocaine-ravaged nose) she was quoted affectionately as saying, "He couldn't make his dreams happen." When he fell into bad shape, she could still feel the old power. It was "like talking to King Lear. It's this man who is raving, but there was this stream of lucidity. To me, he represented the brilliance of Alaska." And he did reel off visionary projects that "should have already" been completed, like a railroad to Siberia, a water viaduct to California. Newcomers "pushed on the brakes," preventing the state from fulfilling its potential with their Lower-48-type zoning and laws. Business should lead, "not politicians who won't talk about what we're going to *be*, through change, only what we want to *have*."

Though he spoke somewhat bitterly of New York and Boston, he'd been born at Doctor's Hospital at 88th Street in Manhattan, gone to Riverdale Country Day School, then prepped at Lawrenceville before entering Boston University—which he quit after breaking a thigh bone and lying painfully in bed for four formative months. When his father, a Russian-born textile merchant who'd manufactured shoulder patches for the army during the war, disowned him at nineteen, "for marrying a woman who caught my eye," Bob found he "was good at two things, people and driving." At his parents' country place in the suburb of Mahopac, there was

a tractor and other machines he wasn't supposed to use, which prepared him for his first independent job—driving a backhoe. He also
worked at the Hammond map store on 43rd Street in the city, fueling
his adventurous itch, and repaired sewing machines at the family's
downtown sweater factory, where the Puerto Rican girls, including
his wife, "got my attention." His father's principal occupation had
become part-ownership of the famous nightclub El Morocco—an
uncle owned the restaurant Voissant—so Bob grew up watching a
lifetime's fill of rich celebrities who acted like shits. He and his wife
escaped west to Missouri, his first new home, where he worked on
farms and roads, till, restless, he called the telephone operator in
West Yellowstone, Montana, for advice about finding a job there.
She mentioned a sawmill; he chatted with them; and the couple set
out in a 1957 Ford, in 1968, for a $2.50-an-hour forklift berth. Dur-
ing the winter he picked up two dollars an hour in the national park
as a snowmobile guide. But by the beginning of 1971, ranger friends
had steered him to Alaska, where he walked around, unzipping his
jacket to figure out how cold "cold" was, or dark "dark" was. Before
making the leap, he tried California, for contrast, for a year during
his first divorce, digging water lines in the slums of Watts and working as a gofer for a producer of wildlife films or a lookout for "sex-
ploitation" movies being shot in the canyons behind Hollywood.
Then, with $1,500 saved, he chose the North, starting as a parts man
for the Caterpillar dealer in Anchorage.

The heavy-machinery operators were better here—tougher in
hairy situations, better mechanics and technicians, and mostly employed near the North Slope installing the pipeline. But Bob hadn't
come for pipeline work. "The pipeline was the only negative I knew,
and like a 4-F Charlie, staying in Anchorage," he fucked the women
left behind by the studs up on the Slope. Instead, he bought a grader
"for finishing-work downtown." Where you had macho dudes bull-
dozing three million cubic yards of dirt, you could earn as much
money as them just smoothing the site nicely afterward. Then from
that he spread out to do the earth-moving too, for roads, sewers, pav-
ing, a bridge or two. "Nothing is impossible. I always seemed to fill a
void. And people may sue me, but I don't sue them." While gunning
to make thirty grand a year, he hauled in $20,000 in his first three
weeks as a corporation. Grossed $250,000 and netted $100,000 that

year. Soon owned forty big machines, a hundred vehicles, counting trucks that he could also lease, and had an aerial attached to his house with which he could monitor by CB radio all the activities of all of these, plus stay cautious financially, as he observed his competitors lose money by "buying jobs," underbidding so they could find employment for their excess equipment.

"You don't make money running a business, but in buying and selling businesses," he said. And of his personal decisions: "I'll never leave Alaska, and I'll never run for public office. But you must prepare for success as well as for failure because worse problems come with success." Yellow and blue Uchitel Construction rigs were still a commonplace sight throughout the metropolis, but what he was especially known for was laying down seven hundred miles of TV cabling in only a couple of years for MultiVisions, the television company he started that brought him notoriety because it carried some pornography, along with the standard dramatic, sports, or newsy fare, not only to Anchorage but by satellite to Alaska's other time zones and to subsistence villages still beginning to get used to radio soap operas and talk shows. On the White Pass Railroad recently, he said, he'd met a Swarthmore graduate, a girl, who liked him—which meant something to him because these educated-type people who used to cotton to him in Alaska lately did not—the controversial "trash TV" man. Being a tourist, she didn't count, but the kind of characters who did congratulate him on his programming when he met them, he disliked. Enjoying argument, he insisted to me that the reason he'd left Boston University after one year was "because the seniors all looked the same; it was the freshmen who looked different from one another." In his economics class he'd asked the professor "whether business was a place for wise men," when an up-curve was always the goal, not "the flat line of serenity." Socrates was a hero of his, though he wasn't sure who came first, Plato or him, and Bob was now a trustee of Alaska Pacific University, in Anchorage.

Direct, impatient, Hollywood-slick or sophisticated, he still liked eagles and other wildlife he saw; in Yellowstone he'd wanted to film the winter herds of elk and buffalo; but by 1977 had brought in Alaska's first twenty-four-hour, over-the-air, cherry-picked, one-channel television feed, a medley chosen by him. Later it was fifty-four channels by cable, with two hundred employees managing the enterprise—twice the number in his construction operations—and complaints, not just for the porn that children in Kotzebue, because of the time changes, were getting home from school to, when children in Juneau were safely tucked in bed, but for the inchoate impact on remote native settlements of suddenly seeing round-the-clock in their own cabins how richly and variously the worlds pictured beyond the bush lived. The commercials alone could be flabbergasting. Now Bob was being "paid to stay away" by Prime Cable, the new owners, but before that the gales of flack from many directions had caused him to prefer the company of his construction crews. Dressed like a truck driver himself, he relished having somebody blunder into the general office on business and ask *him* where he was, so he could pump the guy sub-rosa about "Uchitel's reputation" or maybe confide what his own plans for the meeting really were, "when Uchitel gets back." Loathing middle management, wanting simply "to clone them," because their jobs were to do exactly what he would do if he could be everywhere at once, he hung out instead with the steel-toed fraternity, or else wealthy folk who didn't complain about "homogenized decadence" being brought to pristine valleys.

Like many Alaskans, Bob had a dictatorial streak, and once he was merely broadcasting prepackaged, mainstream franchised channels, not a private medley or buffet of programs he'd selected for his subscribers, his interest waned. Disliking business (he said), he now pushed for the public good—specifically to bring Expo '84, the World's Fair, to Anchorage, instead of New Orleans, where it ended up. Alaskans are masochists, he claimed, so therefore when they threw rocks they mostly hit themselves; also isolationists, so that they affected Outside opinion minimally. Since they'd come here either with a grudge or a sense of superiority, they didn't know how to lobby, except perhaps for money. He wasn't surprised as much to lose that World's Fair fight as at the anemic support he had received. But what rankled more was that his concurrent plans for a gala, world-class celebration of "Alaska 1984," the twenty-fifth anniversary of statehood, didn't come to pass, World's Fair or no. Domed cities for climates such as this, a plan where people defined their citizenship in continental terms, not narrow nationalism, and President Reagan would have met his Russian counterpart on Kodiak Island, where both powers had ruled, to inaugurate a century of peace.

Bob had a light New York accent and a multitasker's attention span, as he signed the birthday cards Pam had procured, plus a condolence note to a dying ex-governor, critiqued a working script for *Voices of the Planet*, and spoke of "the genius of innocence," then the Greeks' ancient greatness but present irrelevance, the importance of bacteria, mankind's destruction of habitat, and larger cosmic ultimates, while giving me copies of *The Little Prince* and *Jonathan Livingstone Seagull*, name-dropping celebrities he'd known in New York or Hollywood, and accepting a phone call from Gonzalez, Texas, where that prizefighter, "Macho" Camacho, whose career he was dabbling in, was training for a fight in Corpus Christi, and whose manager he wired money to after the contracts had been faxed for his inspection. Although he believed in having "plenty of everything," after acquiring eleven hair dryers he'd promptly quit using them, preferring a towel; and when Pam objected to his fuming about that, he told her, "You sound real kind, like my ex-wives." His lavish carpets, his curved-screen Mitsubishi television or multi-use receiver in an oak wall cabinet dominating the sofas, crowding glass coffee tables were luxurious, and next door was a separate red building housing a deep blue heated swimming pool.

"Work fast, charge a lot, and hire other people's wives" was his maxim, he told me, laughing, as we explored the paths he was having constructed through his acreage of woods along the bluff, with maxims of his own devising posted on sticks alongside, besides the botanical advisories he'd paid for. "The first exported TV signal from Alaska that wasn't news," he asserted, had been a Camacho fight he'd promoted at Fort Richardson, the army post here. "The heart sees what's invisible to the eye," was a sample adage, and the theme of the statehood festival was to have been "The Spirit of Adventure: To Try Is To Succeed." I suggested, however, that the appeal of the spot for many roamers was the opportunity to "fail": for nature to subsume them. He had wanted to buy the White Pass Railroad from Skagway to Whitehorse, to operate for tourism, and construct a gondola ride over an enormous scale-model re-creation of the entirety of Alaska, plus twenty other rides—"none you could buy"—for a major theme-park exposition accompanying the anniversary.

Four companies, twenty-seven subsidiaries, three hundred employees: "I had enough. I liquidated everything." But boasting of the

sex and girls he still got, he added that his tastes were "traditional."
What he regretted were "memories lost," such as during his first visit
to Nome in 1971 when several Eskimos invited him on a seal hunt by
dogsled—as they wouldn't now, for a rich man—and "too busy," he
declined. Or the disintegrated dream of Alaska 1984, for which his advocacy committee had evolved plans filling twenty-six volumes, that
the state legislature thereupon rejected funding for. At thirty-eight,
he hadn't yet metamorphosed into a recluse, still wanted the publicity
of a *Vanity Fair* profile. Yet within six years, the police would describe
a body that "had many old cuts and bruises that were the apparent
result of frequent falls, but the blood that was smeared and spattered
on the floor and walls came from his nose." His income was reported
to be $20,000 a month from his remaining investments. A black Ma-
serati sedan with leather upholstery and only a thousand miles on the
odometer was parked in one garage, a Corvette in another.

• • •

CHAPTER 8

• • •

Walruses and Whales

A MONTH AFTER RETURNING FROM the Kuskokwim, we boarded another Boeing 737, converted for carrying goods until only four rows of seats were left. A Nome businessman wore a sealskin coat with a polar-bear collar. Hurtling through the clouds on Bering Standard Time, I listened to the thin metal wall rattle between us and eternity, reminding me of my creaky berths on the old Cunard Queens, crossing a stormy North Atlantic two decades before, when nature also slapped against human certainties.

"Welcome to Nome. Facilities are quite limited," our pilot announced ironically. After the seal-skinned businessman had debarked, the pilot cowboyed up and off the spindly runway, past a talky-looking, tiny-looking, Cold War White Alice advance-warning radar station—the black hole of the jet engine was just outside my window—and over the tundra of Seward Peninsula: settlements such as Iron Creek, Mary's Igloo, Coarse Gold, Coffee Creek, and the Bering Land Bridge National Preserve, to Goodhope Bay and Kotzebue Sound. Kotzebue (pop. 2,700) was situated on salt water on a marshy peninsula at the mouths of two Brooks Range Rivers, the Kobuk and the Noatak. This meant a hunter could go inland thirty miles and shoot a moose or caribou, or seaward the same distance and shoot an "oogruk," a hefty bearded seal, whose hide the whalers traditionally used for their skin boats. A walrus provided still more meat—twice as much as even a beluga whale—plus the tusks and skull that Eskimos could legally cut up to carve three-dimensionally or scrimshaw for sale.

Lacking Nome's gold-stampede origins (and then deflation: its name supposedly a map draftsman's misreading of the handwritten query, "?Name"), Kotzebue was instead a vibrantly unassuming Inupiat community memorializing an early nineteenth-century Russian explorer who searched past here for a Northwest Passage to Europe. Nor did it seem an airless regulation-processing center like Bethel, stranded neither on the sea nor in the wilds. As in Tanana or Fort Yukon, on the great Yukon River, I felt tentative, in the minority, and on my best behavior, far from white-run Fairbanks, so to speak. God knows if there would be a hotel room within a hundred miles if Linda lost her temper with me.

It was February 27th, cold enough to sting the lungs, weigh down your arms, and pinch the muscles in your heart. Along Front Street, the wooden frame houses had caribou antler racks on the roofs. The women standing in the doors, as we drove through from the plane, looked haloed by their white-bear or grizzly hoods, often with the claws left on. But Kotzebue had a twenty-nine-bed hospital (four doctors in and out) and another solid supervisor for its three itinerant nurses, who served the many villages ringing Kotzebue Sound or sprinkled up the fabled Noatak and Kobuk. Martha, who took us in, was a tall, severe-faced, San Francisco ash-blonde beauty, now a veteran of six years living here, and good with a rifle or on a snow machine, as well as the healing arts—and at sizing up men. Pilots would risk their lives, stunting in barrel rolls overhead, to impress her. Others brought her luscious sable furs they had trapped, or delicious cuts of wild meat: not that she didn't also hunt her own. Nonetheless, she'd not picked one of the macho guys to live with, but Fred, a round-faced, gently intellectual Inupiat birdwatcher, who had identified ninety-five species passing through last year. Both on North America's closest contiguous point to Siberia at Wales and as a student of subsistence tactics and culture—strumming for us some of Greenland's Inuit songs—Fred had probably also acquired part of his nimble versatility because for ten years during his childhood he had accompanied his mother when she lived at a tuberculosis sanatorium in Seward, in the south of the state. But after college he'd chosen to return and immerse himself in his ancestry, representing his heritage at statewide "walrus conferences," for instance, where the current population census and harvest statistics were discussed with federal and state biologists and regulations thrashed out both to protect "the resource" and the natives' need for walrus meat and ivory. Martha was more interested in exploring the Noatak, where she had a cabin, but that was up his alley, too.

Kotzebue was a tough town, each house a fortress against the cold—even Martha's mud room felt cold enough to die in, if you were locked out of the rooms beyond—and armed for self-defense at night, when drunks wandered abroad. But the poverty was local- ized among families without a breadwinner. Not only Prudhoe Bay was sloshy with jobs for anybody fit to work, but the Anaconda and Kennicott copper companies were salivating over deposits recently discovered near Ambler on the Kobuk River, much closer indeed. And tin ore identified at Lost River on the Seward Peninsula offered another prospect of big bucks. Or two "fish-pickers" salmon-netting for six weeks in a twenty-foot boat during the summer in Kotzebue Sound might gross $40,000, if they knew how. Robust energy was the currency. Oil and metal geologists needed guys for their field crews who could deal with an unexpected snowslide, or fill the fry- ing pan with Dolly Varden; and even the ancient craft of luring a lynx into a trap paid cash.

The harbor was navigable three months a year, when generator and heating fuel and durable goods were barged in. Then in the cold weather before freeze-up, the waves of the wake of your motorboat lost their rooster tails, Martha said. But even now, through the ice, you could hook up to sixty twenty-pound sheefish in a couple of hours, or twenty dog salmon in just one. Or elsewhere, pike, char, whitefish, lingcod (called "mud sharks" here), and tomcod from the ocean that you froze before you ate them to kill the worms inside. Household running water was piped ten miles above ground from a frozen lake to town, heated twice in boilers along the way. The new senior center had been architectured like a spacious igloo, with a lovely skylight impersonating the smoke hole. We walked across a frozen lagoon, admiring the darkening blues of the night in the east, a peach light to the west, and the town's appealing sparkle behind us. Then back to Martha's low, red-painted log house to look at her angel-wing begonias, asparagus ferns, and spider plants, plus Fred's collection of paddle-shaped Eskimo drums fashioned from walrus intestines stretched over a thin driftwood frame.

Both of them had lately become embroiled in native politics: Fred quitting as vice-president of the health corporation—though still loyally claiming it was better than working for the State—and Martha moderating in that organization's disputes with the federal Indian Health Service. But the doctor who lived next door was cutting his schedule in half to train his dog team for a two-hundred-mile run to Nome. Some couldn't stand the isolation, she said; yet some went native on you. And one of her troubles was that when a patient not hers came back to the area from an operation in Fairbanks or Anchorage without their paperwork catching up to them, they might not be able to tell her what had been repaired or removed, so passive was their relationship to white-man's medicine. She was the tallest, richest woman in town, with a polar-bear hood and the tails breezily tossing on her marten-skin hat—speeding around on the best snowmobile, with a new boat and truck and the Noatak cabin to get away to—pineapples and chutney on her table, polypropylene long johns under her jeans, and fifty-year-old bush pilots sometimes piggybacking or tailgating each other up in the sky just to catch her eye. Yet she was a healer, if they got hurt. And Fred's father was her ballast, telling her skin boat-and-walrus stories: how, if you killed one in a herd, others might surround and try to capsize you in revenge by hooking their tusks over the gunwales. Skin boats were more vulnerable to an attack by a polar bear in the water also, but their flexibility made them superior to the wooden kind for navigating among ice floes, bending with or riding over them.

Kotzebue's cabdriver was its bootlegger, and he buzzed the doorbell with a liquor delivery this Sunday eve. His belly protruded parallel to the floor, but he was laughing because of the joke he'd pulled on a local braggart at the greasy spoon. Everybody knew him and he was boasting about all the women he'd fucked, until the cabbie interrupted: "Oh, I hope not *her*! I caught the clap from her last month!" Then went home, peeled the label off a bottle of aspirin, and sold it to him as leftover pills.

Everybody was worried, however, about the fate of an eighteen-year-old Inupiat boy from Point Hope named Amos, who had unscrewed the plates on his cell window and escaped from Kotzebue's lockup two nights ago, stolen or "stolen" a friend's loose snow machine, and headed at top speed straight northwest across the sea ice and corrugated shoreline toward the Eskimo hamlet of Kivalina, hours away. Villages like Sheshalek and Tikizat came first, and the pressure ridges of the ice, till, exhausting his gas, he abandoned the snowmobile and borrowed or stole a Honda three-wheeler in Kivalina to continue his hopeless flight northwest along the tumbled coast toward Point Hope, a village of less than five hundred souls, about as far again—where state troopers undoubtedly would be waiting for him. Confinement had terrified Amos, the Quaker missionaries and several nurses who had visited him said, and the last time he'd escaped, during warmer weather, he managed to elude capture for two precious weeks with the help of sympathizers. Now, though, the three-wheeler inevitably stalled in deep drifts short of Ipnot, and he must have been forced—no one knew—to flounder through the soft stuff inland for cover in the willows and hills and dig a "wolf hole" to survive Saturday night. Today, on Sunday, a police helicopter spotted the Honda, but not before the winds obscured any tracks leaving it. Since he didn't come out of hiding to wave for help, people could assume he preferred dying under the snow to being caged up again. A mental patient once fled from the hospital in his pajamas and slippers, Martha said, running across the sea ice until a helicopter spotted and lassoed him. And a three-year-old boy had been blown away in a blizzard and whiteout from his backyard here in town, and not found for thirty-six hours, only a few yards out on the ice, but still so securely zipped in his snowsuit that his temperature was ninety-five degrees and okay.

In the morning, Monday, the last day of February, Linda and I ourselves flew northwest to Point Hope in a Baker Aviation Cessna Stationair ($225 per hour) so Linda could do the village's annual TB checkup. It took an hour and a quarter, over the Noatak's mouth and sea ice formations curlicued by narrow leads, icepack pileups, grayish open water, and humpy true gravel beaches fronting tundra spreading to the stumpy ends of the Brooks Range, in the east. Little dabs of settlement at Talikoot, Kilimak, Ungayookot, Ebeokvik, and Utonok preceded tiny, spearhead-shaped Kivalina, where Amos may have received a hot meal and a parka to cover his jail clothing, when his first machine gave out. After that, Capes Seppings and Thompson and the hamlet of Chariot prickled me, gazing down, with Amos's plight.

How far had he got and how badly had his hypothermia progressed? Russia and its Cold War MiGs lay on the left, and the majestic folds of North America's northwest all across the right, with the polar rim of the world ahead, till we slanted down onto Point Hope's rudimentary airstrip, where my eyelids promptly froze shut. Our pilot, a burly, compact, confident man—who later would fly in for Amos, too, after Eskimo trackers replaced the troopers in trying to discern his filled-in tracks and save his life—only laughed. "Don't panic. I'll come back for you."

Luckily, when he roared away, Linda's eyes had not done the same, because we waited a while before a truck materialized to pick us up. The health clinic, in this prideful, prosperous village financed by North Slope oil (although the Prudhoe fields were actually further east than Nome was to the south), had wall-to-wall carpeting in the reception and secretarial areas, a 160-power microscope, and an incubator for culturing gonococci that might be swabbed from a patient needing diagnosing. The high school boasted a heated swimming pool, no less. But consternation reigned for a few minutes when the health aids realized they had scheduled Linda's visit for what was now spring break. Some of the kids she had come to test had scattered to other towns on visits, but fortunately thirteen boy scouts who were supposed to be camping in the bush had stayed around because their snowmobiles had been diverted to the search for Amos. Finally, after Linda was done with them, a caribou hunter caped in white, with a white-camouflaged rifle slung on his back, hitched a long sled behind his snow machine and gave them all a thirty-mile lift to their campground.

"It's not fair to the caribou now, is it, how we speed about?" he confided to me with a grin, a lavish wolf-skin hood concealing his mild face and a raven's-wing forelock of hair.

Then two state troopers carried poor Amos into the clinic, strapped on a stretcher, from a snowmobile sled, with frostbitten hands, face, feet, and a frozen eye. The Kivalina trackers who had helped ferret him out had already given him some coffee, chicken noodle soup, and comforting, but after fighting the straps and cursing, he began to weep, seeing the first nurse: Why hadn't he been left to die? That misery was why the troopers had permitted him to be transported here for first aid—with his stepmom rushing in from home to sit beside him—instead of flying him right back from Cape Thompson to Kotzebue's hospital and jail.

"Trust us," the trooper named Dan suggested to the room.

"Not till a year goes by," an old man answered, and the darkest-skinned health aid nodded, meaning the police as individuals. Linda and I had already heard muttered complaints that our white pilot, in callously flying a normal route instead of low, watchful, and slow, had been irresponsible.

In his second two-hundred-mile dash for freedom, and partly on foot after the three-wheeler stalled, Amos had reached a derelict radar station for shelter. "What eighteen-year-old is going to have a hundred-and-thirty thousand dollars?" he wailed. That would be his bail for the rape, robbery, and kidnapping charges he faced; yet nobody seemed nonplussed by the gravity of the accusations. The nursing was tender; and in Kivalina, sure, they had helped him, he said. His father, arriving, told him not to run away again and that the law should be obeyed; he also consoled the crying stepmom that they hadn't encouraged him either to break out or do bad.

Trooper Dan told me spending this night in Point Hope would be a nice change from his ordinary paperwork and giving driver tests—which was to say, driving lessons—to those of Kotzebue's youth about to venture to Anchorage to look for jobs. While Amos's condition was being stabilized by the health aids, Linda, and the hugs of his relatives, Dan and the second trooper explored Point Hope, and talked to the Episcopal minister. In divvying up such a jumbo region by accretion or by handshake agreements, the Episcopalians had been allotted the upper Yukon, extending down from Anglican Canada, and certain Inupiat arctic villages like Point Hope, where in 1890 they had established their second mission in Alaska. The Quakers got Kotzebue, the Moravians Bethel, and the Russian Orthodox priests much of the rest of the Kuskokwim and Yukon.

Many houses on the handful of short, snowy streets had meat platforms outside with a caribou carcass or two laid on them. Others, four or five seals stacked upright, nose-first, embedded in a drift out front, as if about to dive out of sight for safety's sake. They were bottle-fat, ocean-colored. A polar bear skin was drying on a rack in the backyard of another cabin, the flesh side red, with a bird occasionally darting to pick off fat. Once the drama calmed down and Amos fell asleep, Linda continued her PPD (purified protein derivative) testing for the tuberculosis bacillus of the village children and any adults who walked in. My eyes seemed to be adjusting to a sensible frugality in their production of tears, so I roamed out onto the arctic ice for a few hundred yards, where I could gaze back at the scanty settlement, built either of sea-stained driftwood logs or whitewashed prefab boards, and occupying possibly ten degrees of the three-hundred-sixty visible here in the midday twilight. The landward portion of the Kukpuk River, to the east, was minimally humpy, but its snows, less windblown than what had fallen on the sea's ice, magnified the sun's fitful illumination from below the horizon, whereas a more prismatic palette spread crosswise from the direction of Siberia.

The cold ceased being a novelty after a very few minutes and profoundly frightened me, at forty below—ominous like an undertow in surf when you belatedly recognize it after enjoying yourself, then realize that the ocean isn't exhilarated, as you are by your swim, and may sweep you off and smother you. I tramped to shore, hunched up to conserve the heat and energy I had, and sought out Don Spicer, a preacher from Arkansas and the vice-mayor, who fed me a caribou sandwich heated in his microwave, the meat shot by him last falltime, while we watched the ABC evening news broadcast from New York, we being six hours behind, on Bering Straits Time. Don had been learning Inupiat, and how to catch chum salmon, arctic char, whitefish, and snow crabs, but his son, after trying the life, was going back to attend the University of Central Arkansas next year.

Point Hope, called Tigaraq, meaning "Point" by the Eskimos, who if they live there are *"Tigaraqmint,"* acquired its English name from a passing sea captain in 1826, and within twenty years whalemen, after oil and baleen for corsets, frequented it during the summer season, eventually, by the late 1880s, establishing a whaling station called "Jabbertown" nearby. Whalemen, of course, were as brutal by inclination as the gold rushers in Nome or on the Yukon. In Nome I'd still seen lubricious old photographs of topless Eskimo matrons for sale, of the type miners used to carry back to display to stay-at-homes after their adventures were over ("this is where I got my coffee milk," etc), and on the Yukon heard about Gwich'in Indian squaws and their babies who had starved to death in midwinter early in the twentieth century because they wouldn't put out for a gold-hunter. But from the Kivalina River around the arctic coast to Tolageak, on the Utukok River, the Eskimos were said to have asserted an unusually aggressive degree of control over their lands and villages. They could be scammed but not bulldozed. Indeed, a hundred years later, a white man without a defined function, like me, was not welcome and might have been set upon and beaten up, if not for a tip-off like my being the nurse's boyfriend. Construction crews were deemed commonplace, though, because after a storm surge in 1976, and regular flooding and loss of nine feet or so of beachfront per year, the community center had been moved half a mile in from the historic Point. Spicer showed me new housing built by the Feds, the State, and the North Slope Borough, along with the spiffy school, washateria, sauna, and the 2.7-million-dollar water storage tank for the residents' convenience, pumped seven miles from a lake.

I went on to Joe Towksjhea's snug, friendly home, at Spicer's suggestion. He was an older, worldly guy who, late the last April, in a skin boat manned by seven paddlers and a rudderman, had harpooned a twenty-seven-foot bowhead whale. It was important to the whole village that somebody land at least one whale every spring—a signature event—whereupon template hunks of meat, skin, or blubber were distributed to other villages up or down the coast and perhaps along the Kobuk and Noatak rivers, too, for traditional feasts. Whaling vastly predated nineteenth-century contact with whites, and two gargantuan jawbones arched over the entrance to Point Hope's festival grounds. If nobody speared one, a bit of the town's cultural identity could be dismasted or dissolved. In the bad old days of forced assimilation, schoolchildren might be punished for murmuring to each other at recess in Inupiat or another indigenous language, but lately television had been much more effective at unstringing the coherence of the North. Caribou hunts continued in motorized form, but not previously central, though eclipsed, subsistence rituals like collecting wild murre eggs by the countless hundreds off giddy ledges on the sandstone cliffs of Cape Lisburne and Cape Thompson during the birds' brief hectic June nesting season. Colonies of whirling, "growling," "moaning" thousands had been gleefully, dangerously robbed in the village-wide bash—everybody absolutely stuffing themselves on their only fresh eggs of the year.

Bowheads, like murres, migrated northward for the wealth of nutrition generated when the sun shines round-the-clock. Also gray whales: but being more pugnacious, grays were left alone. The bowheads could weigh a ton per foot and grow much larger than Joe's last one had been. The early migrants were easier to get at because the melting ice at first left narrow passages they had to swim through while keeping their access to air. The wooden frame of the longboat sat prophetically on a whalebone cache all fall and winter, but well before the season, Lucy, Joe's wife, and the wives of the other men in the crew prepared by painstakingly sewing the skins of eight bearded seals, or "oogruk," together in leak-proof fashion to cover the twenty-foot ribbed outline. These special seals can be eight feet in length, twice the size of the ringed seals I saw stacked as larder—nosed into the drifts in people's yards, and shot at blowholes by young men. They could weigh eight hundred pounds apiece, required more ambitious hunting, and their tough hides were also cut into harpoon lines, boot soles, and whatnot. Then, with April's longer, warming days, the men hauled the big skin boat, with their white tents, Coleman stoves, and the caribou skins they slept on, out five miles or more by snowmobile onto the ice, to reach the open-water leads that had split the winter's cap. There, during the thaw, they kept watch night and day for the whales to arrive, hunting seals, perhaps, in the meantime, and watching for a possible shot at a polar bear, prowling too, after seals.

The International Whaling Commission granted an exception for Eskimo harvests of an otherwise protected species because of the argument for cultural continuity, but limited the number of "strikes" now legally made. Point Hope, allotted four the last year, had been granted three for the coming spring. Other historic villages like Barrow and Wainwright, on the North Slope, Gambell, on St. Lawrence Island, and the Little Diomede Islanders, at the choke point of the Bering Strait, had been given quotas too. It was a doubly contentious point, of course, because so many whales struck by harpoons were never captured, even though explosive devices had been fitted onto the harpoon's head, but dove, escaped, and died alone. Since the hunts are unmonitored, the ratio is unknown. Before regulation, the most whales ever killed at Point Hope in living memory was fourteen, although how many more were fatally injured could be anyone's guess. Joe, in fact, after spotting his bowhead last spring, paddling hard with his crew of eight, and hurling the harpoon, almost lost *his*, in spite of the fluorescent float hooked to the line and the explosive tripling the damage inflicted by the spear point itself. But he also had a harpoon-firing shoulder gun with additional "bombs" and floatation aids at the end, so they recovered the whale, finished it off, and towed it to where their Ski-Doos all together could haul the carcass onto the ice, then toward land. But first nine squares of skin were cut from its back for the crew to ritually chew, and a piece of the whale's skull symbolically returned to the sea.

Lucy, Joe's articulately spicy wife, flew back from a vacation in Honolulu the day the whale was speared to help distribute the meat. Not only every local received a token, but each Inupiat village in the region, such as her hometown, Kiana, on the forested Kobuk, where she'd grown up as a "fish-eater," as she put it, not weaned on seals and whales. She even insisted upon using a wood stove for cooking, rare on this coast, although there was abundant driftwood. She'd come to Point Hope as a young widow to help in the school, but now helped organize the three-day *Nalukataq* June festival, when young bloods underwent the blanket-toss to prove their physical composure and delicacies like the whale's flippers and chewy gums were eaten.

"Me, Joe, our cooks, and our boys go down and dance on the oogruk skins."

Other organs and parts were set aside for Thanksgiving and Christmas, and the tail would be eaten throughout the village when the fall sea ice began to form. The last of the whale was not consumed until the wives sat together next spring chewing muktuk (skin), while sewing a new skin boat's skin. Yet each band of hunters, she said, may practice ceremonies of its own. "It's a really big animal and a real godsend to us to be able to feed all the people, out to the last village up the Kobuk." Some hunters employed walrus skins, instead of bearded sealskins, for their boats, and after the bowheads had passed the Point, swimming toward the Beaufort Sea, migrating walruses became the quarry, for their tusks and mountains of flesh.

I didn't just taste the muktuk politely in Joe and Lucy's living room, but accepted the gift of enough to nibble at each of my mornings in Point Hope—a thick black patch of skin with white blubber underneath, like oil-of-the-sea—when my senses were fresh. The same practical talent for improvisation that elevated him to success as a whaling captain made Joe the best spokesman to white visitors from Outside like me: not defensively contemptuous, as some of the other old men were. Apart from the teachers or missionaries, most whites skating through seemed equally offish. A computer guy from Anchorage told me when he was in Point Hope he simply worked till he "dropped" on their electronics, then flew home. An Anchorage municipal accountant did exactly the same, and also a maintenance team of "Bob and Bob," from Barrow, tuning up the big generator. Another outsider was installing improved refrigeration at the school; another at work remodeling the plumbing. Several families told me, though, that they preferred puttering out on their Ski-Doos or three-wheelers, dragging a sled behind, to chop blocks of lake ice for themselves, much as they'd used to patrol the beaches with dogs for drift logs to tug back and buttress their whalebone-stone-and-mud huts, or cook in front of the house with. Before baleen was bought by metropolitan corset-makers to balloon women's skirts—or nowadays as a curio for the tourist trade—these silky-fringed horny slats for sieving krill had been cut out of the beached whale's mouth to weave baskets from, as the river Eskimos or Indians to the south utilized willow withes. Also, the oval tympanic bones were cut out of the whale's middle ears and saved, either to be scrimshawed or kept unblemished as a talisman, palm-sized but similar in shape to a human's external ear.

Eskimo scrimshawing tended not to portray battles between men and beasts, like the white whalers' carvings on sperm-whale teeth, but rather wildlife, such at ptarmigan, gulls, caribou, seals, murres, bears, and whales, like fellow spirits or citizenry. Yet at the cemetery the graves of whaling captains were each marked by a whale's jawbone, and the perimeter of the grounds outlined by many others. Whaleboats were tapered at the bow and stern, with four boards fixed crosswise for the paddlers to sit on. Bolts anchored the ribs to the keel, but rawhide thongs tied them to the gunwales, and the sealskin outer covering, scraped hairless by energetic women like Lucy, became parchment-colored in a year. Although Point Hope is a hundred-twenty-five miles above the Arctic Circle, by seven in the morning on March 1st it was well-lit, while still gelid-looking because of the blizzard-blown drifts surrounding everybody's house; some people hardly bothered to shovel their windows clear. Even indoors at the clinic I'd been sufficiently awed by the cold to become impotent, despite being zipped securely inside a double sleeping bag and talked to severely by a nurse in a manner one would ordinarily respond to with alacrity. We'd brewed our supper on a stove next to the gonorrhea-culturing machine, as a disturbed Eskimo named Roger paced outside the locked door and the CB radio relayed a blow-by-blow account of a health aid by herself in another village trying to help a screaming girl whose fingers had been mangled by a snow machine. Meanwhile, the Ski-Doo drivers were picking up Trader Vic's salad dressing or Norwegian goat cheese at the general store—as befitted a town funded by Prudhoe Bay—but often standing up en route to emphasize their prowess and haste.

I remembered Martha, Kotzebue's heartthrob, telling us about one of the berserk white men who periodically showed up. He was a Vietnam War amputee who filed medical records in her office for a time, but developed a crush on her, then insisted on roaring about the Kobuk River's myriad sloughs or out on Kotzebue Sound on his snowmobile just as if he still had legs. While rabbit-hunting on a wilderness trip, he went through the ice but managed to propel himself to shore with his arms alone—having "floated well," he said, because of being legless—and through the snow to a cabin close by. Martha's having joined the search party that rescued him that time may have goaded him into a needlessly dangerous quest to locate her, out on thawing Hotham Inlet, when she was reported as late in returning from a trip to her cabin. Not being ice-savvy like a local, he cracked through a thin spot on his machine and drowned. Leggy Martha, with straight, carefully combed hair, good bones in her tall Anglo face that, like a nurse's, seemed able to look several ways at once, was somebody a wounded vet might fall hard for in the howling loneliness of the north. Certainly he hadn't surrendered his dream of immersing himself in Alaska's wilds when he lost his legs.

I noticed while walking around Point Hope that the yards with half a dozen bottle-shaped, olive-colored, four-foot seals planted in a snowbank in front of the house—their flippers either pressed prayerfully together or despairingly stretched wide apart—belonged to families with the liveliest dog teams staked in the snow and perhaps several partially dismantled snowmobiles cannibalized for parts. Wary of being patronized, if not frankly hostile, most people dodged questions from a passing stranger, but I did find a college student home from Fairbanks on winter break who was both tolerant of my stutter and confident enough about his white-collar future that he was willing to spare a few moments to talk about seal-hunting.

Sure, he'd done it. You went out for several miles on the ice on your Ski-Doo to where the blowholes were, wearing your white parka, with a single-shot, pump-action rifle and a grappling hook. Then you lay camouflaged in the snow for a long while. After finally shooting one which had hauled out to rest and sun itself, using your spotting scope, you remained still, allowing it plenty of time to die in peace and mystification, not diving in terror back into the ocean under the ice, having figured out what and where its enemy was. Ideally, bewilderment would keep it filling its lungs in gasps, so even if it did slide into the blowhole again, its body would float. He studied me to see if my comprehension was genuine, as he spoke—as young as my students at Columbia University, back in New York—and if so, to judge whether I was just another preservationist agitator here to try to gather ammunition to abolish whaling; then turned away. Harbor seals were already supplanting ringed seals as the species shot, although their skins were not as valuable for working into moccasins and mukluks. Ringed seals, like bowheads, had gotten scarce.

Animals' bodies were borrowed when they were killed, to be consumed, but the spirits, treated respectfully, returned to the place of capture for reincarnation, Joe had explained, especially with the hunter's assistance, as when he'd slipped part of last year's whale's cranium into the sea again. The hides of the seals I was noticing, when they were skinned to be eaten, would be soaked at room temperature in melting snow until the hair follicles rotted enough to be scraped off. Then they were bleached from every angle in the cold sunlight to a comely paleness and kneaded with the hands for pliability before being cut and sewn into footwear and mailed south to stores in the cities, along with five-foot wolf pelts—gray, white, or black—sold whole as arctic mementos, or caribou skins variously worked.

Eight polar bears had been shot by Point Hope villagers so far this winter, drawn hungrily close by the smell of dogs and seal and caribou carcasses. Occasionally you could shoot one out of your window, but last winter it had been the arctic foxes, short of food, appearing in town to surrender their white fur. I went to visit Hubert

Koonuk, born in 1911 but looking ten years younger than that and still an ace bear hunter. More of a loner than Joe Towksjhea, he pursued his passionate specialty far out on the pack ice solo. Had totted up a reported thirty-six in his life, including the fresh one draped dripping underneath his skin boat on its rack at the side of the house. Black claws, slitted eye holes, and the surreally squashed head lacking a skull, and boneless arms and legs dangling down made it look a bit like some Bugs Bunny "bear" that had suffered a comeuppance, except for the steel ring through its nose, by which on his snow machine he had dragged it home. Koonuk's hunts could be perilous affairs, I had heard, involving not only the possibility of the huge, ghostly beast turning the tables and stalking him, but the floe they were on breaking loose and floating away, while the same gale blew his skin boat off it and marooned him. More than once he'd needed to leap into the water and fetch the thing back, or else wait for a plane to maybe spot him after a day or two when the storm cleared.

His vendetta against bears didn't encompass the cultural import, collective effort, or sharing of the meat far and wide of a whale hunt, but brought him personal fame, tasty steaks, and a saleable commodity in the creamy hides. A couple of sealskins were also drying on bear paw snowshoe frames, along with two caribou, curing in the sun as well. Koonuk was a rangier, moodier, pricklier fellow than Joe, and immediately asked me, "What outfit are you with?" A fair question. My state-issued, navy blue, Eddie Bauer winter jacket with the coyote collar might mark me as a kind of wildlife cop nosing around. I explained I was a freelance writer from the East, accompanying a TB nurse, and after stories and therefore harmless. After opening the door, he had resumed what he was doing, sitting cross-legged on the floor, sawing cross sections off a walrus tusk—which was curved like a saber-toothed tiger's canine—to insert for decorative purposes into the lids and bases of several baskets his wife had woven out of baleen.

"So you won't even leave us our stories, will you?" he remarked. "Now that you've stolen everything else? I ought only to tell what I know to an Eskimo!"

Filing and polishing the discs of ivory, with a wide wall-cloth illustrating Jesus herding a flock of sheep behind him, he didn't suggest that she, in the kitchen, produce a cup or a cookie to palliate his sarcasm.

"You see how we live? And we don't talk about how we hunt whales or walruses or polar bears now because they're trying to stop us from doing that. So this is how the Eskimos live. They drink coffee and carve ivory, and then they drink some more coffee and carve some more ivory." He gestured at the muted TV. "We don't see any Eskimos on NBC, you know, but we do see people drinking wine and other things. So we try to drink our coffee like that." He imitated wine tasting. They'd used to get forty-five dollars for a ringed-seal skin, he said, but now weren't supposed to sell them. Yes, the ear-bone of a whale brought two hundred dollars, but how many of *them* were there? Maybe I would buy one of his caribou-skin mukluks at the Anchorage airport when I headed out of Alaska and give the salesman his markup.

Laughing, I tried to persuade him to confirm the figure of thirty-six polar bears that he had killed. His pride in having done so, which people spoke of, intrigued me because in my trips to Indian country in British Columbia and Alaska, I'd never heard of anything equivalent regarding grizzlies. People shot them if they had to, but assiduously wanted to avoid a grizzly, unless perhaps guiding white hunters from the city into their habitat commercially. They wished not to meet them at a salmon stream or berry patch, and didn't enjoy their flesh, like a succulent black bear's. Nor was the hide as valuable in the marketplace. Although not revered religiously, grizzlies possessed an accepted status as natural citizenry, and for a grownup to go after them *mano a mano* as a lifelong quest might have struck others as loony or impious of the natural order. Hubert's solitary obsession was not to speed the polar bear to extinction, but personal ennoblement, and in the sparse setting of the Arctic's beaches, the subtleties of intuition and perception fostered by more temperate climates were hard to come by. Besides grizzly country, where bears were considered part of the dramatis personae of God's world, not to be gratuitously killed, I've been in forests in India where the villagers cohabited gingerly with tigers but never requested them killed. If the tiger itself had not become an aberration and man-eater, that would be second-guessing God's will.

A brutal climate with a minimal cast of characters left little leeway for ambiguity, but the classic Inupiat ceremonial masks used what they had—a plate of whalebone fitted with polar-bear teeth in the gap of the mouth, and fringed with caribou fur. Since I didn't want to lose my foothold in Hubert's house, I didn't inquire why he alone had ranged so single-mindedly and far, but did ask him to suppose that no Eskimo showed up to record his stories, would he be sorry he had chased me off? In Louisiana I'd talked to Cajun alligator-hunters who, wading barefoot and hip-deep with a spear, had pursued the biggest reptiles as relentlessly through the swamps, yet waited in vain for a Cajun-speaker like themselves to come along and write down what they had to say before they died. Thus some had talked to me, even though I was just a Yankee from New York.

Hubert laughed dismissively, posing with an imaginary spear while feeling for a gator with his toes. The white fur had bought his TV, his CB radio and scanner, snow machines, and winter's fuel oil. Beyond that, he left out the primordial battle of beast versus the beast-in-man, but showed me how whale baleen strips, soaked until they grew rubbery, were split wicker-thin to be woven into boxes or baskets such as he was setting the walrus-ivory discs like gemstones. Or, left hard, blue-black, the baleen could itself be scrimshawed, and a nub of polished baleen was sometimes inserted like a jewel into an ivory finger ring. Indeed, pairs of them had served as eyes in those big whalebone masks, with the bear teeth and caribou or wolf hairdos. In the old-time days, more than a thousand pounds of baleen (the word derived from the Latin, *baleena*, for "whale") and ten tons of whale oil to light Europe's cities might be extracted from an average bowhead. So it's no wonder they're endangered.

Sunlight shone through Hubert's skin boat's skin, demonstrating his craftsmanship, and he showed me the hundred-foot retrieving line, studded with hooks, he used for grappling sinking seals out of the water after he'd shot them. In the old days of harpooning, you'd have a line already affixed in them, but now you had to stand on a stool next to the blowhole and grope for them through the opening with a pole that had a prong on one end and a hook at the other, then twitch the line, too, around them. What he'd have going for him was the wounded seal's instinctive attempt to resist the ocean currents sweeping it away under the ice. Instead, it would try to hold a position near its home: that same blowhole it had battered open at all temperatures in order to be able to breathe. Then, when he'd secured several animals to tow back from the ice pack through shoreline patches of water, he might stick a bicycle pump into their anuses so they'd float, stoppering the holes with wooden plugs he whittled specially for the purpose. In the old days, sealskins sewn closed and inflated were the floats that held a harpooned whale up.

The bowhead, with two feet of blubber cushioning it against the cold, a handsomely white-napkinned chin underneath a head about a third of its total length, possessed a skull capable of bashing breathing holes in several inches of ice, broad graceful flukes and an arched or bow-shaped mouth large enough to sieve gargantuan amounts of plankton and krill through those wondrously pliant, but skinny, stiff baleen plates, five or ten feet long, and two hundred or more on each side—that the whalers sold for dressmakers to whet the lust of city men in the form of bustiers and bustles—was a slow swimmer, surfacing predictably every twenty minutes to breathe, and floated conveniently when killed because of that fat content, which lighted the lamps of Europe. At the heyday they were called the "Arctic right whale," "Greenland whale," "great polar whale," as well, in contrast to the grays, which besides their more tempestuous temperament, were a less desirable catch because, wintering in Baja California and swimming all the way back and forth, (not arriving at Point Hope until June), they required much less fat as layering for insulation.

As our conversation petered out, I assured Hubert that I understood it was we whites who had wiped out the whales, not his people, and he continued to wait for an Eskimo writer to materialize for him to spin his white-bear yarns to. Wandering the streets, encapsulated in my protected status as the nurse's boyfriend, I remembered how, in pristine days, shipwrecked seamen on these snowy shores had tended not to survive unless an Eskimo widow took a fancy to them. But since Linda's severest admonitions had not corrected my impotence, here in the true north I mightn't have made good at all as a castaway washed off a stove-in whaler, by the widow route.

I talked to a man with both a whaling skin boat and a little sealing skin boat stored on racks in his front yard. He was sawing a haunch off a naked caribou, under a tarp on his roof. At the June festival, he said, a flag flew for each whale captured that spring, and the best captains, like Joe Towksjhea, had no trouble filling their complement of eight paddlers for next year. He described with a shake of the head how one whale he had killed rolled on its side to meet his gaze unforgettably with its topmost eye, just before the harpoon's bomb he had fired into its back exploded and it tried to dive. Mothers often sacrificed themselves trying to save a calf. References to Eskimo whaling go back four thousand years, according to Richard Ellis's *Book of Whales*, and the young ones, "Ingutak," make the choicest eating, not the big old "Apsavak," even though the latter have feasted the longest at the mouth of the Mackenzie River's great debauchment, which is the culmination of the bowheads' annual journey.

Behind the ceremonial arch of twenty-foot jawbones at the festival site, he told me, were rib-bone frames on which the oogruk skins were customarily hung that were used in the ritual blanket toss—a manhood rite designed to test or display young blades' panache in controlling their bodies' flight, while the women watched: in the old days, a central event. In those days, before tradition, and perhaps divinity, had been bleached out, experienced captains gradually amassed the equipment and gravitas to mount a sensible hunt: whose point was to choose and then land what you killed. But now young bloods with overtime money from the oilfields could promptly buy harpoon guns and explosives, snowmobiles and steel boats with outboard motors, and go shoot seals in the open water they hadn't a prayer of retrieving, or blast whales whose deaths nobody else would witness or count, and no feast result. A culture attenuated became frivolous, a cul-de-sac, with suicide a ruinous endgame on the rivers.

Every town had its own obligatory crazy white man; and this one's guy, a contract administrator, told me angrily, "The last white woman I slept with gave me VD, so I ain't never going to sleep with no white woman again." He was like a part-time trapper and government employee on the Kuskokwim who said he'd voted to keep Sleetmute "wet" so in the evenings he'd always have a tipsy Eskimo or Indian girl standing at his door wanting money for tomorrow's drink. Rows of yellow, sky-blue, or barn-red, three-room prefabs stood on stilts ready for occupancy, near older, log-and-tarpaper houses on rollers that had been moved from nearer the ocean.

Seals with cat whiskers, dog muzzles, aldermen's bellies, and babies' touch holes—eight of them seeming to dive for cover into the snow—signified the home of Laurie Kingik, a majestic sort of man with a cane and huge, somber face, with black-rimmed glasses and a blue T-shirt, an elder of the village who had killed many bears. He "knew them and they know me," he said: a TV drama on for his grandchildren and walrus tusks mounted on the wall. "But you bring a signed statement from North Slope Borough headquarters in Barrow that I can talk to you and I will. Otherwise it's not good enough for me—this local office is maybe okay for some of the others but not for me." There had been questioners, film crews, and his sons wouldn't let him hunt any more, he said. "Not for four or five years."

"Thief!" a young guy had yelled at me, the night of Amos's capture, when it was known that I was after stories and his submerged anger brought out by that. Less appetizing details had emerged about Amos's behavior, beating people up in flight, and he would wind up in Seward, presumably, at the pen. Officially, last year the tally of polar bears killed in ten towns in Alaska had been a hundred-nine, a tenth of them here, more in Shishmaref, Kaktovik, and Savoonga—all places where the wind had pushed the ice floes that they were riding on. Clusters of freight trailers and crates lay around, awaiting the barge season. The green barnlike Episcopal Church and rectory had more presence than my friend Don Spicer's Church of Christ, but he had carved snow blocks as windbreaks for his. He showed me the head of a Dall sheep that the Bombardier snow machiners had carried off from somewhere, as people occasionally did a moose from the south. In the old days they would have had to snowshoe out and spear a seal just to heat their homes. Laurie was a "King of the Bears," yes, but Hubert had killed a whale scarred on its flank with his own nickname, "Eli."

A woman had tied a sash tight around her parka to support the baby tucked inside. But with television came not just consumerism, the preacher said: from the soap operas, divorce. Back in Batesville, Arkansas, he lectured on Alaska and showed arrowheads, fire flints, seal penis bones, and etc. Said how scary it was to be out on the tippy ice floes with his Eskimo brother-in-law; how they sometimes broke off and floated away. The Episcopal minister had had to swim for his life; another guy was adrift for five days till his ice islet bumped up against Cape Thompson, twenty-five miles southeast. As we talked, his small son and daughter were playing "Dungeons and Dragons," featuring a caveman with bow and arrow fighting off snakes and lizards. He said there was a Lions Club, Lionesses Club, a Women's Health Committee, and a Women's Dog Mushers Club. Lots of Bingo. But by whaling season everybody got out on the ice. The helmsman tried to get the harpoonist right on the whale's spinal cord, so he could paralyze it while other harpoons and floats were stuck in. People could drown from even a docile whale's jactitations, flipping a boat over, or when the carcass was hauled by block and tackle onto the ice, but its weight broke through the ice, pitching them into the water.

Since the Russians never occupied these North Slope lands, how could they "sell" them to the United States in 1867? asked a young man, who was drinking Pepsi and watching *Sesame Street*. His father was at a camp meeting elsewhere. "Nothin' much to tell. Kind of scary sometimes," he said, about seal hunting, wrinkling his nose. Spoke of seven Colorado college drop-out types he envied who rented an apartment in Anchorage as a base, then showed up in bush villages like this during the six-month construction period, working like hell on a health-care center, an Alaska Commercial Company store, or a Pioneer (nursing) Home, and flew to Samoa, the Galapagos Islands, or the Biobio River in Chile for a raft trip with the swag they'd earned.

Ian Hunuicutt, the short, dark Eskimo health aid at the clinic, was tending a possible meningitis case this day, and thankful for Linda's accidental presence while she read skin test results by looking at people's arms. Amos's poignant presence lingered in the air, despite his having been whisked back to jail; and there was talk of a child on the Kobuk who'd been badly chewed by a dog team; another had been born with twelve toes. Would they have reparative surgery? Both cases would require, not the village health aid, but a distant district nurse with manifold responsibilities to beat on the bureaucracy. For adult sufferers, to enlist remote hospital facilities and personnel, that special commitment gripping the nurse's heart for weeks after her quarterly visit to a given bush settlement wasn't as likely to take hold.

People didn't walk, they revved their Polaris to go fifty yards, and no longer landed between smudge pots at the air strip. But in America's Siberia, and Ronald Reagan's Cold War era, I couldn't help being reminded of the countless Russian writers who'd been exiled to the same climate across the Chukchi Sea. If they weren't worked to death in freezing labor camps, how was the balancing act each must have managed to perform in order to survive in the hamlets where they were confined? Could I have? Soaking their biscuits in tea to soften the one and thicken the other. Fortifying a stew by pouring in flour; cutting off a moustache because ice constantly congealed on it; trading a precious needle for a goose egg when hunger for protein became irresistible. But privations aside, could they snuggle into aboriginal or frontier society? In the taiga, on the Yukon, so mammal-rich, I thought I could. Here, to the north, the Eskimos knew the early "King George Men"—British whalers—as opposed to the "Boston Men," Americans, primarily New Englanders, who were also hounding the bowheads. On Martha's Vineyard, in museum ships' logs, I've read notations like "Pack ice. Snow. Harry Gilbert sick." "Under full top sail." "Raised Bowhead." "Struck him." "Cutting all day." "Died at 9 a.m. Buried Harry Gilbert today."—and a drawing in the margin of the handwritten page of a flower, plus the day's whale. "Cruising under all sail. Southly tack." "Sight ice in straight." "Home bound thank God. From Arctic Ocean towards San Francisco." "Thaddeus Bodfish master." He mentions a Yukon River Indian with a British sixpence suspended from his nose to mark his allegiance to the King George Men, and after rounding the Horn, grabbing sea turtles from the longboats.

There were the "Russian" Eskimos, and Episcopalian Eskimos, as well, but a dying miner scratched on his tin cup the horror of *"real cold."* Another, having no paper, wrote his will with a pencil on his white handkerchief, after subsisting for twelve days on relic berries, bulbs, and a few frozen dried apples he'd sliced with his axe. *Nulagme* was the Inupiat word for white person, corresponding to *Gussuck* among the Yupiks. As I trudged about, each leading family's prowess was on display, sun-curing in the yard—deboned bears, diving seals choreographed with spraddled-out tail fins, a wide-racked moose head shot in the willow belt riskily south, or a cat's cradle of caribou legs. The prickly regality of hunters like Hubert and Laurie was justified, as they chainsawed snow blocks to set windward of the house, its windows iglooed with ice, or carved tusks into cribbage boards to sell. Whites could yo-yo in and out on the mail plane, but not them.

The sun boiled in a halo of clouds near the horizon. A dump, a mile long and half-burned, stretched alongside the road to the airstrip, where a tanker plane's tail end sat next to the runway, its fuselage five hundred yards away.

"Take care," we said to the maintenance man who drove Linda and me out.

"Oh yeah. Always do," he answered seriously. As a carpenter building federal prefabs had told me, working in these native villages was more interesting than "being a zombie" in the oilfields, where you were a sort of robot at higher pay.

When the Cessna buzzed over and landed, he received and handed over Point Hope's mailbags to the pilot. The town, as we soared off, appeared like a scribble of toy machinery in the featureless wastes—a surface all white except for low rock roughness inland and pressure ridges of sea ice piled along the shoreline or cracking in zany patterns out in the direction of Siberia, where the geography became wholly marine. The sun, veiled now in chilly mists, lay low over the floes and bergs of that semi-mythical territory, because even the Eskimos or our dauntless bush pilot would be forbidden to go there.

I thought of Don Spicer describing how the ice dipped and split under his boots as he ran for shore, when seal-hunting with his new brother-in-law. On the left side, as we flew south to Kotzebue, the De Long Mountains, then the Baird Mountains materialized, both spurs of the Brooks Range, and the Noatak River's mouth.

The bootlegger cab driver took us to Martha's place, where Fred, in cardigan sweater and slippers, with *The New Republic* and *The Economist* on the table, welcomed us in the persona he had acquired at San Francisco State College and then the University of Alaska. But he still wanted to "get as good as Attla" at handling dogs. The relationship of men to sled dogs intrigued him, as did banding or at least recording the waves of birds round-the-clock sunshine brought north for the summer, and bagging a plump russet caribou every fall. And walruses were his job and preoccupation. From the area of Nome alone, hunters had gone out sixty or eighty miles in fast motorboats and killed about seven hundred among the floes in the last season—just two men accounting for eighty. But no herd could absorb attrition like that, as simultaneously the new industrial fishing fleets vacuumed the seabeds they fed from. And since they sank when shot, as they hadn't when harpooned, even the legitimate cultural needs of Eskimo communities, in terms of meat, tusks, and hides, required considerable surplus killing to achieve. With telescopic rifles, lethally fast boats and snow machines, and, for instance, a raw pair of walrus tusks selling for three hundred dollars at the Point Hope store, mediators such as Fred, proud of his own subsistence heritage west of Nome, had to help federal biologists convince Inupiat elders and younger hotheads that regulatory constraints on this central pillar ought to be tighter now. We'd met a St. Lawrence Islander who had participated lucratively, and shot four oogruk in one day, to boot; and it couldn't go on. In fact, Martha's predecessor in Kotzebue had moved to Barrow to supervise the nursing there and married an Eskimo called "Beluga Bob" because of all the beluga whales he'd killed. "Good whaling money!" he'd said, because of what equipment his share of her salary would buy.

The hospital, their cozy cabin, and the beer joint marked Martha's winter life, but being "more native than the natives," Fred said, she would have gone careening out on the ice with the men if that had been deemed proper. Instead she feasted on herring roe squeezed raw from the fishes' bellies (the Tlingits put spruce boughs in their spawning waters, then boiled the mix of eggs and boughs to serve with seal oil, Linda told me), and sheefish, or wild-swan soup. Trolling for coho with salmon eggs, she might hook fifteen in a morning, or, up the Kobuk, three times that many pike, plus shoot a skinny, gray spring caribou if their freezer meat was low: easier for her to do than when their coats got so lovely again by snow time. Fred had only bought her an 85-horsepower outboard because she had to be able to drag it across pileups of ice. That casual, San Francisco-style, reckless air wed to the northern stoicism, in a statuesque blonde, caused plenty of Eskimos to suggest "rubbing noses" with her in bars. Among the whites, the California-mellow, impromptu immediacy served equally well, and we enjoyed her couch, until the workhorse Boeing lofted us back to Anchorage, whose slippery night streets were the scene of down country skids by newcomers from the no-snow states. After margaritas, a green salad, and a bath, as a city man, I found my impotence abated.

• • •

CHAPTER 9

• • •

More Middlemen

SHELLFISHING IN ALASKA IS NOT like lobstering in Maine. King crab pots are seven feet square and weigh seven hundred pounds, and the waters mountainous in a storm. But the midnight sun works wonders on even run-of-the-mill millionaires, who tend to be able to fix as well as afford a cabin cruiser, field-dress as well as plug a moose, sail off Tonga or kayak in Turkey. Even hippies living a chilblained existence on an interior river might catch a flight over Greenland to London, if the late-winter blues overtake them, board the underground for Bond Street, where the furriers are, and stroll from store to store with thirty-five prime marten pelts to sell. To fly to Lagos or New Delhi and be recognized as nothing more particular than an American was part of the essence of versatility here. The oilpatch people posted from Houston or Dallas had brought concerts, theater, ballet, expanded funding for the university, because it was what they were used to, but the climate did not suit bravura in the brim of your hat or Old South snobberies. The military had salted people from all over the country into its towns and institutions, and old-timers didn't swagger in the cold, or imagine they owned much in a state the Feds mostly owned.

But Gary Holthaus, the Humanities program director, remembered the magic of his first days as a schoolteacher in Naknek, a roadless village of Yupiks on the Alaska Peninsula where he felt disoriented when he went for exploratory walks, as if he might drop off the rim of the world, until he began to figure out that the dozens of separate isolated cabins were not organized by any ordinary grid-work plan you might grasp at the start. Each family instead had set their home where it could catch a prevailing breeze or maximize the winter sun. Salmon was the food, driftwood the fuel, so paths to the beach were a priority, and once his sensibility was attuned to the tides, sunshine, and wind, Naknek's layout made perfect sense. Linda's boss, now a medical administrator, spoke similarly fondly of his early years in Alaska as an itinerant doctor serving islands like St. Lawrence, St. Mathew, Mekoryuk, Ukivok, or Diomede; how hospitable the Eskimos were in response to conscientious care—remembering wistfully the unforgettable joyful cry of a teenage girl he had just handed her first pair of glasses to. Suddenly she could see!

Linda's first job in the state, fresh off a cross-continental train after her divorce, had been as cook on a fishing boat out of Prince of Wales Island, bunking in the upper berth of the old Tlingit captain's cabin, where she was safe from advances by the crew but he enjoyed watching her bare legs swing down every morning to put the coffee on. Old crocks she liked, but for Linda and her friends in the front lines of frontier nursing, men in their prime remained quite baffling, provoking through malfeasance or testosterone so many medical problems, from saloon fights to wars that women, via education, nursing, or mediation, exerted their best efforts to repair. Loosely speaking, were they even worth it, or marriage a sanctuary? Her best friend had socked her last boyfriend right in the balls and kicked him out when she suspected him of cheating on her, and Linda, though not violent herself, seemed to draw some obscure satisfaction from hearing about this, as if it were perhaps a payback for the sexual abuse she believed her father had inflicted on her. I reminded her that, with her assistance, I was cheating on my wife, but love trumped adultery in her mind—she was using my name as her PIN in ATM machines, and could come in lovemaking at the urging of my voice. My Ivy Leaguer, college professor, *New York Times* editorial writer, Guggenheim Fellowship arbiter (I judged a competition of a hundred books in her apartment) persona may have been more unsettling than the adultery, because it portended divergence in the future, as my dependence on her out in "the villages" did not. We'd met at a writers' conference in Fairbanks, so mobility was implied, but that can be ambiguous. Here I was, having conned the famous New York editor Tina Brown for an Alaska assignment in order to hang out with Linda, and having long ago rebelled against my parents' country club values, financed by my father's job as a lawyer for Exxon, was nevertheless going out to interview sometimes repellent millionaires with a confidence born of private schooling with the sons of people named Rockefeller, Lindbergh, Wrigley, Tunney, Kennedy, Matisse, the Aga Khan, DuPont, Mellon, and so on.

I went to see a cardiologist named Gary Archer next, who had trained at Johns Hopkins, then done a two-year residency in the mid-sixties at the University of Washington in Seattle, after undergraduate work at the University of California at Santa Barbara, near Hollywood, where he'd grown up. But in 1977, after a dozen years in Alaska, he'd lost his hospital privileges in Anchorage due to a medical dispute I didn't delve into, and plunged into the travel business, where he was already a local titan: three hundred-sixty employees in twenty offices, eight in Anchorage alone. In the past five years his sales had jumped 691 percent, he said, and was aiming in the next five for a hundred offices nationwide. Also wanted to "go vertical," purchasing his own planes, ships, hotels, limos, and lodges. Lacking these, he presently picked a "preferred carrier" each year and instructed his staff to funnel customers to them; but, retaining a siege mentality, claimed to me that "a consortium" of local competitors had banded together to oppose him. He felt like "a platoon of Marines fighting against a bunch of Arabs," they were so scatterbrained. Alaska had been at its best when he first arrived, in '65, "when you could still simply say, get out of the way, I'm coming through." But the oil pipeline brought niggley increments of other regulations, plus a fundamentalist Christian influx lately, which he said bothered him more than the conservationist tree-huggers.

A chunky middleweight with unkempt black hair, an open-collared shirt, a high forehead, and a big, sad, formless, fearful face, Gary drank from a coffee cup that was inscribed "In case of panic grab me first." His head office was in an inconspicuous white house hidden away on a back access road near the airport, where numerous employees not dressed for success or prepossessing worked the phones in a warren of rooms.

"We're at the airport to make a statement. The action is here; we're here; and we've put the word out that we're looking for a hangar. We thought we'd give them a little chest pain," Gary added, speaking continually and often in brutal, quasi-physiological terms, not just about rival agencies. Employees should be "brainwashed— brand company policy deep in their frontal lobes"—and he loved to talk of the "positive incentive" of firings; the very threat was "a strong negative incentive against hanky-panky." "Tits-up" meant being dead, or "worthless as tits on a boar." His executive assistant could "fire three hundred and sixty people," and Michael, Gary's younger brother, "three hundred sixty-one." "I don't care if you're purple or orange or a woman, if you're working for us you don't have to wait for somebody to develop angina pectoris to move up." In the public offices, where Alaskans flocked to get out of town, "our agents wear uniforms so they will identify themselves not as individuals but as members of a team. Otherwise we seriously want them to work for our competition."

His home, up on a switchback of the affluent Hillside District, overlooked the city from a foothill of the Chugach Range. The gate was copper-lined, and two dynamiters named Hoot and Shoot had blasted out an eighty-by-fifteen-by-twelve-foot wine cellar for him underground. His house had six "telephone stations" in it, equipped with headsets, where he could work at all hours of the night. He said the travel industry struck him as the most bullish since Silicon Valley was invented. "And if you want to grow, we'll hire you, but I don't mean the going home at five to play with the kids bullshit. Career gratification must be the center of your life. It concerns the hell out of me if somebody even wants to take a vacation. We want to run for the roses; do not want to be a good small company, but a great large company. Hire very crazy people who have no personal life, and we're thin on management at the top." Consequently, he spent lots of time refereeing, "because a smooth team, that does not make." His gross at the Captain Cook Agency had leapt from $53 to $76 million in the past year.

Nonetheless, Gary did have a fly-in cabin across Cook Inlet to escape to, and he dated the end of Alaska's era of innocence to 1972, when the cabin had first been broken into and robbed. Not that burglaries per se marked the end of a pioneering ethic; crooks robbing the rich in a town like Anchorage would, of course, be as old as original sin. But up till then many people had purposely left their fly-in cabins unlocked and stocked with staples like canned food, a first-aid kit, and barrels of fuel, against the possibility that a fogged-in plane might be forced to land nearby and stay a while with problems ranging from a busted leg to a busted pontoon. Fishermen could be blown ashore, tipped over, wet or out of gas, or a famished hiker on his last legs might turn up in a blizzard, needing heat and calories, from the landward side. So even outlaws would have considered foreclosing the chance of saving a life, by stealing Good Samaritan necessities left in a vacation cabin, beyond the pale. Nowadays, however, a bush plane headed on a sporting trip might land by your cabin and fill up from your barrels just to save money and provision themselves with your beans and booze, too. In Barrow, on the North Slope, at about the same time, he witnessed a similar transformation. What with the oil boom, money in wages or taxes was pouring in, and all the Eskimos were buying snowmobiles, four-wheelers, and other modern doodads to get around. But one fellow still had a last dogsled downtown, and a stray dog loose on the street started a brouhaha with his team, in which his lead bitch was injured. Although a few years before this would have been a commonplace, if exasperating, fender-bender sort of thing, he hauled out a pistol and shot not just the troublemaker but, one by one, his whole string, as if to be rid of canines entirely. Gary spoke of Indians as "nasty bastards" but liked Eskimos, and said both were generally "going to the good," even where more pounds of beer were being imported than pounds of meat.

Before the boom, the whites who'd trickled into Alaska were "a dribble of sociopaths or rugged individualists," but now the city's rich were "displaced from Texas, Denver, or wherever, representing their home companies as in a foreign country," between assignments to Venezuela or the Persian Gulf. Since a travel business thrived on the misery of rootlessness, this was fertile ground, between the climate shoppers and the rolling stones. When you dropped into an office of his, "qualifiers triage the customers in two minutes" into either "the browsers who don't get to talk to a human being," the low-budget travelers whose order would be clicked into a computer while they stood at a no-stool counter by one of Gary's "black-box people that we don't let see a human face," or prospective vacationers of more affluent means, who were assigned a "consultant" at a desk, where they themselves were allowed to sit down and chat about their hopes and wishes. A "Travel Center International" was provided for the Cadillac crowd, where sherry and cheeses were on offer, along with advice and brochures, but his "Corporate Division" furnished the most transactions per hour.

When I peered into a downtown location, all these categories, even the "black box," seemed in desultory mode, yet Gary declared that Alaska offered latitude for his innovations; the established operators Outside "would all have heart attacks" if they had to go up against him. He'd learned not to hire agents who had trained Outside. "We had to say sayonara to fifty percent." He hired locally now for control, and asked himself for my benefit, "Who are the real dudes, the tough guys" who could make or break this place?—yet talking in a slurred, elided baby talk, with that fearful, sad, bully's face. In 1967, two years after arriving to practice medicine, he'd bought a half-interest in the nascent agency from a doctor-mentor at the hospital for $11,000, inheriting the rest a couple of years later, but only throwing himself into the business in the late 1970s, growing it from two to five offices, as the airline industry was deregulated and his hospital privileges were rescinded. Now his 75 percent ownership of Travel Center Inc. included the Touch of Class limousine service, two air charter businesses, three Silvertip fishing lodges, a forty-five-room Lands End resort hotel on the Homer Spit, and two national wholesale booking entities. A legendary bush pilot named Jack Peck, who'd come to Alaska in 1935, had taught him how "to fly and stay alive," and during his dozen doctoring years, along with fishing, it had become his avocation; later implicit to the travel business, ferrying customers to the lodge at Unakaleet on Norton Sound in his twin-engined Otter if a salaried pilot wasn't available. After delivering them, he'd stand on a float and throw in a line before returning.

Paintings of Western homesteads decorated his office, but his round-fronted mansion in the Hillside District featured Italian marble in the bathrooms, a Brazilian rosewood bar in the living room, plus three different TV sets so he could watch all of the major networks at once, and a spiral staircase crafted from rosewood from Honduras, with Tivoli-lighted mirrors on the walls. He "freshened" his personnel by shifting them to Kodiak or Juneau occasionally, he said, but wanted to feed into hubs like Miami eventually and regarded himself as a "consumer advocate," passing along block-seating savings to his "client base." He laughed, mentioning that in his start-up days the first person who taught him about bulk discounts was an eighteen-year-old girl in a sporting-goods store who surprised him by giving him ten percent off when he bought fifty pairs of hip boots. (The next year he bought five hundred pairs at a 40 percent discount directly from the manufacturer.) Moving from medicine to business, he found the hardest transition was the lack of honesty, the lying and secrecy, and handling time zones and jet lag, but was confident that at least a third of the 23,000 travel agencies in America would have to fold if confronted with the sort of business plan he advocated. In fact, he was to die, instead, in a rafting accident a dozen years after I talked with him. But the happiest times he'd ever had, he told me, had been when he was still a practicing cardiologist and he and a girlfriend would rent a pontoon plane on summer weekends to fly all over the bush with his two sons, landing on any lake they wanted to to camp and fish.

Larry Carr, my next magnate, a grocery man with twelve supermarkets, plus drug, liquor, and convenience outlets, though he sold out to the Safeway chain a few years later on, didn't make Linda feel like a gal Friday for delivering me, or call up synonyms for Capitalist, like "fascist," in her mind. He was gentle-mannered, liberal politically, with a rabbity-shaped face and a sweet smile befitting a man whose vocation for thirty years had been feeding people. A month after graduating from high school in San Bernardino, he and a friend had migrated north from California to Anchorage, whose population was then fifteen thousand, and found a laboring job at the army post, Fort Richardson. The friend soon decamped, as Larry had expected to, but, liking the place too much to leave and harboring secret ambitions to become a grocer, he took a job at the Alaska Railroad's commissary, moonlighting at a store in the evening. Then by 1950 he rented a Quonset hut at 13th and Gambell Streets for a spot of his own and hired Wilma, a soda fountain clerk at Hewitt's Drug Store, to help him, who became his wife when she finished high school herself. His corporate headquarters still sat in a square modest building behind the food mart he'd built to replace the Quonset hut, though now he owned three office buildings, two close to the courthouse and full of lawyers, accountants, and the like; in fact he was kicking the IRS out as a tenant by raising their rent. Wilma and he had three children, five grandchildren, and a desert hideaway in Palm Springs to retreat to in midwinter, having brought his parents to Alaska from San Bernardino so as not to have to go back there.

Wilma had moved to Alaska with her merchant-mariner and harbor-master family as a schoolgirl from Prince Rupert, British Colombia. Real estate had now become as profitable as groceries, in their partnership with Barney Gottstein with a Business Park, a 600-acre Bayshore subdivision, a 400-acre Southport subdivision. Barney, born in Alaska, had inherited his father's food-wholesaling business after going Outside to college, at the time Larry launched the Quonset hut store, and the fit was fortuitous. Larry, too, utterly loved Alaska, all seasons, all parts—would charter a boat, with "the wife," to explore Prince William Sound or Bristol Bay, north of Dillingham, or Chichagof and Baranof Islands, and owned a cabin in the sockeye territory of Kenai—plus Fairbanks, where he had opened a store only three years after the first in Anchorage, and then a shopping center. "Their sunnier summers," ten degrees warmer than Anchorage's, made up for the hammering they got in the winter, and it was friendlier, more historic and trusting there, as what he called "the Railbelt between us and them" was a fine place to sell groceries, too. He and Wilma had raised their family for seventeen years downtown, at "I" and Tenth Avenue, underneath the oil-company towers, but being empty-nesters—his eldest son had joined the business, which he conceded might be worth a hundred-fifty million dollars—had downsized to a smaller house at Campbell Lake.

Larry had even run in a Democratic primary for governor once, favoring less helter-skelter zoning to sculpt development, and more humane social programs. Success was a given in groceries. "It would have been hard to fail," when your customer base grew from fifteen thousand to a quarter of a million. He chuckled modestly, though sharing Bob Uchitel's dictum that "you have to love Alaska," and delivered a disquisition on the senators and governors it had had. The enormous expense of merely campaigning across four time zones of land mass made unseating the troglodytes, who often won, an uphill trudge, so Larry preferred chairing the board of Alaska Pacific University. Barney Gottstein, his harness-mate, was completely dissimilar in personality—a workaholic who seldom vacationed at all except to nip off to Hawaii or indulge a daredevil's pleasure in piloting his private five-passenger, twin-engined Beechcraft Baron to old gold diggings and ghost towns about the state, dropping in on customers in the bush whose general stores they provisioned up and down the Yukon and the Kuskokwim or offshore, not caring where the weather chased or stranded him, once they'd hired sufficient office staff.

• • •

CHAPTER 10

• • •

Wolverines and Wolves

L INDA LOOKED LIKE ANNA, FROM *L'Avventura*, though she knew about embolisms, and I detoured from my fifties to thirties again. So many floors we slept on! Sometimes in a private house, vouched for by a phone call from friends of friends, or after a teacher unlocked the school, with the light plant and boiler grinding, the alphabet or animal kingdom decorating the walls. Alaska was such a destination for end-of-the-roaders that you must have been recommended, but minimal acquaintanceship would win an endorsement. Under the heat lamps on a ferry deck, surrounded by sleeping retirees, with moonlit glaciers parading past, or in apartments where other women were sibilantly undressing as we moonily clasped on a couch, Alaska was still not for first youth. Everybody had a back story; the expenses and wagers were high, and crying jags might ensue when the plane flew off. A log cabin turned out to be a bitch to build, rain had wet your staples and you'd spilt your chainsaw gas—could you tie the logs together in a raft? A marital or business tailspin, some stinging dismissal or ill-healed wound, even a motorcycle accident, could have propelled people here: which was all to the good if they'd hoarded a bit of grubstake and heedful caution as a result, because from Florida to Oregon there were easier places to try for a new start. In bleak little towns, individual fractures are thrown into brittle relief. Every other white man had "two or three children two or three thousand miles away," as a guy in the Sea Inn Bar in Dillingham told us. A broken snowshoe or Ski-Doo tread on a finger ridge or pinhead lake could spell frozen buttocks you'd limp from all your life. "And the mark of Alaskans is that they don't intend to stay." He watched us ironically to see if we were going to disagree, but I had a fourteen-year-old daughter more miles than that away, and Linda already felt hankerings toward graduate school back east.

My own uncontrolled crying occurred out of the blue at the memorial service for an ex-governor, Bill Egan, which I had gone to not because of any interest in him, but hoping to at least observe, if not chat up, several prominent power brokers or millionaires who had failed to return my phone calls. But as I sat weeping, sobbing in my pew, instead of intercepting or ingratiating myself with them, I became an object of considerable unease and curiosity—a total stranger grieving more publicly than the governor's family. (The hall was even named for him.) I was crying for my broken marriage and maybe my father's death and that of a dear friend recently, but couldn't stop—so people wondered what cranny of the former governor's life I represented; power brokers covertly stared at me. Finally a burly, comradely Tlingit representing his village walked over, put his arm around my shoulders and said, "He was good to us Indians, too."

I felt better on the street, flushed of tension, and remembered Linda's and my drive from Haines to Tok in that heap of a car we'd had to abandon and hitchhike from, but first burrowing together in deep rainforest ferns and moss, under St. Elias, Wrangell, or Nutzotin Mountain, jaggedly crenellated above our twig-fire supper, and a gray glacial creek coursing past, the skies intensified by the snow on the peaks. I was after true love, and also material for a frontier novel that ended up being called *Seven Rivers West* when it came out a few years later, so I needed to see a string of rivers.

Dillingham was next. March 7th, we flew in a Wien Air plane, boasting the state colors, blue and gold, whereas Alaska Airlines employed silver with blue lettering and the doughy face of "Charlie Fairbanks," a cherubic prospector, on the tail. It was a white-run town of eighteen hundred souls, fifty-five percent of them native, which serviced about thirty other villages around Bristol Bay, and a regional population of five thousand. It had two general stores, though one was empty, a penny arcade, a fishing-net shop, The Sea Inn Bar, and the Cannery Restaurant in the Bristol Inn. Except for herring caught for their roe for the Japanese delicacy *kazunoko* in April and May in the corner known as Togiak Bay, it was all salmon here, and all five kinds of salmon to some extent, though twenty million of the twenty-five million caught would be sockeye (reds), and ninety percent of these in a three-week period peaking around the Fourth of July. The catch was by gill nets, and the thirty-foot boats and yearly location permits near the mouths of the Nushagak, Kvichak, and Togiak Rivers cost over a hundred thousand dollars, but the captain could clear fifty to a hundred thousand in a season; his crewmen each made perhaps a third of that. Three-hundred-foot commercial nets strung from shore cost by permit half as much, and subsistence nets half as long were free to those with heritage rights. The cannery workers earned six dollars an hour for twelve-hour days from mid-June to Labor Day, though helicopters were also lifting a lot of fish directly from tenders out in the bay to the air strip, where they were promptly flown south.

We'd missed by one day the annual Dillingham Beaver Roundup, when besides skinning contests, there was arm-wrestling, snuff-spitting, beer-swilling. Ken Taylor, a state biologist, said the cat and dog families—wolves, lynx—were easiest to skin, but beavers have shoulder muscles attached to their undersides, so it becomes more time-consuming and complicated. In Louisiana I'd traveled with Cajun trappers who tried to keep the nutria—a related southerly furbearer—they caught alive all day by only cracking their heads enough to put them into a coma, so their bodies would remain limber for skinning at night. (It created a pile of groaning beasts in the boat.) Otters, however, had the most complex muscularity and points of attachment.

Taylor said, when I asked, that only half a dozen of Alaska's eighty or so game biologists have ever been to Africa; the rest were "intimidated," except for one guy who went every year. A Tlingit fisherman, Bill Demmert, told me he ate only the sockeyes, although he caught king salmon and humpies (pinks) and cohos (silvers) too. "Unlike an Eskimo," he specified—Bristol Bay being Yupik country—he dried them first for twenty-four hours in the wind so they would be less oily. Even our X-ray technician from Communicable Disease Control, Tom Sanders, said he took a three-month leave every summer to participate in the sockeye bonanza, and Barbara Campbell, a friend of Linda's from the Juneau area with a lucrative

North Slope job, returned to her Auk Bay home to hand-troll for king salmon from a twenty-foot boat in Hobbit Hole, off Elfin Cove, on Chichagof Island. Many boats from here, after the sockeye spawning surge (sixty-two million fish were estimated to boomerang through Bristol Bay in the rush), moved south after humpies, and processors competed for the salmon market by the appearance and condition of their fish in cans, or fresh or frozen, the quality of handling or quickness of their jumbo jets.

Charlie Blood operated the Bristol Bay Rural Education Center, for these thirty villages, in fifty-five thousand square miles—the size of Iowa—and an extraordinary ethnic range, from the Yupiks of Togiak, to the Tanaina Athabascans of Nondalton, to the Aleuts of Perryville and Ivanoff Bay. Courses in gold-panning, anthropology, fishing, or detective novels led to Associate in Arts or teaching assistant degrees. Ken Taylor, as regional biologist, had a smaller area, eighteen thousand square miles—like two Vermonts—to supervise, with ten villages and probably two hundred part-time trappers, whose primary livelihood was, of course, fishing or canning, he said. He'd allowed them a one-month season and a ten-beaver limit and eighteen hundred had been trapped; then censused the remaining population from the air by counting food caches in front of the beaver houses (otherwise a counted house might be "dead"). The twenty thousand caribou in the Mulchatna River herd he counted from aerial photographs taken in June by following thirty radiotagged cows to the rendezvous grounds where they gathered after calving, and adding an estimate of the bulls, which though they remain higher up at that time, join them in a verifiable ratio in the fall. He said caribou inhabited climax vegetative terrain, and moose at its successional stages—a moose to about every square mile and a quarter where they have food—but neither live on the Bethel-like tundra around Togiak (which is not far below the mouth of the Kuskokwim).

Dillingham itself had pretty shade trees and an air of permanence which reminded me of Aberdeen, the coastal town in the State of Washington, where my mother was raised. But spruces grow only to an altitude of three hundred feet, willows and alders to a thousand or so, and timberline separates the brown and black bears, with the latter therefore sandwiched between mountain and shoreline grizzlies, either of which will happily grab and eat them. Wolves were shot at a rate of one per thousand square miles per year here, and occurred at better than ten times that level, no aerial hunting being permitted. Wolverines live near glaciers at the heads of the rivers and other remote redoubts that trappers avoid—though in fact they are easily trapped and come down to eat porcupines where there are trees. Even ptarmigan tracks he could follow in the snow from a plane. The Togiak National Wildlife Refuge, nearby, was now slated to hold in abeyance 3.8 million acres, two-thirds with a wilderness designation, including a hundred-forty-one bird species so far recorded, counting the stray migrators from Russia, Japan, New Zealand, or South America. Ten thousand emperor geese staged and fed in Chagvan Bay during their migrations. Big walrus haul-outs existed between Kulukak and Togiak Bays, and sea lion rookeries. Eight villages of forty-six hundred people lay within the wildlife refuge and did subsistence fishing, and on three river systems—the Togiak, the Goodnews, and the Kanektok—plus smaller, fertile spawning waterways, ducks fattened on the eelgrass and rafted up for their enormous flights. Eskimos made rain parkas out of seal guts; but "all you had to do for meat was go upriver."

I talked to David Fisher, the refuge manager, who had a Cessna and pilot to help him, trailer housing, and a half-time clerk. Moist muskeg and alpine tundra, up to five thousand feet, were belted with bits of spruce or willow-alder growth and isolated mining activity, notably a platinum find in Fox Gulch on Red Mountain in 1926, from which 320 tons had so far been extracted. Ken Taylor told me he'd taken only bears' hairs off tree bark, etc, for dietary sampling, instead of more invasive techniques like knocking them out to draw a vial of blood. Said he had noticed the more experienced bears, when fishing the salmon rivers, although they chomped down on any fish darting upstream, if it turned out to be male, they'd discard it, let it float away, and grab the next, hoping it was going to have a belly full of roe to chew. Younger bears avidly seized any scrap of fish they caught or found, however, and clambered onto the bank to tear meat from bones. He acted out with one hand how a bear employs a paw to do all this.

People ordered in a thousand-dollar grubstake on the October barge before winter, but the "N and N" General Store, with benches in front, was the hangout, besides a Seventh Day Adventist Center,

a little Baha'i Temple, and a mini-Foursquare Gospel Church, dat-
ing from Aimee Semple McPherson. The hospital was a converted
orphanage, circa 1918. No nurses' uniforms, just RN nametags on
sweaters. A place redolent of many dramatic, transient romances and
religious epiphanies. We saw two red retrievers who had achieved co-
itus on the main drag, but now, facing in different directions seemed
desirous of becoming disentwined if they could figure out how. White
men here acted either too tough or too waffly, but Johanna Bouker—
coordinator for the University's Rural Education Center and Charles
Blood's assistant—took a shine to us in a manner as comfortable as a
shoe, in a well-settled town where we were treated a bit brusquely,
snootily by other whites. I walked to "The Flats," wind-blown, snow-
blown, just before the spruces start, where the airstrip was. As at
other airstrips, Dillingham's had a wrecked (Convair) plane lying in
the woods, multiplying the endeavor's uncertainties. I saw two eagles
stooping after ducks. The town of Aleknagik, pop. 150, was asking
the State for a $150,000 hovercraft to take its kids through a lake
outlet to school instead of using the road around. And oil, along with
the 1971 Alaska Native Claims Settlement Act, was the golden goose.
It was also supposed to fund a thirty-eight-foot, ten-million-dollar
hydroelectric dam on the Quigny River, powering the TVs and dryers of the town of Togiak, population 470, but thus ending its salmon
run. We stayed at Johanna's, as newcomers paired in a love affair,
locking fingers as we strolled, engaged with Alaska. Dillingham was
not a plungers' town. The cannery investors had always pulled their
money south and out, and the hoi polloi who they shipped in and out
from somewhere like Seattle to work with the local natives for the
compact, feverish, high-summer season, did not create a boomtown
in Dillingham, just a comfy middleman's supply base.

If somebody local got bored or crazy-seeming and couldn't stay
put, they might simply go "upriver." The Nushagak, the Togiak, and
parallel north-south rivers led to numerous lakes and then the Ahklun
Mountains, a watershed that if you climbed across became the headwaters of feeders to the Holitna River, winding down eventually
to Sleetmute, Crooked Creek, the Stony River, or other mountains
descending to the webwork of the Kuskokwim, then, climbing again
beyond that, the Yukon's fabled arc—gold country, starvation country, honeycombed with crusted hopes. Johanna had been born here in

1940, the only all-white child at school, except for the territorial marshal's son, who was so picked on that he used to hide underneath the
building. But it was also the kind of tiny town where at Christmas-
time everybody gathered at Loews Theatre and put their names into
a hat, to be drawn individually, and whomever you drew you had to
give a present to. "Upriver" was where the outlaws ran and where
the wild Indians lived, who used to chase Johanna when they came
to town. *Beards* meant "upriver"; and once the marshal brought her
father two heads in a pail to try to identify. Her father, a pilot, married a local Indian woman in 1958, after Johanna's mother, a schoolteacher, died, but she had probably lusted after him ever since he'd
first arrived from Minnesota twenty years before. This lady, Johanna's
stepmother, with her son, had lately been murdered in Anchorage.
Her father, John Walatka, had dropped out of high school back in the
Midwest, and started living at the nearest airport, then became a stunt
pilot and mail pilot, and married and had three children—whom he
abandoned when he flew off to Alaska along with a teacher from
town, who left her own family too, and married him after Johanna
was born. At first they'd landed in Dillingham "just to gas up." John
didn't think he'd like the sea air, but was hired immediately for quick
fish-hauling jobs, and gave many natives their first airplane rides.
The canneries hired him as a private pilot, paying him like a "high-
bullet" boat captain at the end of the salmon season, whereupon he
would fly hunters and fishermen to the upcountry lakes for their ex-
cursions—in fact, he finally died of a heart attack at sixty-five while
hefting a rich customer's luggage out of his float plane at a hunting
camp. (Fishing itself made him nervous, however. He once jumped
out the front window of their house in his sleep after dreaming that
the fish were running and their family's beach net wasn't set.)

Johanna, long before, had been permitted to go to school in
Anchorage at twelve; then the University of Washington. In 1972,
at thirty-two, she returned, married to a man who was to manage
the village's electrical utilities, its population having more than doubled, to nine hundred. Having since redoubled, the town was "rawer
now," she told us, except for the absence of sled dog teams and those
wild "upriver Indians," although with the new flood of fishermen,
more teachers and nurses had arrived for the hospital and school.
"Heavyset," as she politely put it, the nurses married native men and

stayed forever, supporting them through the long winters when they couldn't fish.

Her father had worked for Wien Air, too, but kept leaving its stifling Anchorage office to bush-fly hunters or cannery executives again, and kept a beach-setting permit her family still used, paying $30,000 a year and $40,000 for the site on the beach, though it sometimes distressed her to watch her kids wading in mud and learning to curse. Said so much money flowed that her kids found hundred-dollar bills in the parking lot of the Willow Tree Bar, where the Eskimos and fly-by-nights drank. (The Sea Inn was for long-termers and locals.) A Yupik from Togiak might make $75,000 to $100,000 in a summer's fishing season—often paid in hundred-dollar bills—so there was no impetus for family heads to send their sons off to be educated. As it was, the women were the ones who pushed for that, or did it, wanting to manage their village's affairs, teach, and influence the corporations set up under the Alaska Native Claims Settlement Act.

Charles Blood added that Dillingham residents, at the captain's level, could make $150,000 or $200,000 in a summer, and fly to Florida with their seven kids, buy a van and tour, buy a speedboat, buy an organ, a video tape recorder, buy new movies instead of bothering to rent them. But then they may not have paid their taxes before they spent it all, and, out in the bay again, they'll find that while they were working, the wife and mother-in-law maybe got so drunk together that their infant daughter drowned in a slop bucket. And you'll have another domestic assault case.

Johanna said she missed the fishing camps her father serviced on lakes in the Katmai National Park and Preserve, where classy folk like Adlai Stevenson and Laurence Rockefeller stayed, not to kill any animals but just to look. "Some people can't stand to see an animal alive," she complained. And that "only watered-down versions" of the caliber of the old Alaskans showed up nowadays. People used to have a skill of some kind to offer—"you had to be able to sell yourself or else you just grew a beard and went upriver."

Historically there were no drugs in the Arctic among the indigenous groups—who didn't ferment berries, for instance. But their shamanism could generate an occasionally comparable hysteria, controlled or uncontrolled. The Tlingits' practice of slavery did not spread north; nor the ritual execution of a captive for entombment under a house post when a new one was constructed, as the Tlingits did. Perhaps the fearsome climate precluded superfluous displays of cultural ferocity. It had been the end of the road for many a white drifter, but now a peak of opportunity for young, white, liberated, credentialed women fitted for what was becoming an impromptu meritocracy, and native women too, who accepted the scholarship opportunities and took over post offices and town clerkships, yet withstood the dizzying deterioration of the menfolk around them, of which suicide was only an extreme manifestation.

While Linda worked, I went and talked with David and Mary Carlson, a childless couple in their eighties. He arrived on a monthly mail boat from Dutch Harbor in the Aleutians as an out-of-work schoolteacher from Minnesota during the Depression, having also tried Juneau first. The job he got was on a cannery-owned sailboat, seining salmon, then trapped up the Tikchik River and its string of lakes during the winter, earning enough to buy the little house on the hill they still lived in, forty-five years later. He'd considered he had a sweetheart back in North Dakota, who was going to come out and marry him. But she wasn't too keen on Alaska, suggested Mary, and on the train ride out west from the Dakotas, met a man from California whom she married instead. Mary herself appeared on the scene as a nurse from Philadelphia, in 1939, to work in a hospital for terminal TB patients and frostbite cases, intending to return after a couple of years to the University of Pennsylvania again for graduate work. But she was introduced to David one night by flashlight—the village, unincorporated, had no electricity—although her friend, who was doing the honors, assuming she would be most interested in *another* man, kept the beam always fixed on *him*. So she fell in love with David's voice, not seeing his face. A Cuban doctor, New York-trained, who supervised, a Dr. Salazar, passed him the word that he was liked, and by 1941 they were married in the very sitting room where we were having our talk: Mary saying that she was lucky to have a husband who was "a homebody, not gallivanting." There were town meetings to organize a fire department, an electric co-op, a cemetery committee. The house was crowded with plants in fat pots, and books, a piano, a warm stove, and warm furnishings. The Carlsons sat with lumberjack shirts over their pajamas and strips of cardboard on the floor to absorb the dirt of their boots. They each received a state "longevity bonus" of $250 a month, in addition to federal social security, in a program that was instituted to encourage old people to stay in the state, not slide south in retirement, leaving the state wholly "young."

David fished commercially for seven years, then helped found and run the Fishermen's Co-op Trading Company as a shopkeeper for twenty-five years, an organization patterned after Irish co-ops started after the Potato Famine and which aimed to cut the markup on Anchorage prices for food and dry goods from 100 percent to 30 percent, he said. (Complained that with the N and N privately owned store taking over, the markup over Anchorage was back to 100 percent.) When only a hundred people lived in town, you had to speak some Yupik and go to the Russian church, till the English-speaking Church of Christ was established; then the Baptist; the Seventh Day Adventist, the Assembly of God; and the Moravians', which was the one the Carlsons chose to join, although from Lutheran-Presbyterian backgrounds. The cannery companies had managed to restrict fishing to sailboats by claiming motors would disrupt the salmons' spawning rush, and since they owned the fleets of those, bringing in crews to work them, excluded outside competition. But the sailboats had a way of blowing onto sandbars and tipping over in tempestuous weather when overloaded with the catch. One year seventeen people drowned, and Mary made him quit. In 1938 he'd earned eight cents per salmon; in 1939, twelve cents. In 1952 motorboats became legal in Bristol Bay, outsiders came in, and the canneries began paying by the pound. Now, thirty years later, the going rate was about sixty-five cents a pound or three dollars for an average red salmon. Until 1955 there was no bank in Dillingham, so the canneries gave their workers coupon books (in some towns, aluminum tokens) to use in local stores. Because international waters started only three miles out, Japanese ships could swing in close, however, and gobble tons, until 1976 when a two-hundred-mile limit was imposed and enforced. Now the Japanese tenders come to *buy* more than to fish. The change greatly stimulated the American catch of herring in Togiak Bay, as well, which jumped from under a hundred tons to a range of ten to twenty thousand tons. Another recent change was the switch from mainly canning fish to immediately freezing them and flying them to the outside world in DC-3s or Hercules jets, along with fresh salmon, cleaned but not processed. In 1978 sixty-three percent of Bristol Bay salmon were canned and twelve percent frozen. In 1982 seventeen percent were canned and sixty percent frozen (the rest left fresh, or salt-cured for export). Until the middle-1920s the two or three principal canneries had only needed to rig fish traps in the rivers to supply their operations; any boats were supplementary. But now that salmon were lofted whole to Tokyo or Paris almost as soon as they were caught, the hugger-mugger of motley cannery workers shuttled in en masse to work like hell, except for a weekly blowout if they could hitch a boat ride to town, was reduced.

Mary, born in 1900, had wanted to be "a Nurse on Horseback" for the Frontier Nursing Service, an outfit famous at the time for serving the mountain hollows in Kentucky, like many other nurses who ended here (like Linda, indeed). She arrived on the S.S. Yukon in Seward on St. Patrick's Day, 1939, then flew in a Star Line Widgeon on skis to here, in her hat and suit, crammed next to an Italian gentleman in back who had a piglet on his lap and a bottle that he wanted to share, and they were met by an Eskimo dogsled that jostled her every which way. Only three nurses staffed this TB-warehouse hospital, one for each shift, but to spend your life as a nurse is "a life of service," she said—"good service to mankind. You can go to sleep with a clear conscience." Said she'd postponed marriage for so long because of a wretched family life behind her. At the hospital, the patients were only given rolls of toilet paper to spit into, but one young Inupiat, George Agupuk, in Kotzebue, was so talented that he drew on the toilet paper, and a nurse, noticing, helped and encouraged him, and he became a famous primitive artist with a New York gallery.

She and her friend Edra Pfeiffer were the only nurses who married white men, and both thereupon quit when they did so, after just a couple of years, and then persuaded their husbands to stop fishing as well. Edra's, though, contracted TB and died of surgical complications down in Seattle—maybe she shouldn't have sent him Outside. Mary's Swede, David Carlson, was called "Slow Motion" in Yupik by the Eskimos, Mary told me, because he was so deliberate. But they'd bring a piano into the movie house for him to play, and have a community sing. Courting her, David would borrow a dog team and mush the seven miles to where the hospital was (after the doctor let him know she was interested), and they might go to a "box social," a dance where boxed suppers were raffled, each prepared by a young lady anonymously and wrapped with ribbons, and her young man would try to guess which of the bunch had been made by her and bid high to obtain it. They still had no phone or running water; said the proposed sewage plant was presently the dog pound; raw sewage ran straight into the bay; so they were glad not to be contributing to that flow.

The itinerant nurse here, pragmatic and husky, visited the villages of New Stuyahok, Manokotak, Egegik, Igingig, Koliganek, Togiak, Goodnews Bay, Ivanoff Bay, and Portage Creek. Her office boasted *National Geographic* and *Forbes* magazines. Her supervisor, taking a sabbatical, had gone to New Zealand for a year: no brighter lights for her. Edra Pfeiffer, from Spokane, arriving as a TB nurse in 1944, had married Heine Hildebrand and fished with him, until they started Hildebrand's Dry Goods Store. But he died and she married Mr. Pfeiffer: who duly died, too, of a stroke. And so she'd run the store for three decades, carrying on alone, while resisting her sister's admonitions to come down to Washington's milder conditions. Edra seemed an everyday sort of elderly woman, compared to Mary's animated curiosity and humanity, and said the men napped in the winter, "if they *stayed in*. I guess it will never be anything but a fish village. I often wonder what is making it grow. Really there isn't too much here, you know. It depends on what you want out of life." She paused in talking to me to sell a woman a sweater zipper, a man a $5.50 belt. The tall grass, shade trees, and boardwalks made for an appealingly quiet town that the residents were glad to see the fishermen clear out of in the fall, and the fishermen—turning their boats out to sea—were glad to leave behind.

The quietness made me stutter worse because there was more focus on me as newcomer in conversations; less action, information, and accoutrements to ask about. And when I stuttered, I automatically, immediately dropped my eyes, as I had been doing for forty years or more in order not to witness any smiles or pity, confused astonishment or subdued laughter on the other person's face, although some people might laugh in an attempt at sympathy, not mockery, because they didn't realize I had a handicap and was stuttering, but thought the jerking of my mouth and head must also be laughter. Though understanding this range of reactions—from Schadenfreude to coolly dismissive to demonstrative empathy—I didn't want to see it, at least until the other person had figured out what my difficulty was and what they wanted their considered response to be. Having an impediment wasn't always a disadvantage; it could break the ice in a helpful way, arousing a bit more trust or fellow-feeling in a stranger, especially if he or she had hang-ups too. But if I heard their words without seeing their faces, my gaze being defensively averted to save myself the possibility of being hurt, I might not register the details of appearance a writer should. In our tenderness, I spoke fluently to Linda without a stutter, as if healed, although the magic seldom extended to conversations with others sitting with us, and in order to escape the humiliation of stuttering in ugly helplessness in front of her, I would generally stay silent.

We were treated to a ride up the one patch of road Dillingham had, to Wood River and Aleknagik, the first in a whole zigzag or Mad Hatter series of skinny lakes piggybacked northward of where we were, which, like the larger Iliamna Lake on the Kvichak River not far away, provided the sockeye ideal spawning conditions to make Bristol Bay a bonanza for the industry. (In Iliamna you might catch fifteen-pound rainbow trout which had fattened their whole lives on salmon roe and dying salmon flesh.) Our hosts, however, were local boosters hoping for publicity for spending projects they had in mind, like the hovercraft to save certain white schoolchildren a bus ride, much as the village of Twin Hills, pop. seventy, near Togiak, had six or eight children but a new gym in their school and even provision for a high school expansion, and the children of South Naknek were flown every day to Naknek for classes. Their pitch was wasted on us, since Linda's heartstrings were tied to native villages, where health issues were marbled through a wider cultural devolution, morale cracking and crumbling, which led to frostbitten children and young men flinging themselves in the river.

I went to talk to Ken Taylor, the crackerjack state biologist for this area, again. He said he resented a new "remote parcel" program, which gave people the right to build wilderness cabins in the midst of moose wintering yards or caribou calving grounds, using the Fish and Game Department's own habitat maps to choose the locale, but not other input from its experts as to particular harm that could be done. These were on state lands and otherwise, however, he resented the feds "locking up" huge tracts of federal land. Said Alaskans should own all of Alaska and simply sell their oil to the rest of the country at an eight percent royalty, as Iowans sold corn. He also objected to the Marine Mammal Act, which he said resulted in "no management of the animals." Only natives could shoot them, but there were no bag limits, sex limits, or seasons on seals, walruses, or bears, so the easier, close-in creatures were the ones that got killed—the fertile female polar bears on or nearest shore, where they gave birth and trained their cubs, and the fertile female walruses floating on pack ice, not the mature male bears and walruses, which ordinarily were farther out but were the specimens that should be "harvested."

In addition to his landward duties, he managed Round Island, near Togiak and Kulukak Bays, the one state-owned sanctuary where walruses routinely hauled out to sun and rest, when it was ice-free, from May to September—as many as twelve thousand at a time on the lee side, while four or five hundred sea lions made use of the windward beach. One mile by two, and rising close to a thousand feet, it sheltered more than a million nesting birds as well, the only predators, besides a pair of ravens and a pair of eagles, being about a dozen foxes with five or ten kits, which starved during the winter, aging fast (at three were old), after stealing and burying eggs not only from the birds but from each other. Russia, he said, had many more protected walrus sites, with a sixteen-mile, versus half-mile, boat-free zone, and airplanes taboo within ten thousand, versus two thousand, feet. Taylor, at thirty-five, said Round Island was "like Africa" in its thronging wildlife. He'd once visited there but hurried back to take his first job here, which then fell through, and had always regretted his haste. Once saw fifty gray whales all together migrating past eighteen walruses sunning on a rock, and a single sea lion scouting cautiously past, plus the thousands of birds. Walruses breed on the icepack north or west of Round Island and the females with pups tend to stay at the edge of the ice, where they can rest close to their clamming grounds and avoid the danger of pups being inadvertently crushed by galumphing males, larger than the mothers. Stronger swimmers, the males congregate on the island instead, but leave on weeklong feeding cycles, foraging way out, then returning to haul on the beach for a couple of days. A walrus scientist, he said, once fashioned a mask from Styrofoam, with tusks attached and a brown hardhat and cloak, in order to be able to approach the animals close enough to affix radio-tags to them. But to see out from under the helmet he needed to tilt his head at such an angle that his tusks stuck forth in what in walrus-speak was an aggressive posture. Although young walruses fled from him, aghast, a big dominant male charged—he had to quickly strip off his disguise. Another scientist, studying the handful of foxes—which uncharacteristically consolidate into a pack, with an alpha male and vixen, in order to survive— accidentally broke a leg on his database animal, and pinned it together like a vet to continue. Taylor himself also kept track of the eighteen-thousand-head Mulchatna caribou herd, named for a river that drains the Ahklun Mountains between the Kuskokwim and here. So a wallboard in his office was marked with pins showing where aerial surveys have determined their high-country locations. Yet despite his love of the state he "missed the four seasons" and had bought a strip of property on the Mississippi in Wisconsin, where he could retire and enjoy them in another decade, just returning for the hot money of the summer sockeye bonanza. The Kvichak River, connecting to Lakes Iliamna and Clark—where the rainbow trout grew to fifteen pounds feeding on salmon eggs and the flesh of their expiring parents—was the greatest sockeye nursery in the world because of the conditions it afforded their one-to-three freshwater years, before, as smolt, they headed downstream for the sea, whereas the longer, more complicated Nushagak River was hospitable to all five species, including the "humpies," as they're called because of the shape their backs assume at spawning time, a type that prefers the brackish mouths of rivers and intertidal tributaries. Humpie eggs hatch in about a year and the smolt go out to the sea from the estuary almost immediately, when two inches long, and in another year or so return to spawn, already weighing five pounds, two feet in length.

The spirit of an animal, in Eskimo lore, appreciated being hunted with a beautiful implement, and after its body was killed, being permitted to transfer to an unborn creature, which when hunted in turn, remembered how it had been treated before—becoming easier or harder to secure as a consequence. So there was a gulch between the old ways and how even Eskimos fished and hunted now.

CHAPTER 11

• • •

Salmon and Dogs

J OE RUNYAN FLEW BACK TO Tanana in a little overstuffed Cessna
with his girlfriend, Sheri, her small daughter and son, and his
long dogsled and sixteen huskies. He'd just finished eleventh in the
eleven-hundred-mile Iditarod Sled Dog Race from Anchorage to
Nome—had been named runner-up to a Norwegian for Rookie-
of-the-Year—and now hadn't been charged the ordinary charter fare
to be ferried home. The race generated enormous excitement in all
Alaska, of course, starting in downtown Anchorage and lasting for
twelve days or so, featured on any news broadcast, and in Tanana,
population 370, the town fire engine drove to the airstrip to meet
him, when the pilot buzzed the town.

Joe unloaded, waved the plane off with thanks for the break
on the fee, and hitched up his team to drive in triumph in front of
the engine, with its siren sounding, down Main Street to his home.
Another fifteen dogs were chained on gang lines in his yard, so he
said hello to these, and to a doctor friend from the Indian Health
Service, who'd walked over from the clinic to congratulate him, and
Stan Zuray, who'd watched Joe's place for him and who the previous
year had finished ninth in the same race and achieved Rookie-of-the-
Year. Sheri said she might be more tired than Joe, from the continual
partying and social events during the thirteen days he'd been gone.
Although an Eskimo family had hospitably opened their house to her
and the children, she had caught a cold, but gamely hosted yet another party that night for their boosters and friends here.

Tanana was an Indian town, in these early 1980s, about half-way up the great bend of the Yukon River between salt water and Canadian (or "Klondike," in the old days) territory. A substantial, six-hundred-mile tributary of the same name flowed into the main-stem valley half a mile across from town. Tanana comprised perhaps a hundred twenty-five houses, cabins, shacks, or huts, and the salmon runs, as always, were the staff of life—fish in superabundance at the height of their runs in the summer being sun-cured or smoked to last till next year. But in the last census, only twenty men had listed themselves as "trappers," the traditional occupation since first contact with Russians or English-speaking white men a hundred-fifty years before, whereas the local school had twenty-two employees, which seemed quite indicative of this era of giddy, fearful changes in store for many of the Indians in the state.

Alaska, like America, had been a magic name, but also "The Last Place," as people said lately who weren't here so much because it was a land of opportunity as because they disliked the rest of the country, yet didn't as a rule propose to do much of anything different here, just climb out on a limb and saw themselves off. In the northern interior one could run into a state trooper, a school superintendent, or a game warden responsible for territory equivalent to six Vermonts. White people arrived to opt out of the grid for a spell to discipline or distract themselves, as a challenge or an escape, to procrastinate, or simply volplaning, putting miles under their belts, enlarging the theater of their lives, fulfilling a personal dream they didn't expect to pan out but would regret quailing out of. Per capita income and divorce rates were the highest in the country. Statistically, nine times the national average of adults had a pilot's license and the proportion of people over fifty was the lowest. Hoosiers, Tar Heels, and Buckeyes whose foreheads wrinkled when they recalled being born on the wrong side of the tracks: their fathers' drunks, their mothers' bruises—Alaskans were generally a goaded group, masked by the beards they grew to ward off mosquitoes. But the Indians were native, not trippers, and floundering for footing, having had the rug pulled out from under them, as the advent of satellite TV made painfully and daily clear to anybody too dull to have realized this by grammar school.

Joe Runyan was not one of the thirtyish whites who show up so equivocally that people joke, "What was his name in the States?"

He wasn't wanted for something or edgy from Vietnam combat or a nervous breakdown somewhere. On the contrary, he was unusual for being a bit of a world traveler, with brief tours, after an Idaho boyhood and graduating from Oregon State, of India, Latin America, and Africa, and had a cosmopolitan air, a liking for languages, and energetic curiosity. He spoke of "the vortex of money" the oil boom had inflicted upon Alaskans, both native and white. Said his dogs had "a waterbug energy, a genetic imperative to pull," and were "so imprinted to pick up a human's moods" that they could lose a race only because their master grew discouraged. He'd missed the tenth position, $2,000 in prize money, and Rookie-of-the-Year by just an hour, and felt himself getting stronger, not weaker, by the end. (Indeed, he was to win the Iditarod race in a later year.) At thirty-four, he was a long-jawed, lanky, black-haired man who, even among these Yukon River types celebrating with him in Tanana, stood out for his size and vigor. Said he'd spent the first week on the trail "learning how to run the race." A dog driver "can operate them forcefully" for sixteen or eighteen hours a day, traveling at five miles per hour, or else "harmonize with them and their sleep patterns and work them only twelve hours a day but go at nine miles an hour"—which, over eleven hundred miles of mountains, river valleys, and arctic coast, should win, he said. One "ought to balance, harmonize, and work with the dogs' own magic and integrity. A lot of guys take the magic out of them, and then you never get it back."

Stan, his sidekick, originally an inner-city white kid from Boston, who had done so well last year, had ended up with thirty-five dogs (counting puppies) but couldn't raise the eight or ten thousand dollars necessary to finance all the expenses to try again. Many contestants write begging letters or go door-to-door for sponsorship among corporate entities of Fairbanks and Anchorage, but Stan lived with his wife, Helen, on a homestead forty miles cross-country from Tanana and sixty miles up a tributary of the Yukon, called the Tozitna River. Between them, Joe and Stan did more fur-trapping, dog-running, salmon-netting, and forest-traveling than any of the locals now, and, having proved their chops, both said they would have moved on if it weren't for the dogs—Tanana being a town renowned for its dogs. Joe compared dog mushers to "the Masai"; they valued a person's status not by his house, summer garden, beaver catch, or bank account, but only his dogs. And the two of them strolled about the dog lot, feeling different animals' hips to figure which ones to put more meat *on* by putting more meat *in*. Sled dogs are mostly smallish huskies with Labrador and hound strains bred into them for speed. Yet they don't have a whole set of speeds; they appear to run around the same pace for a hundred-mile as for a thousand-mile race (apart from a few specialized sprinters for short events). Each lived on a short chain at all times except when pulling a wagon or sled; their exercise was channeled to that, and it became a question of stamina, which is to say, feeding and management and assurance by the driver, plus previous conditioning and juggling the makeup of the team, replacing the leaders with swing dogs, according to what they were good at—finding a trail, breaking a trail, intelligence, or a brave heart, or competing at the home stretch. In the grueling hours of a race they must be coaxed to eat and drink, with water warmed, food from "banquet bags" spread as tidbits on the snow beside them, maybe beaver meat wheedled from a trapper, chicken and other butcher's trimmings, a road-killed moose from the game warden, chum, or "dog," salmon from a friendly Indian family, with juice and meat scraps added to the water pans. Each dog is harnessed to the towline by a "tug" rope near the tail and a neckline at the neck, so by watching these a driver is able to tell exactly how hard every animal is working, and in rather short order it will meet its maker if it does not.

Though Stan had constructed what several people said was the best home place in the area—greenhouse, workshop, root cellars, meat caches, and even a "church"—he told me he and Helen wanted to move to the banks of the Yukon and start over so they would have enough fish at hand to feed half a hundred dogs and go into raising them in a serious way. The "Tozie" or Tozitna was only fifty to seventy feet wide at the point where he had built his cabin and, since the last year had been lean for salmon, it just couldn't support thirty-five dogs, plus those of the neighboring homesteaders up or downstream, and the several dozen folks who lived on the Tozie's two hundred miles, and their gardens, fertilized with salmon (on half an acre he grew fifteen hundred pounds of potatoes), and the wildlife eating salmon that they grabbed. He'd ended up needing to shoot twenty-five of his dogs, he said, chain-sawing their frozen bodies to fit into the winter dog pot and sustain the survivors.

The Runyans did live on the Yukon, at Tanana, and also had a summer fish camp on an island fifty miles upriver at a rapids near the village of Rampart, with harvest rights Joe had paid $17,000 for. There he caught and sold, fresh or dry, thousands of pounds of salmon—planes landed to fetch them—and could raise sixty puppies on fish flesh, with a couple of pigs, also fed on salmon, on the side. Here in Tanana, amidst the March snows, an outdoor bin was still stacked with last summer's fish. Yet Joe, too, fed his dogs on dogs. Here he was in this center of dog-raising for profit, theoretically, except that the dogs weren't selling lately; there were "thousands of pounds of dead dogs in this village" yearly. "Why not use them? The team does real well on them." Since the Indians believed it was *Huklani*, or "bad medicine," to feed dogs to other dogs, the whole town's came to him for a dollar apiece when they got old or didn't pan out. Cardboard boxes of frozen bodies sat in the yard that he would cut into three-pound cross-sections—hair, bone, and all—with his chainsaw and put in the twenty-gallon black bean pot simmering on a tripod over a driftwood fire.

In winter, if he was not running dogs, he and Sheri, his partner, went sixty miles down the Yukon to their trapping camp to trap marten and beaver; and in the spring, his favorite season, he went southeast across the big river half as far to Fish Lake for "Spring Camp," the traditional exuberant duck hunt, fish fry, and greens-eating binge in the succulent marshes, leaves germinating. At first the lake was silent; then, as the temperature broke, you saw the early, stealthy hawks arrive; and the precocious songbirds, noisy with joy; then the fat, honking white-fronted geese ("speckle-bellies"); and rafts and hordes of ducks, gorgeous eating, along with the fresh whitefish, pike, and needlefish. His Athabascan mentor, Lester Erhart, taught him to prop the first geese he shot into lifelike positions, using sticks, out on the ice as decoys to draw more in, then lie in a snowbank overlooking a spring hole, covering himself and his rifle with snow, and mimic their calls. Erhart (whose son had recently finished fourth in a dog-mushing sprint in Fairbanks) would get so emphatic calling geese that his elbows flapped. They went in dragging boats on their sleds to paddle home in, but one year Joe mistook poison hemlock for wild celery and almost died, while his companions continued netting whitefish around him because there was nothing in particular they could do.

Sheri Mitchell, Joe's partner, had arrived on the river with a husband as well as her kids, but he had gone back to "the States," as people expressed it here. She was stylish-looking, educated, on the order of certain faculty wives or the centerpiece of a Vermont commune I used to go to, whom I'd dubbed "the sweetheart of Sigma Chi," and like Joe, adaptable, good at whatever she did—such as building a raft or a fish wheel on the river in a pouring rainstorm, or marinating and smoking salmon strips the natives were willing to pay her eleven dollars a pound for, preferring them to the ones that their wives prepared, and sewing three-skin marten hats worth $250 locally, again because they were the best in town. She was teaching her skills to some of the wives.

Stan and Helen had a two-year-old daughter named Monica who'd been given to them by a native woman when their own baby died. They lived in a trailer on Runyan's land when in town, and he told me he mainly ran dogs during beaver season, but did trap an average of forty marten, four or five foxes, three or four wolverines, and several lynx in a typical winter. Joe called him a "master innovator" because on an income of $2,000 or so for boat gas and lantern kerosene, for the past ten years he had truly lived off the land and its rivers, eating wild protein, besides what he grew. Stan said the natives who were angriest were the ones who lived most like a white man. And indeed a reason I'd come to Tanana was because it was supposedly home base for a nucleus of radical young Indians, and one Eskimo activist from the North Slope living by the Yukon with his Indian wife, with secessionist proposals for native sovereignty, but they were all out of town hobnobbing passionately in Juneau or Fairbanks, espousing the cause of subsistence living.

Stan had spent some time in college but kept dropping out, sailing on a trawler out of Scituate, Mass., till 1972, when he decided to fulfill a dream and go west to Vancouver; then, consulting a map, way north to Manson Creek, at the end of a dirt track toward the top of British Columbia. By trial and error he built a cabin in a secluded spot on the Omineca River and lived alone that winter. This was an old gold-rush village, one of the most remote in the province, where I've been, but a previous settler got exercised at the number of "American hippies" infiltrating to escape the draft in their own country and clearing cabin sites and planting marijuana, and called in the

Mounties. Though it was a hundred miles to the nearest police post, a detective showed up dressed as a fisherman and chatted around, spotting the illegalities for a raid and arrests. Stan escaped because he was new to the country and lying low the way many people do upon first arriving in a wilderness, new to solitude and self-reliance. That spring, he went east for his brother's wedding, met Helen, and drove back with her, but after his experience in the Canadian woods, pushed on up the Alcan Highway to Fairbanks instead, going straight to the office of the Bureau of Land Management because that happened to be an interval when homesteading lots of five acres were being given away, and he nabbed his on the Tozie for just forty dollars in filing fees. Within nine days—"a nine day wonder," he said—he and Helen hired a plane to fly them in; and now he has fifty miles of trapline trail, two hundred traps, and "flows through the woods, doesn't walk," said his friend Runyan.

Alaska is a destination created out of anger and quests, with frequent infusions of both, where people decide how much wildness they want to have, maybe content with a suburb of Anchorage. But "when the birch leaves are the size of a squirrel's ear, there will be no more frosts," and even city costumes could take on a questing élan. For Stan on the Tozitna, an orgy of homecoming ducks and geese marked the spring, too. Then at falltime, after the fish runs but before the freeze-up, when the wolves had more coat but still had to follow the riverbanks, before the ice "gave them more trail," he'd lay his first traps, while other furbearers were fluffing out. Indian activities like this had lapsed. "They're aggravated inside. Don't know what hit 'em. The work on the Slope has changed people." On the North Slope at Prudhoe Bay, a busboy earned $47,000 a year, an oil-rig mechanic $70,000. Mostly windowless, it was a life lived within modules, till he flew home across the Brooks Range to the Yukon's trees, and what was he to spend it on, after the sno-go, outboard, new TV or radio-telephone? And the State came in with oil-royalty money and construction crews to build a City Hall, City Garage, sewage treatment plant, generator plant, water system, a skating rink for the new school, a longer airfield with hangars, and threw up HUD housing for natives desirous of it, which necessitated parceling out fuel assistance grants because HUD houses were heated with oil stoves instead of good sensible wood stoves, and brought in what Stan called Tonka

Toys: Caterpillar tractors, fork lifts, dump trucks. In accent and face, he reminded me of other acquaintances from Boston, but with a wilderness freedom and brutality about him, as of a man who had lived for a decade by the accuracy of his gun, and who when he saw he had too many dogs, ran them in a series of teams, winnowing out two-thirds one by one, taking the less diligent out of harness to shoot and feed to the others. He treated us to a ride behind Joe's buoyant Iditarod team, bounding gaily along, after warning us that despite his best efforts it might kill us if the sled hit a tree.

A fellow named Alex and his young girlfriend, Kate, showed up, a bit blinkingly, at the party for Joe. She'd flown in ahead, but Alex was straight off the river, having made a two-day dogsled journey from a tributary of the Yukon called the Nowitna, where she and he were spending the winter alone. Alex had crossed illegally from Hungary to Austria in 1966, then got to New York and "misspent" the next seven years as a TV repairman there, before plunging "straight to Fairbanks from 86th Street." He'd sacrificed a little time practicing the same trade while finding his footing, which he claimed now had been superfluous—then invested the past seven years on the "Novy," all but this last one alone. From age six, reading books like *The Pathfinder* and *Robinson Crusoe*, he had dreamt of living as a trapper in Alaska, so taught himself the craft with no coaching from Indians or other old-timers, exulting, he said, even in his mistakes. Wolves and bears held a special fascination. He liked to provoke encounters with bears, to shoot and examine them, or meet them on a trail and not shoot them, merely poke his rifle muzzle against the bear's forehead and wait for the bear's reaction. If he photographed an animal he considered he'd already "taken" it and wouldn't shoot it thereafter. But wolves he howled to, after digging a snow cave to hide in near one of their rendezvous points, in order to draw them close so he could shoot one. If he howled just once they'd know where he was from a mile away. But after three years, and three pups shot, the ploy worked no more. With bears, even when one tore at his tent to get at the food inside, he studied it before shooting through the fabric, though missing, perhaps, because its shadow had deceived him.

At the party Alex met Ken Lilley, whose cabin he'd stayed at, midway up the Yukon, and thanked him for "one fish and one onion" consumed. He became shaky with excitement, after months in the bush; stayed up talking all night, as if trying to accomplish a whole year's worth of conversation in nine hours or so. For his first four years on the Novy, he said, he had lived in wall tents, till he made absolutely sure where he wanted to build his home cabin, but now kept three cabins, which were from one hundred-twenty to one hundred-eighty miles upriver from the Nowitna's debouchment into the Yukon and controlled a hundred miles of trapline along its main course that were just his. The tributaries he left as a kind of nursery—didn't trap them—and tended to "rest" half of the hundred main-stem miles each year to keep the furry populations high. In the summer, apart from laying in salmon for his eight dogs, he prospected to the high headwaters country, looking across toward Denali National Park, partly for gold but primarily reveling in the newness, liberty, mystery of roaming wherever he chose to turn and never meeting another human being, in settings where probably nobody had set foot since the stampeders at the dawn of the century. His dogs came, too. He'd gotten "addicted to dogs," after using snow machines his first few years and having two of them go through the ice underneath him—floundering for shore, for kindling, dry matches.

Whereas the Alaskan March cold nipped off my pleasure, my sensibilities, enthusiasms, energies, and panicked me if I walked out of town a little, as though I were afraid I might not make it back, Alex was utterly at home, in his bear and wolf skins. The Nowitna is some five hundred miles long, curving back close to the head of the Kuskokwim River, in the Kuskokwim Mountains, and exploring it was mostly a matter of affording the time. In describing experiences, he sounded as methodical as if fixing an implement, step by step, explaining the path events took: on the working of a bear's mind—its pauses in scratching or chewing his tent's fabric, the way the threads hung from its teeth when its muzzle intruded inside, and how when his gun misfired it withdrew its head with immediate caution at the click but remained just outside, the sun etching a strong grizzly shadow on the tent wall until, carefully re-aiming at this outline, he shot a neat hole through his tent, yet the shadow of the head stayed for a moment as before. He'd blasted the shadow, not the head.

The first feds had shown up only a couple of weeks ago, licensing him to remain in his cabin in what was a national wildlife refuge for five more years. "But no matter what they do, they can't take away those past seven years!" Only once in all that time did a plane land on the river in front of him and some stranger climb out to introduce himself. Rather, he was harassed occasionally by the whine of wolf hunters' planes buzzing round and round, monotonously searching for a shot at a pelt which otherwise might make part of his own livelihood. For months on end, being two hundred-twenty river miles, but only seventy by air, from Tanana and its refueling strip, their exasperating sound might be his sole contact with humanity, because if they bagged meat or fur, they'd land on skis and fly off again. In fact, five years had passed before he even met his nearest fellow trapper, although they'd seen signs of each other's existence and established tacit boundaries where their traplines met.

Kate, much younger, with a sort of clean, open face, said the winter was passing quicker than she had expected. Alex came home most nights from running his traps, now that the cabin was toasty warm, with a stew on the stove awaiting him, but wouldn't let her do much more than clean, wash, and cook—not skin his catch, not listen to music on the radio ("to save the battery"—presumably an element of self-discipline) or the news, because it was "depressing." They might squeeze in a bit of music and dance around the cabin before "Trapline Chatter, Your Gospel Radio Voice of the North," on KJNP, came on. It was all easier, warmer, less lonely than she had expected and had taught her to be alone with herself. She read, learned to knit, crochet, and do needlepoint, though the house always smelled of the dog pot and of Alex's skinning and drying skins.

She'd known him from Fairbanks, the summer before, when he went through the trailer parks, Winnebago by Winnebago, peddling his wolf and wolverine skins. During this winter he'd flown out twice for ten-day periods to sell furs and purchase supplies, leaving Kate to take care of the dogs. She'd felt content to enjoy the silence and privacy for the first few days, until each time she suffered an accident while exercising the dog team and checking his closer traplines—once the sled hit a tree and she was banged up, not so bad she couldn't get home, but enough that she was frightened to think how quickly she could have died alone of the cold if the collision had been more severe. Now, briefly in town with the days lengthening, she was both sticking with him through this spring and summer and feeling, expecting, herself to be through with Alex after that—not wanting another winter when she would not be allowed to listen to the radio for more than a quarter of an hour a day or do more than cook and clean house or share more than a small fraction of his exultancy. Alex mentioned, however, that he might wind up in a protective role here, as a ranger.

This seemed another provisional alliance, of which Linda and I saw so many. Almost everybody in their thirties appeared to be provisionally allied with somebody of the opposite sex. But only in these ultimate frontier areas was the pattern likely to be the old-fashioned system of a bold young man with a helpmate female. Mostly, through Linda, I was meeting women who had fine, well-paying careers— nurse, teacher, social worker—and were living with men marginally employed at temporary, tentative jobs, sometimes because they were Native Americans grasping for a life ring, at sea in a world topsy-turvy, sometimes white exiles from the Lower 48 at loose ends. In Alaska people operate at the end of their ropes, and during her TB survey of Tanana, in and out, Linda bonded more at the clinic, the school, and social services office than with the dog-mushing cadre.

• • •

CHAPTER 12

• • •

Exxon and an Odyssey

I N ANCHORAGE, THE CORRUPTION WAS so blatant it amounted to a form of innocence. Governor Bill Sheffield flew in three oil company airplanes to visit with Secretary of the Interior James Watt in Washington, or on to Houston to collect campaign contributions for himself. But some Mexican-Americans were being added to school staffs, as at least more sympathetic to minority issues than the usual Midwestern whites cycling in and out to pay off a mortgage on the farm. And to the city's mélange, women's lib activists were added to the bitterly disaffected Vietnam vets and disillusioned counterculture types who both had found that by the 1980s the nation's mainstream had rejected hippie values—not just the kooky ones but egalitarian altruism, as well—and Army or Civil Service straitlaced sorts, too.

Breakfast at Hogg Bros. Café, behind a bar; then the Garden of Eden for lunch or supper; and the Bush Company, for topless grunge, or the Pines Monday nights, when the dance floor became a boxing ring where tyros fought in street pants or borrowed trunks, refereed by a mayoral campaign manager. "Stick and move! Stick and move!" shouted their fan clubs.

Linda disliked the macho violence, naturally, whereas I didn't, having written a boxing novel twenty years before, but she liked how I transferred the animal personae from my daughter's early-childhood stories to our love games, then opened myself in flat-out surrender when she chose to straddle me.

I went to visit Father Michael Oleska, an Orthodox priest at Alaska Pacific University, a vigorous, opinionated man of thirty-six who taught linguistics and counseled students. His wife was Yupik and his face, otherwise severe, broke abruptly into kind, amused lines when Anastasia, their oldest of four kids, wandered into the room. From Allentown, Pennsylvania, he had gone to Georgetown University to study Arabic originally, before finding his calling and switching to St. Vladimir's Seminary in Crestwood, New York. In the summers and after graduation he went to Kodiak and Sitka Islands, the Kenai Peninsula, and Bethel and Dillingham. Father Epchook of Kalskag was his wife's cousin, and he wore a moose horn cross carved by Epchook. Alaska had about twenty thousand Orthodox parishioners in eighty-seven congregations, served by seven non-native priests, nineteen native priests (some still trilingual in Yupik, English, and Russian), and Bishop Gregory, a fifty-eight-year-old from Kiev, at the old cathedral in Sitka. At Kodiak a local seminary had been established, where twenty native students were enrolled. St. Herman of Kodiak—a Finnish priest who arrived on the island in 1794 and was glorified in 1970, with the Archbishop of Leningrad in attendance— was Alaska's contribution to Orthodox Christianity's sainthood: not martyred, but a cleric who stayed at his post protecting the islanders from persecution by brutal Russian sealers as best he could after other priests had become so disheartened they gave up and went home.

The Russians, though, Oleska said, made one Aleut a major-general; others whaling captains, not merely seamen—and teachers, priests, mapmakers. Aleuts explored much of Alaska's northern coasts on behalf of the Russians, evangelizing where they could, and translating for the Yupiks. Alaska had had twenty indigenous languages, and among Protestant missionaries, the Moravians behaved the most flexibly toward native communities, he said: the Episcopalians and Presbyterians tended to be the worst, except that ministers who had been born in Europe were more tolerant. In the 1830s the first books were translated into Tlingit and Aleut, but both cultures needed to go underground to survive the pressure of colonization, compared to the more isolated Yupiks. As recently as the 1970s, divorce had remained unthinkable among the Yupiks, only known to exist Outside, but now was playing out daily on the television in their living rooms, and English inescapably ubiquitous. Orthodox priests were officiating to an old-fashioned working class, because the native villages were "like company towns, where you can never finish paying your bills, are always in debt." One of his educational functions was helping teachers' aids become credentialed teachers, so that the cycle of transients from the Lower 48 being shuttled in and out of villages could be interrupted by hiring lifelong local mentors. Often this was mostly a matter of intervening to be sure all their assorted credits from summer programs were counted properly, until the parents newly elected to a given school board could act.

"World class" was a favorite Alaskan phrase, as in "world-class platinum operation near Goodnews Bay," "world-class molybdenum mine at Misty Fjords," "world-class lead-zinc deposits at Red Dog in the De Long Mountains"—having come so far to feel different. I watched James Watts hold a press conference, with his carnivorous grin; then went to Outer Continental Shelf Sale #57, of 418 tracts of 2,304 hectares each, in the Norton Basin—underwater, in other words, in the general neighborhood of Nome, which was held in the ballroom of the Sheraton Hotel. On the podium as co-toastmasters were bland, bespectacled Alan D. Powers, the regional OCS manager of the Minerals Management Service, and Vernon Wiggins, James Watts' personal watchdog in Alaska for the Interior Department. Vern had a boyish, aggressive voice, a Boss Hogg physiognomy, an expression of strain, as if from moving his ambition and bulk around the platform, and a hunterly squint, as though he were peering past a shotgun barrel through a duck blind. This was an auction where sealed bids had already been submitted, however. Refreshments were provided by the Schlumberger drilling equipment corporation, and a mirror overhead doubled the anthill atmosphere.

"Al, you and I get to be on the stage with all these good-looking women," Vern announced, beginning his stump-speech boast for the Secretary about how Outer Continental Shelf lease sales were being tremendously accelerated under the Reagan Administration. Kathy Martin, the lady particularly referred to, had brown hair and a comely, graduate-student face, which wore the fixed smile of somebody talking to a man she doesn't want to be talking to. She represented the Office of the Solicitor. There was also a pleasant woman coloring in the blocks of marine prospecting leases as they were bid for, in yellow, angularly chickenpox blotches on a large map of Norton Sound. Three other women opened the sealed envelopes with paper knives and arranged the offers for Vern or Al, as M.C., to recite.

The price of benchmark Saudi oil had dropped the day before from thirty-four to twenty-nine dollars a barrel, and offshore work in these waters would of course be considerably more complex and expensive than desert drilling.

I heard soft-spoken Texas courtesy all around—that momentary, Southern focus upon the person at hand—until these silver-haired oilmen with their protégés, attorneys, geologists, assistants, and counselors sat scribbling with their briefcases on their knees on the ballroom chairs like university students while the bids were read. The Interior Department's buffalo logo on the podium pointed optimistically left, but the numbers were such that only sixty-four of the four hundred-eighteen potential tracts, or fifteen percent, had actually attracted hard interest from any of the eleven companies participating. The sum of the high bids was three hundred twenty-five million, of which nearly three hundred was from Exxon, with a little help from its friends like the French company ELF. Exxon, sometimes with bids twice or three times as high as the closest rival, had walked away with the show—perhaps embarrassingly so. Had it gone too high to make up for having been outbid by ARCO and British Petroleum for Prudhoe Bay's enormous North Slope reserves a few years ago?

The Interior officials were on the spot a bit also, with these "moderate," "modest" results, as Alan Powers phrased it carefully when he noticed I was eavesdropping, not free to speak his disappointment. "You never know. You never know." They'd already faced accusations of hastening the auction ahead of prudent scheduling, when the industry could have prepared better for it, in order to beat out several Eskimo and conservationist lawsuits alleging irreparable damage to the fisheries and marine mammals in case of a spill. The oilman talking to him, representing Bunker Hunt's Placid Oil Co., remarked that it was "nice to go to work when you don't have anything to do." But a Yupik Eskimo standing nearby interrupted: "Norton Sound is our supermarket! Our garden!"

All of Exxon's team of accountants, lawyers, and geodesists sat in white shirtsleeves alongside their chief, J.D. Langston, the VP for Exploration USA. "If you win, you've overspent," he observed to the kibitzers who were gathering. Now naturally the center of attention, he was a white-haired, low-keyed man with a face that appeared much rearranged by the process of living—a much-traveled, practiced face. Langston said his geologists projected that the five major "structures" he had bid for had better than the "fourteen percent" chance of profitable extraction the government's own scientists predicted. "We bought a ticket to explore. It's a high-risk frontier area, though fortunately shallow water." Ice-breakers would be needed and the drill rigs brought from California. He believed that future energy shortages in the world were going to make the petroleum reserves a company owned more valuable than conventional wisdom recognized. As for the Eskimos: "We'll work with these people and in two or three years we'll all be friends. If we make any sort of discovery, it'll be the best thing that ever happened to that area."

Although I was opposed to the sale as a conservationist, my father had worked for Exxon before his death in 1967, and my first ocean voyage had been as a guest on the bridge of a tanker from New York to Galveston at the age of fifteen, so I felt a subterranean liking for this unflashy, sophisticated Houston man who answered the murmurs that he might have overbid because of the Prudhoe Bay sale he had underbid on, by reminding the crowd, "There's one thing worse than overbidding and that's walking away with nothing at all. We came to buy." But he admitted the sealed-bid system favored the Government because if your initial offer was too low or high, you couldn't adjust it. With his tight, high-performance team around him, he walked unshowily toward the lobby, making me nostalgic for my father, who had lawyered at headquarters at 30 Rockefeller Plaza, as I headed back to "L" Street, admiring the snowy maw of valleys in the Chugaches, and ravens on some roofs even in the center of town.

• • •

My favorite among the millionaires *Vanity Fair* had hired me to visit with was Pete Zamarello, age fifty-five, and born of Italian parents on the Ionian isle of Kefallonia, at the mouth of the Gulf of Corinth, close to Odysseus's mythical birthplace on Ithaca, as Pete pointed out. No running water or electricity in his mountain hamlet; they drank rainwater collected in a barrel off the roof. Starting at seven, he'd toddled down a goats' path to the port town and obtained six years of schooling. "It'll take you five centuries to get over a beginning like that." But the cause of this early move down the mountain to the sea was that his poor father—for idealistically protesting against the royalist dictatorship suddenly established in Greece by Ioannis Metaxas in 1936—was seized by the police, forced to drink three pints of castor oil, and sit naked on a block of ice for two hours while the hair was sandpapered off his head. After this public atrocity, and anticipating worse, he signed on to a freighter's crew and decamped to jump ship in America, passing word to his son Pete after several years to watch for a chance to follow suit whenever he could.

Pete still sends a hundred dollars every New Year's Day to each of twenty-five people in that mountain hamlet on Kefallonia, and spent $25,000 recently to repair the village church. Meanwhile, however, by 1941, when Hitler invaded, he'd found himself starving in the widespread famine that followed, and joined the Fascist Youth for the meals provided, then worked at a German munitions factory based on the island, learning German, Italian, Spanish, Portuguese, and Rumanian from his fellow forced laborers, until the Nazis tumbled out of Greece in disarray, and their last job was demolishing the mines, bombs, and shells that they'd made. He went to Athens to enroll at a telegraph operators' school, but because of his weak underlay of primary education could only land a job on a Panamanian ship. It was sufficient to deliver him to the New World, though, and specifically up the Hudson River to Albany, New York, where he walked down the gangplank on December 23, 1955, answering "Heil," from his German days, to the immigration officer's "Hi" on the pier, because he didn't know English, but finessing the encounter even so. He then got down to Manhattan, to Jerry's Luncheonette on 47th Street off Eighth Avenue, which was run by Greeks from Kefallonia, and where he soon fell in love with a Polish-Irish, Hell's Kitchen-raised girl named Pat, who still was his wife three decades later. Pete didn't linger as a counterman, but went at carpentering immediately; then within three months had become a contractor, undertaking $20,000 to $30,000 jobs and living with Pat in Union City or Jersey City or West New York, New Jersey. ("We nearly bought that house in Fort Lee," she reminded him.)

I'd spent five months on the Greek Island of Samos in 1965, which lent us some initial rapport, as did my being a New Yorker, when we began talking in his spacious, well-appointed office, with expensive chairs and Eskimo-crafted ivory displayed in lighted cases.

I'd experienced the hardscrabble rituals of those sun-shot mountainside villages, involving not just the fresh yogurt and fish peddled on donkeys every day, but a choked-down wartime bitterness. In my era it had been the scalding aftereffects of the Greek civil war that followed the Second World War, when Communist guerrillas battled right-wing authoritarian rule armed by America, and the cruel humiliations imposed upon the losers were still detectable even to a foreigner. His father had been a prewar radical, and Pete had experienced both Nazi occupation and British bombings to blast that munitions plant. He'd also remodeled a couple of restaurants in Manhattan, on Lexington Avenue and on University Place, before launching himself clear to Anchorage, three years after jumping ship in Albany, with a two-year-old daughter in tow, who was his only child and had precipitated his fortunate marriage. Pat's mother had died when she was twelve, leaving her to raise five younger kids, although so neglected herself that the previous year she had needed to pay for her first tooth to be pulled by a dentist on Ninth Avenue near John's Clam Bar on 43rd, where she was already picking up tips. Thus large families were not her idea of fun.

Pete had been wearing loafers, stepping off that plane in Alaska during an economic slump; and now the Zemarellos owned the largest house in the state, he told me, 18,700 square feet, at 31st Street and Turnagain Arm. He was also the largest private landholder, with one thousand three hundred eighty-seven tenants and thousands of acres in the Matanuska-Susitna valley and the Kenai Peninsula, and properties in Juneau and Washington. He'd just sold a 48-foot yacht to buy a 92-foot one in order to sail back to Kefallonia in triumph eventually. When he'd slipped off that Panamanian freighter in Albany, he had known his father was already an American citizen living in Alaska, after being wounded in the leg on the Allied side during World War II, then stationed at Fort Lewis, Washington, and operating "Washington's Best Restaurant" in Port Angeles. But Pete told me "mostly craziness," not the father he scarcely knew, had brought him here; and just as in New York, he threw himself into carpentering right away, first at Fort Richardson, for the army, while building two houses on spec after-hours at the same time, as if on a second shift. He skipped lunch to save money, claiming he was on a diet, until a black co-worker began to say his wife was packing too many sandwiches for him to finish by himself: "Please help me out!" Recently this same woman, after all these years, gave Pete a call, saying her husband was dead and the bank about to evict her from their trailer house. He drove over pronto, saw the trailer, the paperwork, continued down to the bank, barged into the president's office without an appointment and informed him he would withdraw umpteen million dollars from all his accounts if anything like that happened, writing a check to erase the mortgage, and stormed out again.

"They have to put up with me," he said, meaning rich guys who'd never known poverty. Said he was helping to build an Orthodox church and had given fifty acres to the University and ten to the Roman Catholics, but only the Russians seemed grateful. Claimed he never sued individual tenants here and forgave old people their rent. In Seattle lately, while he was pacing up and down outside a department store waiting for Pat to finish shopping, he'd experienced a minor epiphany. A beggar selling pencils asked him for some money and he gave him a dollar, then continued walking—but abruptly swung around. *I'm a millionaire. Why am I giving this shivering gray-haired black man a dollar bill?* He handed him a twenty, then a hundred instead, and hailed a cab, rode home with him, saw the room he lived in, and paid the landlord three month's rent in advance.

Inviting Linda along, we went to the Sorrento Restaurant, across from the Fireweed Theatre on Fireweed Street, for supper, with Pat and his two top yes-men; it was owned by a Greek, like all the Italian restaurants in Alaska, he said. Pat, vivacious, humorous, and shrewd, had a sharp face grown plump at the sides but a kind of latent animation in her body that was still attractive to him. Her hopes of becoming a novelist had just been dashed, she said, when her typewriter with her manuscript inside its case was stolen, but she knew the day's London price for gold, and received daily reports on her gardens at her Hawaiian penthouse, her Tacoma and Palm Springs condos, and the Alyeska ski chalet. Her favorite spot, however, was "about one mile from the Columbia Glacier, where you feel like a shrimp in a shrimp cocktail."

A bodyguard from Kefallonia, in a trucker's jacket with a Zorba-the-Greek mustache, sat observantly drinking coffee but eating nothing at a corner table in case he was needed, and when Pete remarked that the temperature was warm, fans were turned on. He owned twenty smallish shopping centers now but was aiming for a million-square-foot mall, three times the size of Alaska's biggest now, he said, and a sixteen-story office tower, graced by a greenhouse club on top. Also he wanted to start a bank. Twenty years ago, while his mother was dying back on Kefallonia, a banker had refused to loan him a thousand dollars so he could fly home. "I don't trust Italians," the stuffed shirt had said. Fermi, Marconi, Galileo, Leonardo, Michelangelo, Aesop, Archimedes: "and the only thing people know about the Mediterranean is the Mafia?" he demanded. The net worth of his companies was around two hundred million, his executive vice-president, Mike David, estimated at the table, but their sights were set on a billion within a couple of years. Pete's first real score had come from North Slope oil money on leases privately bought with some partners. Then he built two restaurants with that and was off to the races, although when stymied for local credit by prejudice (Bob Penney still called him "Mr. Monopoly"), he'd gone, in the early 1970s, to Beirut and Tehran. He lost a quarter of a million dollars in the Iranian revolution, and found Lebanese Christians "were the most worthless people in the world," but described flying with a Saudi prince from Spain to Morocco for lunch in the man's private Boeing, with two bedrooms in the back. Prejudice costs American businessmen loads of money; "and they set obstacles for me, but they didn't watch me and that's how I fooled them. Going overseas. The languages were not a barrier to me."

As a champion of underdogs, he used only union labor, thought dishwashers should earn as much as carpenters and carpenters enough to buy presentable houses of their own. His pay scale for staff was what people needed individually, making of them as much of a family as he could, since Pat hadn't wanted another bunch of children to raise, and if he brought in "Arab money" in order to do it, okay. His mild, muted, tenor voice and manner of pressing a pen or a ruler against his nose as he talked, clearing his throat lightly and frequently, contrasted with the alligator shoes, expensive rings, and gold bracelets inlaid with his initials in diamonds. His skylit office, stylishly carpeted, cheerfully decorated with green plants, a rainbow of tropical fish, and the walrus-ivory carvings he'd recently been collecting through an agent similarly seemed to belie the force of his views. Although a Republican, he thought Ronald Reagan's economists such as Milton Friedman "should be Hollywood comedians and work for Bob Hope and Red Skelton." Yet the current Democratic governor had "crossed me on the Whittier prison deal—I'll bury him in the next election." He predicted ever-better prosperity and property values for Alaska (already "per capita income two-and-a-half times Kuwait's"), but a general collapse in America by 1990 and the secession of the West from the East.

Like Bob Uchitel, though less so because he was still in the thick of things, he fretted about the fate of world peace, as a mover and shaker should. His memories were full of war: the "wall of fire" the German ack-ack batteries put up against the British dive bombers trying to blow up the armament factory on his broken-limestone island, where he'd worked as a very young boy. He must have watched fifty of the Brits shot down, he said, and although he disliked the Nazi conquest, he'd hated the Metaxas dictatorship which had tortured his father and which the German invasion had overthrown, as well. He was not sorry to see the Germans evacuate in defeat, except that soon an ugly, sadistic Greek junta took control over the country, with Western backing, after winning the three-year anti-Communist civil war. Although Pete wouldn't have favored Communism, needless to say, sporadic persecution of pro-democracy liberals, too, continued from 1952 to 1963 and 1967 to 1974 by "the Colonels." For example, an illiterate fishmonger he knew happened to pick the wrong newspaper out of a trash barrel one day to wrap his wares in, and was consequently executed as a supposed radical, along with two hundred-fifty other men, in reprisal for the Minister of Justice's assassination. This the Brits and the U.S. tolerated, and the Brits in any case he intensely resented for giving the Ionian Islands, which had been a British protectorate since 1815, to Greece in 1864 instead of to Italy.

He said that at fifteen, when he was starving in the aftermath of the German invasion and forced to join the Fascist Youth to eat, he'd read Knut Hamsun's *Hunger*, but found it wasn't true: not like Tolstoy's *Resurrection*, Victor Hugo's *Les Miserables*, and Dostoyevsky's *Underground*. And Pat, like Pete, suppressed pained thoughts of home, in Hell's Kitchen—hadn't returned for the past nine years, but acknowledged with a grim nod that it was time. Though Linda's disapproving presence in the restaurant, askance at the Zemarellos' wealth, had put a damper on some of Pete's exuberance, it revived back in his office again, in talking of building a twenty-acre building on a hundred-acre lot, including a skating rink and parking for five thousand cars: two three-million-square-foot malls. He wanted to build two or three thirty-to-fifty-story high-rises—"but not monuments; money-makers." You couldn't lose in Anchorage because property appreciated at 15–20 percent a year, but steer clear of Fairbanks, and once he got his bank rolling he wanted to retire to the greenery of Washington State—such a contrast to the desiccated landscape of Kefallonia—and keep his yacht down there, or in Juneau. Although below the waist his body had subsided a bit toward lard, his meaty torso looked dynamic, like a Mediterranean strong man's, a shipping owner, perhaps, oriented to the bottom line. In London he hung out with "Syrian Jews," he joked, to give the lie to whispers that he had access to "Italian money." Besides Beirut investors, he'd found a Rumanian in Anchorage to speak that language and do deals with. New York or Swiss time is so much earlier than Alaska's that when you went to work in the morning they were either locked up for the day or deep into a martini lunch. Insomnia was therefore a job description for financiers here. You did your phoning while the city slept, then got out to your job sites early to energize your foremen.

Linda and I drove from Pete's to the parking lot of the radio station KENI, with its panorama of both Anchorage and the dominant mountains. Also to Captain Cook Memorial Park, overlooking Knik Arm, for the glint of the sea; and to the Alaska Pioneers Home, on 11th Avenue between "K" and "L" streets, slipping inside for a glimpse of the sourdough faces on the couches in the lounge, because we were alike in cherishing a soft spot for them, if not for the occasional contemporary buccaneer like Pete. As a Kazantzakis fan, I'd responded to his intimations that tragedy often underlies exhilaration, that life is comprised of pendulum swings, and work was our salvation—for Zorba, Pete, Linda, and me. She would pile up field work, academic degrees, and a tenured professorship, and I was sufficiently busy with other projects that a quarter-century would go by before I even transcribed these handwritten notes about "Slavic Christmas" vs. "Gussuck Christmas" and Halibut (fishermen's) jackets and Ketchikan sneakers (boots). In fact, at the airport I watched a departing young man ceremoniously deposit his rain gear and rubber boots in a trash can before boarding his flight Outside from this gigantic cul-de-sac.

• • •

CHAPTER 13

• • •

Tugboats on the Tanana

I FLEW BACK TO NEW YORK that early spring to resume my fractious but loving fifteen-year marriage to Marion, who, as managing editor of *Commentary* magazine, had been helping during the 1970s and early 80s to invent, incubate, and nourish the nascent Neoconservative movement, which cheered on Reaganism, mocked environmentalism and Gandhi, vilified the Muslim world, but didn't attain its full flowering of influence until the George W. Bush presidency and the invasion of Iraq. Even Joe McCarthy was resuscitated for favorable reexamination. Thus our marriage was squeezed in a vise of political pressure, and Marion had her own collection of male friends, whom on occasion she vacationed in Europe with. My next-to-last book, in contrast, had been about the Sudan, but for a variety of reasons, sentimental as well as inertial, we were to stay together for several more years, until our daughter's sophomore year in college.

I love New York more than any other place on earth, and my wise and notably witty wife had helped me construct a platform of stability for the three of us for more than a decade, midwifing my early essays back when her magazine was as famous as *The Nation* or *The New Republic* for being liberal. She had been roaming European capitals for *Esquire* herself, in her halcyon days, writing two film scripts for Robert Frank, and translating stories, such as "Yentl the Yeshiva Boy," for Isaac Bashevis Singer.

Yet at fifty-one I was spending as much on airfare as I'd used to live on for a year at thirty-one; and by July was flying back to Alaska again—that brand-new state with the bracing-sounding name. Three ten-story refinery tanks at a Texaco terminal in Newark were ablaze, as my plane climbed away from LaGuardia, so black smoke covered Hoboken, the Bronx, and northern Manhattan. It seemed by then a great relief to break through this, plus the cloud mass capping it, as well as away from the telephone, my career, my personal difficulties, into bright sun, the clouds like arctic floes below me, peopleless except for the contrails traced like dogsled trails across them toward a prismatic spectrum of colors on the horizon. Marion and I had achieved our best conversation in weeks, as usual, from the airport phone booth—the way we had come to do at partings, free at last of each other's fears and vulnerabilities, the face-to-face political or sexual tension. We wished each other safe passage, with love, while I would be away, our grudges notwithstanding, and I'd watched with rueful wistfulness a woman nearby kissing her baby's head, tears in her eyes, as she watched an inbound plane enter its slip. "John's home," she whispered.

Flying anywhere generally costs less per hour than talking to a psychiatrist—and what a tonic it is. The faces to Minneapolis were businessmen returning with contracts or loans they had wanted; then to Seattle my seatmate was a brisk woman who had just completed her third training spell at Litton Industry headquarters and was as unfrilly underneath her frilly blouse as our chicken Kiev was cold under its feverishly microwaved surface. Japanese was playing on a headset channel, reminding me of a cousin who had survived the Bataan Death March, only to die in detention, as we climbed higher than Everest between the two cities. At Seattle the business suits scuttled off officiously, to be supplanted by jitterily jean-clad, provisional souls, Alaska-bound roughnecks who looked like hijackers. Would they have a home to come back to, if they did this; or measure up, if they were testing their manhood against anecdotal challenges? Would the money-bet pay off; would wages for gutting salmon in Bristol Bay or wrenching pipeline in the midnight sun be as high as rumored? The 727—held up to collect as many servicemen returning to base by connecting flights as possible—was a package of lonely gazes till we met the glass eyes of those Dall sheep, white goats, beige caribou, and white bears in the cases greeting debarking adventurers in Anchorage. Linda was waiting; and we suppered on crab, overlooking the

Knik Arm of Cook Inlet, next to a tableful of bearded young specula-
tors. The city was expanding so fast power outages were occurring,
and a single suburb, Eagle River, would soon surpass Juneau in population. Fondly, she watched me scribble down terms I didn't know
like "Pott's disease," TB of the spine, or "tuberculoma," a TB lesion
in the brain resembling a carcinoma on first examination. The bad old
days of a white trapper passing a "squaw" and her children starving
to death in the snow were seventy years past. Native American men,
on the other hand, had been spiraling into this spate of suicides, a
seizure of despair so simple to consummate among a river or a hunting people there seemed no way of halting the contagion. From the
same villages women were completing educational programs that enabled them to manage the municipal finances, or traffic at the airstrip.
Teaching math, or office work in a city, was open to them, and possibly marriage leading to the Lower 48, although now, in 1983, some
of these marriages from the sixties and seventies, perhaps to white men
who had been social activists moved by the wider civil rights struggle,
were souring in disillusionment on both sides. But the women were
equipped to move on from divorce like anyone else—employable by a
company or the government. No need to return to their home villages
in chagrin, like some of the girls did who may have simply climbed
into the cockpit of a float plane with a flirty bush pilot one day instead.
If these didn't return, they wouldn't be at the university either, in all
likelihood, but waitressing in a bar. However, not suicidal, like the
young men who hadn't advanced in school, yet didn't want to run traplines all winter like their grandfathers, and had watched the prettiest
girls in the village, whom they had crushes on, carried off by white
men—whether construction workers, minerals surveyors, fisheries scientists, Air Force privates, or social therapists—or hope to be.

Linda and her cohort of young feminist nurses could handle
foul-mouthed, unwashed, knuckle-headed macho men, old or young,
with delayed and cursory treatment at their clinics—but male despair, as opposed to male aggression, was a mystery to them. Asthma,
epilepsy, kidney stones, a burst appendix with lethal fever, a snapped
chainsaw or an ATV that had flipped over, a man whose ass's cheeks
had frozen solid, hip-deep on a hike, they could deal with in this
"Last Place," as people liked to call Alaska with a chuckle, or transient Romeos whose very presence indicated a problematic history

"Outside." But coursework in nursing school and cycling through a psychiatric ward or a stint at a Harlem methadone program—which Linda had put in—did not prepare you for the collateral damage of a culture's collapse, and it wasn't what Valium had been invented for. In Angoon she'd sat for hours with elderly Tlingits, hearing their stories not merely for their pleasure in half-a-century-ago, but hers— in retrospect, of course, the hidden anthropologist to come. Alaska plays for keeps, with its white-outs and fog multiplying the ordinary factors of luck and risk, but intrinsic despair is what a good many Caucasians, too, had decamped to the place to escape.

Linda was on vacation, and I was on assignment for *House and Garden* magazine this time, so before our serious business we rambled south from Anchorage for a few days to the hippie promontory of Homer on the Kenai Peninsula, where artsy northern California had a toehold. Anti-materialist but attuned to property valuations, trustfunders pretended not to be, and did fish taxidermy for tourists at seven dollars an inch, then perhaps woodcuts in the winter. A proposal to extend the sewer line was opposed by neighbors who preferred to live like homesteaders without a telephone. Baptists stood at the schoolhouse door passing out Gideon Bibles to kids boarding the bus, and dared the Libertarians to sue. The Spit extending into the sea was where people who had bet wrong lived in their cars or squatted in Visqueen tents on a no-man's-land of sand: "Spit Rats" thwarted by "Not Hiring" signs around town, a freebooter touch eyed charitably or smugly by the "Last In" residents who had acquired enough acreage to build a spec house with their earnings commuting to North Slope jobs, week-on, week-off, with a Sohio or ARCO free plane ride. We met Barb Campbell, the twenty-seven-year-old architect who did that routine as a mechanic for ARCO—tall, with glasses, jerky, compulsive motions but no practical use for the high salary she made, yet a frenetic quality to her focus on work, who said "men don't dust well" and scratched and bit her lovers yet hoped to marry a good breadwinner who would support her—in the meantime hand-trolled for king salmon from her boat off Juneau during her off-weeks in season, averaging four a day, and investing in property.

I'd heard more Vietnam War vets worked near Barrow on the North Slope, proportionately, than anywhere else in all of America. The brutal climate may have salved wounds a bit, whereas Homer's mild weather and mellow ethos encouraged men to go in for coed camping and saunas, avoid anguished, bristly egos, wear their beards mutedly slim, be agreeably chameleon, and maybe have parents in Florida to run home to when winter came on. Like other pieces of Alaska, it was a Shangri-la people had migrated toward when they didn't like the rest of America, but didn't propose any invigorating changes beyond a personal phase—women driving rigs, delivering mail, up-slanting to high-paid bureaucratic jobs, if Homer became a bedroom suburb of the city or the fishing industry, or just an outpost of Oregon. There were "boozer losers," too, and a man who'd survived a boat wreck off of the Aleutians by wriggling into his survival suit in a minute flat, and hobby hunters who would fly out to a pretty lake somewhere, from a high-powered regular career, to shoot a moose or caribou "to satisfy that inner Injun."

The Sterling Highway, north again toward Turnagain Arm, led us past black, turquoise, and aquamarine rivers, in a funnel through the forests. Resurrection Pass, Tin Can Ridge, Chickaloon Bay. We saw gun mounts along the Seward Highway for shooting down shelving avalanches before they fell, and stopped at Portage Glacier in a foggy storm to watch the sudden godly blue of calving bergs through the mists—unearthly indeed. Then to the noted saloon, The Birdhouse, whose walls were upholstered with ladies' undies and bras, its queasy floor a memento of the last earthquake.

Back in our basement, I explored her body once again. My wife, in the East, was in love with a Cornell political scientist and editing essays arguing that environmentalism was a hoax, so I had been unfaithful a good deal lately, but wanted not to be with respect to Linda. That tously black Irish hair, yet smooth skin and pragmatic hands. She'd shown up at my dormitory door at seven thirty the morning after my stuttering presentation at the symposium lectern at the Fairbanks writer's conference, and we picked up from there. Yet my concentration as a writer sometimes baffled her, as if she couldn't connect it to her own perfectionist exactitude with sputum cups and syringe needles. And one time when a sea-kayaking episode was in the offing—the kind of short adventure her previous Alaskan boyfriends might have jumped at to demonstrate their bravado but I pulled back from as too dangerous in the riptide currents off Admiralty Island—she didn't object to my chickening out so much as to my telling her that "I have other books to write." Since this happened a quarter-century ago, it was factually true, as I meant it to be, but she was offended, translating me to mean I thought my life more valuable than other people's, and into the dippy craft she jumped, enduring a hairy time. I was approaching my second divorce; thus scarcely ready to marry again; whereas Linda had gotten over her first during her interlude in Alaska—leaving it behind by cross-country train from Massachusetts, and reaching the recuperative stage. So although we enjoyed sexual acts with each other we'd never performed with anyone else (and my sweat smelled sweet, she said), we felt the friction of being at different stages.

The next jaunt was north to Talkeetna, a launch point for ascents of Mount McKinley, but for us en route to the Yukon. Talkeetna seemed a crisper version of Homer, in its populace of transient transplants from hither and yon, plus seasonal residents after the good life, and mountaineering guides and hoteliers—more like Aspen than Oregon. But rich guys flew in, leaving their families on Martha's Vineyard, to bet their lives on the toiling scarps of the massif of Mc-Kinley—a cathedral presence, surplice-white, even a hundred miles away. The Alaska Railroad had situated a train station here, and many of the trippers hauling hundred-pound packs off the platform spoke European languages. Helicopters buzzed overhead, lifting these enthusiastic souls, in due course, to staging areas seven thousand feet up, on a shoulder or a flat. Though I enjoy the train route to Fairbanks, sitting in the bubble-car, we were driving instead, replicating our luscious seven-hundred-eighty-mile jalopy lark from the ferry landing in Haines to Anchorage, while tenting in the deep moss in each other's arms under the St. Elias Range. But this so-called Richardson Highway, leading on past the entrance to Denali National Park, was so gentrified we were actually kicked out of a camping spot by a Marin County-type weekender couple who claimed we were too close to their driveway, and didn't we know what private property was? We gassed up at a filling station where the absentee owner flies up from the Southwest in the heat of summer, flashing an Uzi and a Glock, so he can shoot his moose nineteen times instead of once.

In Talkeetna we stayed with Ed Craver, an Iowa farmboy, and his schoolteacher wife, who had been growing vegetables and raising Greenland sled dogs on a patch of land next to the roiling susurrations of the Susitna River, curling by—one of my favorite major ones, and by now I'd seen the Colville, the Copper, the Porcupine, besides the Kuskokwim. I sat communing with Ed's slinky big brown lead dog, till Linda felt a trifle jealous, forgetting I was closing on finishing the novel I'd already been working on for twenty years called *Seven Rivers West*. Both Ed and his wife were likable company, generous hosts, but their marriage was on the rocks, so it was not the most propitious moment. He'd also given up his half-dozen dairy cows and shot a lot of his dogs, surrendering the notion of running his team competitively, although he took us for a brief wagon ride behind those that were left. Marriages smash up in Alaska frequently. Just to my town in Vermont alone, two women have recently returned after twenty years of trying to make theirs work, bitter because the glue couldn't hold against the play-acting. At Halloween, one said, when her children went door to door, they met a man with his pistol drawn. More than elsewhere, people in Alaska could define themselves simply by where they lived.

The helicopter noise of industrial mountain-climbing, the celebrity photographs of Warren G. Harding and such in the Fairview Hotel lobby, couldn't dilute the potency of Mount McKinley's vibrant presence, with Foraker and Hunter its sister peaks. The Cravers' friends dropped by to help them through this raw period, and several engineers on the railway line who remembered the farm in its heyday tooted a greeting as they chugged by. Since I like railroads nearly as much as rivers, to lie at night in between the two, with furry Greenland dogs around, was a delight, and the vegetables garden-fresh. But we were headed for a still more boisterous river—the Tanana—a tributary to the great Yukon, in order to witness another sort of commercial venture: barging fuel to an Air Force base at Galena, where frontline interceptor jets were based against the possibility of Soviet nuclear bombers sneaking across the Chukchi Sea from Siberia to slant south toward America's cities.

We continued up the road, past Gold Creek, Chulitna, Hurricane, Honolulu, Summit—the country becoming less peopled once we left the buzz surrounding the continent's highest pinnacle behind. Roughshod truck tracings led off indeterminately toward homesteads or placer workings, harsh and sparse, where frost cracks in a creek bank might have exposed a streak of color, when earlier mining operations had been thought to have played out.

Nenana, our destination, population five hundred, had been the railhead for freight shipped from the port of Seward, far to the south on the Kenai Peninsula, and intended for the Yukon's web of waterways. In 1907, "St. Mark's Indian Church" had been consecrated here, and by 1923 there were five thousand residents, when President Harding drove a golden spike to link the rails with sixty miles of new track to the mining community of Fairbanks, then only twenty years old. Anchorage, at the head of Cook Inlet and with rudimentary footing as a port, was even a decade younger than Fairbanks, so the alternative hubs for provisioning the Yukon watershed's gold strikes and prospecting ventures were either still through Skagway, toward Whitehorse and the Klondike in Canada, or else for supply ships to sail clear around much of Alaska to Norton Sound, offloading onto riverboats where the Yukon finally debouches into salt water, a twenty-eight-hundred-mile lug from San Francisco.

We parked at the dock where the *Tanana*, the Yutana Barge Lines' largest of five push boats, was tied up. After introducing ourselves and displaying my accreditation from *House and Garden* (which, like the *Vanity Fair* assignment the previous winter, had been obtained for me by an editor-friend at the Conde Nast company), we carried our gear aboard; then ate Denver sandwiches at Mom, Aggie's and Babe's Café, washed down afterward with beer at Moocher's Bar. Yutana advertises itself as "Serving Interior and Coastal Alaska since 1916," but of course there have been ups and downs. When large-scale gold extraction ceased on the Yukon, the railroad itself operated provisioning barges to maintain a summer freight service to river communities, after various shoestring pioneering boating entrepreneurs had gone bust, but stopped in 1959, when Yutana's Cold War contracts to fuel the little air base at Galena enabled it to pick up the slack for other roadless hamlets along the Yukon, as well. No bridge even crossed the big river until recent oil drilling in the Arctic necessitated a haul road and pipeline.

Moocher's was quiet, as our putative shipmates looked us over to size us up. But around eight o'clock, across the street at the Corner Bar, an altercation began. A guy named Mark hurled a stool at a Pac Man machine, busting the game, during an argument with a man named Billy over Billy's wife. "She's been fucking everybody in town while you were away!" Mark yelled.

"Why pick on poor Billy?" a middle-aged woman remonstrated with him, as a tall, jaunty-looking black state trooper arrived on the scene to listen to Mark's alibi that, hey, he "never saw it"—the Pac Man device—while the owner's son-in-law insisted he was going to have to buy them a new one anyway, which, working on the North Slope rigs, as Mark did, would take about a month's pay.

A local fireman told Linda and me that he'd been frequenting "this crack in the road" for seven years and loved the conjunction of river, rail, and highway. Several Indian girls with curly, shoulder-length black hair, in jeans and jean jackets, bellied up for drinks again now that it was safe, including the wife the fight had started over. She was heftier than the trio of others; looked somehow more opulent and arresting; and her short, raspy-voiced mother, also a patron of the Corner Bar, kept informing us all that "I used to whip her ass! I used to beat the shit out of her!" Delightedly she repeated twice, *Beat the shit out of her!*" Another girl, less well endowed, laughed and said, "Give me a bow and arrow and I'll drill her for ya."

Nenana boasted a low brown county courthouse, two tourist gift shops by the railroad station, another café, called Hooker's, across from Moocher's Bar, with dogs waiting in the pickup trucks parked behind, and the historic Episcopal mission church, as well as a Bible-believers' fundamentalist one. The few streets were lightly dotted with log cabins or plywood frame houses—a sixty-percent Native American population—and a waterfront slough that was all barging facilities or railway spurs, four hundred miles up from that original seaport at Seward. Our *Tanana* itself, the namesake of the turbid brown river revolving just in front of us as well as of the Athabascan village downstream a couple of hundred very twisty miles, where it emptied into the Yukon, was a thirty-year-old, twelve-hundred-horsepower craft that had replaced the older *Nenana*, now a museum display at Fairbanks's "Alaska-land." The *Tanana's* twin boat, the *Yukon*, had burned in an engine-room fire a few years before, having always evinced "a troubled personality," whereas the *Tanana* "hummed along," according to Charlie Huilicha, its pilot.

At thirty, he was from Chester, Connecticut, on the Connecticut River, but now ran sled dogs on a looping trapline with his brother, Karl, in the winter, near the town of Ruby, which we'd be passing in a week or so. Ruby, like Circle and Eagle, two other white men's towns, lay on the south bank of the Yukon, facing north and with mountains behind it further blocking a good deal of the winter's sun, whereas the Indian towns such as Tanana, Beaver, Nulato, Koyukuk, Kokrines, Stevens Village, and Fort Yukon were located on the north side, basking in their southern exposure. Karl's regular job, said Charlie, was carpentering for the mining outfits that were still scrabbling with earthmovers and flumes at sediments near Poorman, Long, or Sulatna Crossing in the Twin Butte hills in back of Ruby. Karl's hobby was building moveable boathouses he could drag behind a tractor to whatever creek the purchaser wanted it on. Although the settlement at Poorman had a bush airstrip for resupply—or you could land a pontoon plane at Ruby on the Yukon—heavy stuff was Yutana's province, while en route with its bread-and-butter deliveries to Galena, half a day downriver from Ruby. Three hundred airmen had been superimposed upon the original three hundred salmon-fishing Athabascan inhabitants of Galena in order to service three F-15 interceptors, on a five-thousand-foot military runway that constituted America's outrider outpost against any Russian Dr. Strangelove.

Lou Towne, our engineer, had worked on the *Tanana* for all of its thirty years, and Keith Horton, the captain, though only two years older than Charlie Huilicha, for fourteen. Eunice, the cook, was a twelve-year veteran; and the rest of the crew encompassed two mates, a second engineer, four deckhands, plus the waitress, Jo. Gold-painted moose horns were affixed over the pilothouse, and with her large officers' messroom and galley, she was "a pretty boat with a good personality," as Charlie asserted again. His first company boat, the *Independent*, out of St. Michael, near the Yukon's mouth at Pastol Bay, had "had a personality that attracted storms. Soon as she'd stick her nose out into Norton Sound they'd start ablowin'."

We got delayed a day in "tackling up," or hitching onto our barges, by a couple of emergencies. Two tank cars had derailed in a canyon south of Healy on the railway line, thus holding up the fuel we were supposed to pump into our barges for delivery. And—more dicey—a new competitor's tugboat, named the *Bingo* and transplanted from New Orleans, of all places, had run aground on two sandbars—both "a dry bar and a wet bar," as Charlie put it—then had partially sunk in sixteen feet of water, above Eight-Mile Island but below Squaw Crossing, way down the Tanana River from where we were, but blocking the best navigable passage through a hodge-podge of drift piles, blind channels, and boiling shallows. Its hapless crew were novices to the Tanana, which they'd just entered and which was going to require a total of eighty or ninety savvy bank-to-bank crossings, depending upon conditions, in order to stay within the depth of the current while ascending from there to here. Each crossing had a nickname but no permanent buoys (or use for our radar screen), just sometimes an empty Clorox bottle or piece of red tape tied on a tree, if you noticed it, to occasionally mark a passage.

The office's immediate concern was whether one of their boats, the *Kantishna*, homeward-bound, might have violated maritime law by ignoring a distress call. The *Kantishna* had indeed steamed by the action, but about two hours before the *Bingo*'s MAYDAY, MAYDAY was broadcast. They'd noticed the *Bingo* was stuck and listing fifteen degrees or so, with valuables like the radio being taken off in the launch to stow ashore and the heavy deck freight being crowbarred around for refastening. Although this was a bad one, groundings weren't so uncommon that at that point perhaps dumb pride and the potential legal jeopardy of asking for salvage help had prevented these *Bingo* interlopers from officially hailing the *Kantishna*, when lives weren't at stake. At least Yutana hoped the Coast Guard—now officially notified—would take that view. However, with the situation deteriorating, it should be a lucrative proposition to send the *Kantishna*, together with a second boat, the *Rampart*, back down, their barges carrying winch-equipped Caterpillar tractors, to try to raise and right the *Bingo*. The *Rampart*'s captain and pilot had invited me onto their triple-screw, nine hundred–fifty horsepower, twenty-year-old vessel, with a crew of seven, but soon flew off instead in a chartered Cessna to reconnoiter the project—in daredevil fashion, taking off from the curve of the river underneath the highway and railroad bridge, like stuntmen. The *Pat*, the company's other push-boat, was dry-docked in the slough while its drive shaft, which had been bent on a snag, got straightened out.

These various crews, finding themselves fortuitously in town, held an impromptu AFL-CIO Alaska Riverboatmen's Union meeting, then dispersed to a miscellany of trailers and crash pads till management reached a decision. The *Tanana*'s two fuel barges had been loaded and their flat decks utilized for stacks of lumber, ATV vehicles, cases of beer and other canned goods, and assorted civilian freight to be delivered along the Yukon. The pilot's skiff, with a kicker on the stern, perched on the bow of the *Skagit*, the lead barge we would push, in which he'd dart or drift in front of us, chatting into a hand microphone with the captain while scouting the currents' whims at every bend, the lay of the river as it gobbled tributaries, the placement of waterlogged trees upthrust, maybe overnight, from the bottom. A deckhand would sit on that forward bow, also with a walkie-talkie, taking soundings or warning of immediate obstacles in the swirl. And the captain could talk by CB radio or radio-telephone to the different riverboat communities he serviced, other boats, and three times a day to Nenana from as far as eight hundred miles away.

Linda and I bunked on the *Tanana* but ate moose stew at Hooker's Café, adjoining the red tin front of The Corner Bar, where the fight had occurred the night before, and across from Moocher's green adobe façade. Our captain, Keith Horton, introduced his wife, Sharon, who was eight months pregnant, and his brother, Glen, who acted as assistant engineer on the boat. Jo, the galley waitress, was divorced from another brother, back in their hometown of Bay City, Michigan, where her ten-year-old son was spending the summer. Keith resembled John Lennon a bit, with his gaunt look, sandy beard, and metal-rimmed glasses, but chewed his words at the corner of his mouth in the Michigan accent. While still in his middle teens, he had first ventured up to visit a relative who was stationed at a White Alice radar base on the DEW Line. He stayed to work at a sawmill, as he had done in Michigan; then switched to a job on the railroad for the glamour and travel, until, noticing these riverboats at Nenana Junction, he made sure to grab a position as a deckhand when one opened up. And before marrying Sharon, he brought her not only north, but to the river itself for the long-drawn, thousand-mile freight round-trip to Fort Yukon—past Rampart, Kings Slough Cabin, Purgatory, Swede Boys Camp, White Eye, Johnnie Frog Cabin, the Chandalar and Christian rivers—with Bearman Cabin and similar landmarks, to be certain she "liked Alaska," as Sharon expressed it. Since Linda and I, separately, had visited the doughty historic outpost of Fort Yukon, intersecting with the Arctic Circle, and Alaska's first English-language community, which was established by the Hudson's Bay Company in 1847 (Russian traders discovered the mouth of the

Yukon in 1834), we were easy to talk to, lending an ear to either gender. In fact in the wintertime we'd flown on a TB assessment to that bleaker settlement of Tanana.

Wages were okay, said Patrick, a deckhand, except that the river was open only for four months a year, which meant that with time added for "housework and hullwork" afterward and beforehand, you barely qualified for unemployment payments during the cold. He'd spent a hundred bucks the night of the fight trying to get drunk but had still returned to his bed on the *Tanana* sober. The Corner Bar hung up a ship's bell that people could clang when they wanted to buy everybody a drink—only he liked to ring it with his feet, standing on his head. It was placed low, however, so drunks might sound it accidentally, in passing. Since he was anti-union politically, he'd spent the hour of the Alaska Riverboatmen's meeting with us and the row of Indian girls combing their wavy tresses on bar stools, who, if not playing pool, were gazing lackadaisically out the window for the confab to be over. Another deckhand—like Patrick from California but aged twenty, Patrick said—after wintering in Oahu, had taken one of them, aged thirty-eight, as his girlfriend. He himself "must have had fifty or sixty different jobs" in the fourteen years since he'd turned sixteen and left home in Los Angeles. Had been in Alaska six years, three of them on the boats, after peeling logs here in Nenana for a dollar a foot, then quitting that to enjoy life on the river for half that pay. "Jack of all trades; master of none." He said the natives generally didn't like to work for white men at a white man's rhythm, but "sixty percent" of each group got along with the other, "and the rest don't fight."

Matt, the second mate, arriving from the union meeting, glanced at the women fingering their long hair in a row at the bar and told us he had "lived with half the girls in town, but can't settle down." Had vowed that by thirty he was going to, "but turned thirty a month ago." His job was mainly throwing mooring lines, operating forklifts, and managing the barges' valves for pumping the oil in and out, so he'd sat for the tankerman's exam to upgrade his license and maybe move up in the world. "But will that pin me too much to the river" for the new, bank-clerk girlfriend he had also just graduated to? "Everything's quite fine, except for me," he added, before turning to his whisky glass to tie one on.

Captains wore Navy-like scrambled eggs on their Yutana Barge Lines caps. But the pilots seemed more carefree—using Bayliner's Mosquito two-seat workboats with a Mercury outboard hitched to the stern but the rudder's wheel in the bow, to freelance in front of the flotilla. The *Rampart*'s pilot and the *Kantishna*'s first mate— a tall, beef-red Vermonter in a red fedora—had gone fifteen miles up the Tatlanika River, a clear-water tributary, last evening in the late, lingering July twilight, after the *Kantishna* pulled in, and had caught themselves about a hundred grayling, at one of those fishing holes where the eyes of the last fish you hooked baited the next to the line almost instantly. Yet then they found they'd gotten too drunk to clean them all and so abandoned the entire pile to the bears, and corkscrewed on downstream and home, hungry—being still too soused to bother eating, they imbibed another bellyful instead.

Carol, who cooked on the *Rampart*, was nineteen and had been brought up from Arkansas on the Alaska Highway by that pilot, to serve at first as the Moocher's barmaid, facing up to the crummy drunks who smarted off. She told Linda she'd left home earlier at sixteen, when she could quit school, but this last time, at least her mother wished her luck, although didn't take the trouble to be at the house when Carol stopped by to collect her stuff and for a goodbye hug; just left a note. "I write her more than she writes me," and had taught the mom to drive. Carol, however, had never known a town like this, where she said the Indians lived off government checks, girls sixteen had two kids, and people drank for something to do, although they scraped their men's fur catch during the endless winter and sewed beadwork for the tourist stores. In the summer they dried the salmon they netted, and played softball. People were divided into Christers or drinkers, with nobody in between. As a barmaid, she'd witnessed bad fights among friends over a pool game or a bar towel carelessly flung, and tried to ease an incipient squabble out the door and over toward the Corner Bar for somebody else to handle.

A colony of cliff swallows had constructed their gourd-shaped nests under the eaves of the old railroad station, lending the town the blessing and panache of flight. But huge, hide-shaped strips of moss or grassy rootings overhung the eroding sandbanks of the river, as we finally cast off at 8:20 a.m., Wednesday, July 20th, after the status of the moribund *Bingo* at Squaw Crossing had been resolved. With her crew safe and still in technical possession of the craft, which was no longer wedged as a navigational hazard in the passage, she was to remain the property of her owners, the Coast Guard had agreed, and not for salvage. So Yutana, but not our boat, would be hired to help them.

Streaks on the water's surface showed Captain Keith Horton where the current was, although ruffling up to signal a shallows. He followed the flow, taking the long way around most of the bends, as it chewed at each side of the river in turn, but pointed the prow of the frontal barge out of the curve before the *Tanana*'s twin propellers lost their purchase and we skidded close to colliding with the bank, or slid too far to keep within the current's five-to-seven-knots-per-hour boost. Deadwood lay strewn at sixes and sevens across sandbars materializing inconveniently midstream; or jouncing stubs and spars poked out from the bottom like horse's heads, galloping relentlessly, till they would get scrubbed away. The banks were an atrocity zone for standing trees—havoc and slaughter wherever the river inched toward gripping them, though some survived at crazy angles if the roots had found a hidden boulder that had not been pulled loose yet.

At Shirttail Channel—seven miles and forty minutes below Nenana—we passed several Indian fishing camps on the east shore, each with a fish wheel placidly turning. Maybe twenty feet high, these water wheels, set upright, rotated with the river's push to scoop up any spawning salmon swimming upstream on a tangent to connect with the wooden blades, producing a sudden Ferris wheel hoist for the fish, till it was flipped backward into a basket, then dumped into a collecting bin, where it twitched, smothering in the air, and eventually somebody would grab, gut, and fillet it, laying the strips with others to dry red on racks in the sun. Each fish camp had a few white canvas tents or log lean-tos for the family to live in, and Keith took care not to damage a fish wheel with our outwashing wake as he maneuvered past.

Three miles below Shirttail Channel, at Soldier Slough, Charlie Huilicha, our pilot, lowered his launch. Troy Dana, second mate, a twenty-year-old who had wintered in Seattle and was spending only his third summer on the river, went out on the front barge to monitor the fathometer pole rigged there that registered depth readings electronically for Keith in the wheelhouse, but needed to be lifted manually if obstacles were sighted in the water. A white windsock flew from each of the barges, alongside the fathometer pole, and a red metal flag warned others that our load was fuel. A hundred-twenty-six feet long and thirty-eight wide, the *Tanana* was pushing nine hundred-eighty-eight tons altogether, counting two military trucks and the diverse military crates cabled on top of the fighter fuel. From the bridge, each of the boat's propellers had its separate throttle and rudder, aided by levers to the flanking rudders; and below the bridge deck was the Texas deck, my favorite vantage spot (so named supposedly because on the Mississippi's tugs and riverboats you could see from there to Texas), and then the main or working deck, where the many bitts and coils of rope and fenders were, not to mention the galley's door.

White birch and black spruce lined both banks, all different ages according to what the river had wrought. It chomped on trees like a horse crunching carrots, or else tipped them whole into the roil to travel beside us, the branches jutting up like a brown shark's fin. Clouds built up on some of the knolls to make them look like snow peaks, or else turned bruise-blue, or pewter-colored. Sawmill Island stood two miles below Soldier Slough; then the deadwater of Totchaket Slough eight miles beyond that, at Pritchard's Crossing. The complexities of Twenty-four Mile Slough followed soon after, and in another mile, Sawmill Slough, and, next, the braidings of Minto Slough, at an abandoned Indian settlement twenty-nine miles below Nenana, where beaver swamps and shortish streams congealed. At Campbell's Crossing we tied up for lunch.

Charlie's instructions from his workboat, angling to and fro in front of the *Skagit* barge, which was itself a hundred-seventy-five feet long—although, like the *Tanana*, it drew only four feet of water—via speakerphone to Keith in the wheelhouse went something like this: "Steer to the starboard of that bunch of boils at the end of the island." Or, "This bar is a little lumpier than it has been. I'm going to take you on the other side of the drift piles." Or, "You've got all good water down to this wet bar here. And the wet bar is sixty feet up from that dry bar with all those snags on it." Although his skiff resembled a kind of river bug weaving ahead, he tossed round red buoys into the rapids or eddies occasionally as markers, if words couldn't be exact enough, which he circled back to retrieve after we had slid by that particular peril. We were always hugging one bank or the other, wherever the current was freshly chewing. We went where it chewed because the depth would be there, then crossed again when the thrust changed sides.

At Campbell's Crossing, where we ate tacos and calzones, the water was a luxurious fourteen feet deep at the bank, yet ripply-calm, fronting a wide willow and sedge flat where salmon entered the watercourses every summer to spawn, and fishermen, like grizzlies, sometimes pursued them. In fact, although we were alone, while stretching my legs along a path by a creek, I found a nine-shot twelve-gauge Smith & Wesson police riot gun that somebody must have laid in the grass as "bear medicine," then forgotten where—an unlovely short fat killer pump gun which fires slugs, not birdshot. Alaskan fishing can have a proper tingle of danger associated with it: as I think a blood sport should.

Eunice, an imaginative cook, was seventy, also from Michigan to begin with, and told Linda she had worked on these boats for a dozen years, the first ten as a waitress. And seven years ago, she remembered, the *Tanana* and its barges, returning a bit tardily but empty, had been caught by the October freeze-up, and headed into the nearest slough to park for the winter, where a helicopter fetched the crew out—she went to Anchorage—then flew them back in April a week before break-up. Her daughter had cooked on a San Francisco tugboat that powered "gi-normous" loads to Alaska (even the North Slope opens to resupply by ocean barging for a brief spell in midsummer), then switched to the Yukon River's tugs; and when Eunice's husband died, suggested she join her.

Rathborn's Island was another nine miles downstream: after which we steamed alongside Crescent Island and into a nice straightforward stretch, until German's Crossing, duly to be followed after a while by Martini's Crossing. Then, about three-thirty p.m., we rounded the U of a bend studded with islets at the tricky upper and lower McKinley Crossings, watery with marshy runoff from the northern shoulders of satellites of the McKinley massif: to Seagull Island, and Trappers Point. This led us to the thicker, more congested bend in the river called the Big Wow Crossing, from gold-rush and paddle-wheel days, when sightseers floated down from Dawson in the Yukon Territory on the boats of the Northern Navigation Company to ogle every tributary between Canada and the port of St. Michael, which was sixteen hundred miles, leaving out detours such as our Tanana.

Thunka, thunka, thunka protested the smokestacks, according to which screw was being strained. Afterward Keith's brother Glen climbed up to the bridge from the engine room for coffee and a chat. He was a bulkier, slower, quirkier, more punctilious version of Keith, and formerly a movie house maintenance man in Bay City, who may have wanted a larger theater for his life to play out in, like a lot of the people who pile into a pickup truck to drive the interminable vistas of the Alcan Highway. Many Texans, New Yorkers, New Orleans, or Las Vegas folk define themselves by where they live, but the wager can be giddier and the exit farther in Alaska. At the snaky, flush Tolovana River—which collects two others before it empties into the Tanana—we saw the ruins of the old roadhouse where dog teams, mailmen, placer miners, and packet passengers had stopped, winter or summer, for caribou and homebrew. The roof was falling in, but the log walls still looked a healthy yellow, and hay grew in the clearing for vanished horses here, seventy-six miles below Nenana.

After the Upper and Lower Tolovana Sloughs, where we'd stuck close to where that river's volume poured in, we carefully rounded an island to Davis Crossing, alongside a log like a moose in the water— its roots sticking up like antlers—and toward Sand Crossing, which was recognizable by a certain sweeper—a tree now hanging semi-horizontally over the tumult, but still leafy and partially attached to the disintegrating bank. A second reference point was the personably hieroglyphed white skin of a birch, and then a swale growing to grass in an oxbow bight severed by the river. Deadfalls, stubs, snags, and thickets of distinctly different ages registered not only the switchbacks we accomplished but punishment the river had dished out, because although meteorologically it was a device for moving water, geologically it moved dirt. At Caribou Crossing we paused for a swimming caribou, cutting the engine and drifting sideways anyhow until the currents firmed up to define themselves again. A white rainstorm was blowing past close, black, precipitous bluffs, with Deadman Lake behind them to the north. Three peregrine falcons put on an air show, while a bald eagle got into a scuffle next to another cliff, over an island, with four nesting gulls, who chased it.

The Kantishna River, for which our sister tug was named, debouched robustly into the Tanana from the south, a forceful waterway draining the northeastern heights of Denali National Park—Mounts

Mather and Brooks, Peter's Dome, Wonder Lake, and elements of McKinley itself, through settlements like Fish Camp, Diamond, Bear Paw, and Toklat, where dreamers had shaken their gold pans over sluice boxes, or perhaps launched a back-slope glacial ascent. Respectfully adjusting to the Kantishna's nudge, added girth, and velocity, we crossed the Tanana to the Burke family's busy fish wheels, tying onto their dock for a six p.m. supper. The wheels creaked, windmilling gravely in the water, with a seagull perched, waiting hopefully for innards, on the frame of each. The Burkes rigged pails ingeniously outside the blades to dip up water and wet any salmon trapped in the collection trough, keeping it fresh. We bought and grilled a couple to thank them for the mooring.

Our deckhands, Mike Killian from North Carolina, Harley Pauley from Fort Worth, Texas, and Mark Cline from Tenino, Washington, were eighteen or twenty—Harley still wearing braces under his mustache fuzz—but looked five years older because of wear and tear. Mark told Linda he was "nineteen and away from home," wrenching his arms in driving motions as if he wanted to hit the road and go back. They'd set easy chairs out on the bows of our two barges to lounge in while watching for the welfare of our fathometers or using their boathooks to fend off flotsam concealed by the gray river's creamy foam. The black anchors and anchor chains, front bitts and coils of mooring line kept them company, besides the grandest of primeval scenery and Keith's weather eye, from his five front windows. Their paint work on the white boat was shipshape, but they reminded me of Carol, the Arkansas waif of about the same age who was cooking downriver on the *Rampart*, which had been chartered, along with the *Kantishna*, for $10,000 a day to raise the sunken *Bingo*.

Going around several provisional islands sprinkled near the Kantishna's mouth, we took the Flag Crossing back to the Tanana's south bank; then, by and by, via Scotchman's Crossing, returned to the squishy north shore, with the Dugan Hills in the distance, for a considerable segment, past Junction Island, clear to the Double Jennie M. Crossing, meaning a transit both before and after Jennie M. Island itself. Waterspouts decorated the horizon ahead, plus a shelving of cloud formations on the skyline. Lightning was crashing on the radio, where other boats sharing our frequency, not just up and down the Yukon but fishing out on Norton Sound, were experiencing storms.

We shied off from Giroux Bluff, yet, opposite the twists of Baker Creek, slid close to a small willow stand not far from where the Zitziana River comes in.

"Always changes," Keith said. Saunders Crossing, tight and shallow, lay to port of a specific beaver meadow—the river's recent exploits being written on the face of the woods. Bank beavers were noodling in the channel. Lou Towne, engineer of this boat for all its thirty years, entered the wheelhouse for a coffee break and told me he used to keep a house in Nenana, but lately wintered with his Eskimo wife in Seattle instead, picking up machine-shop jobs, because a daughter and son lived there—the daughter a proofreader, the son a policeman. Another married daughter had stayed in Alaska, in Valdez. But Lou himself, who'd arrived to start with on an army tug, said, "There's no place now in the state where I would want to live." He would prefer Long Beach, California, or Honolulu, he suggested, with a sweet, rather disappointed but reflective smile, uncertain what to make of the turns his life had taken.

At Manley Hot Springs Landing, to our starboard, a brave Winnebago had driven to the end of the farthest dirt road west out of Fairbanks, a spot otherwise deserted except for one decrepit building. A stocky woman waved at us with frantic enthusiasm, so, laconically, since no one else did, I waved back, as if I were an old river hand. Hot Springs Slough followed, creek-fed, flowing in, but commanded by a lengthy, lovely, thousand-foot bluff called Bean Ridge. Then Severides Crossing—the pilot boat out diligently—led us to Fox Farm Point. (As Holland had its tulip craze, Alaska sprouted a plethora of fox farms during the 1920s for the fur-coat fad, which quickly in the Hungry Thirties went belly-up, the poor beasts starving if abandoned. And photos display other entrepreneurial notions that flickered out, like reindeer harnessed and trained, or hot spring spas bricked up as a cash cow for the wretched winters, before bush planes could whisk any miner out to warmth and company.) More red-rock bluffs on the north side led to extensive thickets of moose pasturage opposite them, where the river broadened again, with anonymous islands and flats, until at last we reached Miller's Camp, where we tied our stern to a tree trunk at ten forty-five p.m., dusk, pointing downstream, and walked a pirate plank to a clay bank six feet high, having covered a hundred-forty miles in ten hours from Nenana. The

Skagit's fathometer now read twenty feet of good water, but the site, like so many landmarks named for white men who had lived here on the Tanana, was deserted.

Linda and I were sharing one of the four cabins on the Texas deck, under the wheelhouse and over the galley. While I was on the bridge a lot, she'd been keeping company with Eunice and Jo in the messrooms on the main deck. It constituted a reversal of roles for us, since ordinarily she worked when we traveled and I was along for the ride, so she began to want more of my attention. We slept a nice chunk of hours, however, because there was no point in the boat starting before the fog burned off the river, around eight thirty once again, six hours after daybreak had occurred; and unhurriedly we'd consumed hotcakes, eggs, Canadian bacon, and muscular coffee. Keith began his first crossing by sighting on Bruno's Rock, where falcons were nesting, then finagled us between a chain of hefty islands via Patterson's Crossing. We were wending through "Cosna country"—Cosna Bluff and Slough and the outlet of the Cosna River: forty miles up which, Keith said, a twelve-family, fly-in commune had recently been established by what he called "professional people": a dentist, a teacher, an airliner jockey. But the meager ruins of the original Cosna homesite, plus another homestead called "Joe's Jacket," facing it across the Tanana, testified to how fleeting their plans and hopes might be.

After Vachon Island came Bareass Bend, a pleasant sort of beach dubbed that by the Yutana crowd when the tug *Nenana* had caught by spotlight the Indian crew of the tug *Taku Chief*, a long way from their home base down near Juneau, bathing. That was a boat which traditionally made the last trip up the Koyukon River to Huslia in September, then hunted moose on the way down, heaping the deck with them. A ton of Indian lore, of course, had been lost along the Yukon, and was being plumbed for, but it's also easy to forget the innumerable loose-cannon whites—raftsmen, mushers, sloggers—who even before Nome and Dawson scrambled toward El Dorado wealth in "strikes," maybe just as a painkiller. Then the pain of dying fireless, meatless, or in a cave-in was worse. On this one barge line three old captains had recently retired, erasing decades of expertise. And thus the thirtyish skipper and pilots, the deckhand turnover, and newly minted second mates like Patrick trying to keep up with present demands. Six-and-a-half feet tall, sketchily bearded, having averaged about four jobs a year since leaving school, Patrick was adorned with a female demon on his left biceps and a male devil on the other, plus the tattooed legend, *Born To Raise Hell*. The hell-to-pay attitude enabled the state's scrofulous politicians like Senator Ted Stevens to flourish in power, and the perennial Congressman, Don Young, whose summer cabin at Fort Yukon I'd seen burned to the ground by local Gwitch'in Indians.

We skirted the opening where the Redlands, or Chitanana, River entered, with its impressive sand bluff and trees poking every which way out of the demolished surface mat of roots and soil. Then around Hathmeyer's Bend. And Hooper's Bend. And the relic cemetery of a settlement at Patterson Creek and Harper Bend. On past Murray Island, Star Point, Green Slough, and several provisional raggedy islands, where we tracked Tillie's Crossing (for "Old Man Tillie") to Fish Creek Island, and sailed behind it to tie up at Fish Creek itself, to savor Eunice's outlay of cooking again and angle a bit for pike. Mark Cline caught one a yard long, its ventral as red as if colored by the salmon fry it had been eating. Hay Slough, nearby, was where gold-rush teamsters had grown feed for their horses, and Squaw Point, beyond, narrowed the passage for salmon that had entered the gray Tanana from the yellow Yukon a dozen miles down: a narrows where in immemorial summers the Gwitch'in from the area had gathered to net a winter's worth, amidst the multitudes that wriggled by.

Squaw Crossing Creek and Slough and a defunct cabin marked where we hazarded a semi-circular passage around a kidney-shaped island, through much delta mish-mash and a weltering maze of mud and water to Station Rock and Eightmile Island, where the *Bingo* had strayed into a blind channel, grounded, churned, and sunk. "Pretty lumpy in here. Lumping up," Keith remarked as he listened to Charlie, scouting ahead in the launch, convey instructions. Repeatedly we needed to shift our speed and drift or slant. His souring, sober look added ten years to his face, with its brown beard and pocked skin, but he was actually a kind, quiet man, not rattled by momentary errors. Squaw Crossing had acquired its slurry or slipshod name from an incident when white tug men had spotted two Indians, stuck in a jonboat, and the man of the pair was simply standing in the craft, wielding a pole, while his "squaw" waded out in front, pulling on a rope knotted to the bow.

"Do this one low instead of high. Guide by that split sweeper," Charlie suggested by speakerphone, because the navigable splinter of headway had changed since their last trip down.

"Where the sweepers are, that's where we are," Keith explained: sweepers being the half-capsized trees signifying where the river was presently hitting the bank hardest and digging a channel for us. He told me about an episode near Minto last winter when a trapper badly burned his hands by filling his Coleman lantern with white gas outdoors in the bitter cold, where he stored the stuff. Later he brought the thing inside his warm cabin and lit it. Thereupon the expansion of the fuel in the heat caused it to explode.

The hapless *Bingo*, though pathetically askew, fortunately was not blocking an essential passageway. We waved and radioed to the *Rampart* and *Kantishna* crews, laboring to free and right her. An aged, weary little St. Louis-built chugatug, bought on sale in New Orleans as "The Merry Maid" last spring and trucked from the Mississippi to Seattle, cut up and barged as freight to Alaskan waters, she'd been reassembled by welders to ply the Yukon in a misbegotten financial or romantic fling. After wending upstream to Tanana, then trying to enter the wrong approach to Squaw Crossing, she'd promptly grounded on a sandbar. The people aboard had managed to unhook and float their barge to shore, pushing it with the pilot boat, and moor it to a tree. Then crudely they'd dug their tug loose from the bar, using shovels and poles but mostly by straining the engine, propellers, and shafts. After gradually moving it from there to sixteen feet of water, they anchored, congratulated themselves, ate something, and collapsed into bed to rest—but shortly were grabbing life jackets or survival suits, hollering, breathless, and tumbling off the deck, as the *Bingo* began shipping floods of leakage, listing, filling, and sank from cracks in her hull and a damaged propeller shaft.

Since they were in safe hands, we continued past Six-mile Island and Mission Island into the wide, deep, potent, silty-yellow multiplicity of currents of the Yukon, opposite the village of Tanana, about eight p.m., where we tied up to get rid of some freight and walk the modest box of streets, indulging in a beer from the speakeasy: the place being officially dry. Our friends, the dog-mushers, were all out of town at their fish camps, catching salmon like most of the other residents at this high season, or else, if they were teachers or nurses, had flown Outside to visit relatives. I'd thought the town disturbingly demoralized, compared to Fort Yukon's pep, upriver. Only snowmobile trails led out of town, though people had doodlebugs for shuttling stuff around during the summer and plenty of the older Indians seemed to have retained their equilibrium. Their low-slung log cabins indented the riverbank above flood-line, and the government had thrown up a few administrative prefabs back by the three-story log boardinghouse and general store, run by a marooned, disagreeably wordless white man. Sled dogs were staked next to dog-hovels all along the beach, in this off-season, howling competitively in bouts of yodeling, each team joining voice to outshout the others. Eunice took a brace of king salmon from Sheri Runyan's refrigerator and left payment for them tucked in a hiding place.

Since our incomes were on a par, Linda didn't like to appear like a mistress, which offended her both in the old-fashioned sense and as a feminist, and on her professional tours obviously could not. But in Anchorage, driving me to see peremptory, manipulative millionaires—who often fancied themselves emirs of the north and eyed her in that mode—or now on the boat, where my attention was glued to reading the ripples of the river, like the stripling Sam Clemens under Mr. Bixby's tutelage, it was a problem. Later, she would write books of her own, but at this point the friction of our age difference, which in love-making could act as a frisson, rubbed sorely when I scrutinized wet bars, dry bars, sweepers, and eddies instead of honeymooning. I'd flown over the Yukon watershed to get to Bettles—five hundred miles up the Koyukon and gateway to the Brooks Range—and had admired trackless tributaries like the Sheenjek on maps, but this was my first and hard-won riverboat trip. I'd never managed to go up the Congo or the Amazon, but every bend of the Yukon had encapsulated or capsized somebody's golden fantasy. "Tobys Cabin" and "Vincents Camp," near Galena, were noted on our chart, for example, like numerous others, and the old rivermen transported out countless prospectors who had little more than their blunted picks and shovels to pay the fare, but also the beaming guy in filthy clothes suppressing his grin, with rawhide pokes of gold dust concealed underneath his clothes.

But the Tanana hotel proprietor, chewing his fingers, talking to himself and staring fixedly as he rang up a grocery tab, was a contrast too: the standard white guy who's sunk a bundle into Indian country and gotten stranded. Then there was the snickering pair of fly-in whites at the speakeasy who'd drifted up here on pontoons from the city to slum for a couple of days. Their laughter was over the plight they were imagining for a hippie—a "yellowback," as they called him, because apparently he'd told them he had protested against the war in Vietnam—whom they'd met at the Anchorage airport and given a free lift into the wilderness. Couldn't afford to charter a plane, but he had his dream spot picked out on the map, around the head of the Nowitna River. "And a helluva walk out, if he ever gets out. The Big Mud River, Titna River, Telsitna River, Niggerhead Creek. The map says it all, but he had his bug dope and a gallon of chainsaw gas, a tarp, ammo, rice. Maybe a prayer wheel will save him, if he's a Buddhist. Lightin' his incense! You'd need snowshoes in the summer to wade outa there!"

Linda asked whether they were planning to return soon for him.

"No, he's an adult. No law against hitchhiking. No, you'd never find him. He was going to move. If he doesn't starve he'll hoof it out—find a moose that wolves aren't finished with—had a frying pan—and a voice like a violin that the cats still yell out of."

We bridled, and finished our beers, although no more startled than during our last visit, when we watched the Iditarod racer throw chunks of his own dogs into the pot for his surviving team, as he whittled it down, if they hadn't pulled hard enough on a twenty-mile conditioning run—unhooked and shot them right on the trail, he said, in front of the rest, before mushing them back to town.

We had our Cold War jet fuel to deliver, however, and so bright and early retrieved our mooring lines and slid into the confident grip of the mid-Yukon's currents: no need for Charlie to scout in the pilot boat in front. Standing on the *Skagit*'s prow was a banner point of the whole year for me, to survey such a magnificently unpeopled panorama of this mythic concourse, wilder now in aspect than it had been for a hundred years. Long and Leonard Islands passed, and Bull Island, before the Tozitna River poured in from the north—the trunk of a whole food-tree of moose and beaver meat in the wintertime, up its tracery of creeks, such as the Bluebell, Hellbent, Slate, Wells,

Reindeer, Spruce, and Tozimoran, the Wrongtrail, Ptarmigan, Bandana, and Dagislakhna. Circle Island, Sword Point, and Basco Island followed. Then the Atutsak River, flowing from the south, toward Little Joker Island and Whiskey Jack Slough. The Blind River paralleled it to Swanson Slough, underneath Gold Hill, and Swanson Island, but was better hidden.

In fact, an F-15 abruptly popped over the trees with a vanishing roar and terrain-hugging twitch, causing a beachcombing bear to lumber forth in dismay. Lancaster Creek, on Gold Hill, still had some hydraulic dredging going on. Also Grant Creek, just above the settlement of Kallands, where we unloaded a Caterpillar tractor and several weighty coiled draglines, at a workings under Lynx Dome. One of the tin-roofed cabins had belonged to a trapper who this spring "turned up missing," as people say here. Perhaps to attempt to demystify the formidable landscape, the miners had named some of the features Blueberry Ridge, Illinois Creek, Brant Island, and, higher, Buster, Mason, Dixon, and Henderson Creeks—preceding Lange Island, Clay Island, Cronin Island, and Weir Island. But these last few fronted the famous Palisades, which are chalky two-hundred-foot cliffs being steadily undermined by the scouring river and therefore occasionally disgorging mammoth or other spectacular Pleistocene bones to splash into the water, unless somebody rappelled down from above in time to grab a protruding tusk or skull. Nobody lived nearby to intervene, no beach lay below as a catchment, just the current's cauldron, so I scanned the wall of earth excitedly but uneasily, afraid I'd spot an invaluable relic emerging high up, on the verge of falling, amid those perpetual trickles of dirt.

Past Chicken and Montana Creeks, Patrick was splicing cables and fashioning monkey's fists for our heaving lines, below the capstans and winches on the *Tanana*'s forepeak. "I never wanted to be a boss. Or even wanted to be the best worker the bosses had," he said. Jo's T-shirt read, "I got Lei'd Hawaiian-style," with flowers. They told me financing on the river was so tenuous the *Tanana* was actually owned by the City of Nenana and leased to Yutana. We "drifted the bends," gearing to neutral in the widest currents till Keith wanted the propellers to grasp a passage again. As the river cumulatively shoved its bends downstream and threw material from one shore against the other, the water kneaded the sandbars, with gray silt pluming, tailing, off them.

From the Kokrine Hills, Sunset Creek, and Lady, Burns, and Chokoyik Islands, a settlement called Joe De Louis followed one called the Birches. Then, between Kathaleen, Edith, and Florence Islands, the Nowitna River, an important if corkscrewed tributary, joined us from the south. Moose Point faced Mickey Island, and Hardluck Island, the Big Bend, and Kokrines Village; then Fox and Ham Islands; the white cliffs of Horner Hot Springs, and Shovel Creek. Night was settling, but luminously, the right-of-way quite ample. We kept skating along until the Melozitna, a complex, canyoned, hot-springed river, joined the Yukon from the north, near Bootlegger Slough, and opposite the sprightly hillside miners' town of Ruby, whose lights we much admired. Before electricity and mail planes, hot springs like Horner's could seem unspeakably soothing hangouts in the dregs of February to regretful prospectors with bleeding hemorrhoids, far from hope and home. Some had migrated clear down to Tenakee Springs, on Chichagof Island, a warm, stone-enclosed pool reachable by ferry from Juneau, where Linda and I had lazed.

By seven-thirty a.m., past meaty sloughs harboring moose calves and bear cubs for a trapper to live on, we'd reached the Yuko River tributary, facing a sandstone bluff, and Dainty Island, and Whiskey Creek. After two more hours of traveling—by Fish Island, Bear Bluff, and Kala Creek—we looped our lines around the bitts at Galena's dock, hooked onto the Air Force's hosing, and started the pumps, four hundred-thirty river miles below Nenana. The Yukon, half-a-mile across at Tanana, was three-quarters-of-a mile wide here; and the country on the south bank was already flattening out, as it would mostly remain for the last six hundred miles to salt water.

Galena's name derived from a lead ore discovered by whites on a nearby tributary; and the ancestral Indian community had been pushed almost into the water by new, spraddled-out, plywood, antiseptic, oil-furnace housing associated with the air base. A dike separated military operations from the civilian quarter, but the landing field predated the Cold War, to World War II, when the Soviets and the U.S. had been allies against Hitler and Hirohito, and America ferried replacement fighter planes to the Russians across Alaska—Fairbanks to Nome, then Siberia—with Galena for emergency landings. People told us we had "just missed the air show." Two jets had flown close over town upside down. At the post office notices announced a vacancy for court clerk and salmon-counting and Head Start government jobs. Also, an evangelist who billed himself as "God's Fishwheel" invited parishioners to come, and a public letter from a charity in the Lower 48 that had sent a $30,000 check for a church to be roofed asked now for photo documentation that the project had indeed been completed. Frequent rotation of personnel lent the streets a less jittery feel than Tanana's. That is, people might want to leave, when you talked to them, but crabbily, not desperately. Schoolteachers, storekeepers' assistants, Air Force dependents, talked wryly rather than bitterly about the posting; they'd be out by and by. But Linda pointed to a specific saloon where thirty-six different individuals, including her boss in Anchorage, while on a field trip, were thought to have contracted TB from exposure to a certain man behind the bar: a Typhoid Mary on the Yukon. We'd just boated in seventy-six thousand pints of Michelob beer, according to the *Tanana*'s manifest, as well as twenty thousand gallons of de-icing alcohol to the Station Commander and two hundred twenty-four thousand more of "DFA," or Diesel Fuel Arctic, to the Transportation Officer.

Sourdough beards, as painted as a trademark on Alaska Airlines Boeings, resembled Santa Claus's, but the real thing on the street could look hangdog, or like a highwayman's, a hangman's, stained Airedale-brown by snuff or chewing tobacco, and grown longer in the winter for warmth, as the guy got fat. After the 1897 Klondike strike and others at Nome and Fairbanks, ne'er-do-wells and greenhorns poured in to prospect, as smaller waves did again after World War I and during the Hungry Thirties and to recover from World War II—men needing to heal, lie low, start afresh: end-of-the-roaders who were not content with the Adirondacks, the Ozarks, or Cascades. Back-to-the-landers, self-dramatists, counter-culturalists, whether tree-huggers or wolf-pluggers, were propelled to the ultimate place they'd heard about, to trap arctic foxes or roughneck in the oil patch, and if they had no elsewhere to go back to, you might wonder why not.

Pumping the barges dry required a good ten hours of careful deck work, while Linda and I chatted with callow privates (I'd once been a callow private myself) or the elderly Indian ladies who'd been left in town to watch a house while their family was out at a fish camp and to feed and water the sled dogs chained thirstily along Galena's beach, howling—each having worn a trench in the sand around its post. Our *Tanana* moved six miles upriver to Campion Depot to complete the job, unloading a front-loader and forklift and dump truck, too, we hadn't got rid of before, plus pipes and airplane fuel; then moored for supper and to sleep at Beaver Creek. We watched seven sandhill cranes flying under a trumpet-colored sky, and myriad bank swallows seething along the Cave-Off Cliffs, which were calving rubble into the unruly river, because the same soft earthen material ideal for hollowing nest holes out of was munchable, as well. At a fish wheel presided over by an Indian family at Bessy Slough, Eunice purchased several hefty greenish black and red king salmon, their bodies bent, their toothy mouths freshly sculpted into the anguished grimaces of suffocation.

On Dainty Island, next morning, we saw two more fish camps, notable for the basketball hoops nailed up for kids to practice on— *they* were scything grass. The fish wheels had been sparred outward on rafts from shore into brisker water off a point where salmon naturally congregated before swimming around. Fish wheels weren't free; a permit cost about ten thousand dollars for each, as if for a boat, because money was earned from a public resource. Willows flourished along both banks, until a cabin appeared, set on a birchy bench under spruces on a ridge, with tall yellow-white Grass-of-Parnassus, yarrow, Jacob's ladder, purple fireweed, violets, lupine, and rhubarb blooms, a children's swing, and a woman moving about doing chores, looking naked underneath her bib overalls, with a loose automobile seat to sit on and contemplate the river, and a traditional half-moon cut into the door of the outdoor loo.

Charlie knew and named the families in every shack we passed, including those defunct and abandoned, or a newcomer's raw hut improvised beside a bear-proof log cache, such as a firefighter, who had flown from Montana in a hotshot Forest Service crew (I'd once been in one of those also), was throwing together for himself, deciding he wanted to stay, but was "drawing mixed reviews." Charlie disparaged "drum-beating Indians" also, who irritatingly pressed their legal claims and asked "What tribe are you?" as if white people were divided by tribe, too. Melozi Island was handsomely wooded, across from the blue-water Melozitna River, with a short misty canyon in view, which wound majestically northeast into the mountains but had had fewer settlers living up it than most sizable tributaries because its rapids were so hard to navigate that you'd have to fly both yourself and your kit in, at prohibitive expense.

Ruby—a hilly scattering of low wooden buildings in a scoop between two bluffs—had become effectively Charlie's hometown, so he waved to and named people ashore for us, like the shapely lady on her way to her outhouse, nine kids seesawing inside a spare fish wheel, a guy riding a three-wheeler whose dog team, Charlie said, "needs new blood, he's coasting on his reputation," and the Peters couple speeding from the town dock out to their fish camp on an island. The 1913 "Ruby Roadhouse" saloon confronted "the Bible Church," and on the steep brief roads climbing uphill from Front Street, metal-sided newish houses adjoined spacious log cabins with green-glass sun porches and handmade birdhouses on poles in the yard. "Makes you feel younger when you're walking down," Charlie remarked. In a tall tin smokehouse two barrels of driftwood were curing dozens of racks of "eatin' fish." But he mentioned that some-times the chum, or dog, salmon and kings chose to run up oppo-site sides of the Yukon—which lent an advantage to the subsistence fishermen who simply used a net. Fish wheels were much harder to move. The government had given out $15,000 grants for people to try to design a special raft on which chum could be dried and pul-verized for dog food out on the water itself, and also for a kind of underground chicken coop to provide fresh eggs year-round for even an icy community such as Ruby was.

Because we stopped to deliver an ATV, Charlie had a chance to speak with his brother, who trapped furs with him south of Utopia Creek on the Little Melozitna River all winter. Charlie, after spend-ing four summers on the Yukon's waters now, sported the air of a riverman, not a machinist, like Lou, our engineer, or a captain on the bridge, like Keith. "I'm finding fours and fives and sixes," he'd chant into his walkie-talkie, while swinging his skiff contentedly ahead of the *Tanana* at the brink of a slough. "But now it stops and falls down"—where the channel resumed. "Watch your digits!" he'd tell the deckhands, meaning their fingers, when the hawsers were be-ing spooled in. "I guess everywhere there is water there'll be pike," he had remarked when Keith's brother, Glen, caught three green-marbled, bear-mouthed, shark-toothed, two-and-a-half-footers, each of which had managed to tow his canoe about a bit in the flow of Fish Creek. New engineering techniques for extracting riverine gold from sedimentary layers that the old-time prospectors couldn't get at were exposing "another generation" of alluvial deposits to those who'd restaked clever claims in the valleys webbed behind a town like Ruby: Timber Creek, Sulatna Crossing, Tamarack Landing, or wherever else aroused sneaky splurges of speculation, to dredge and sieve played-out sidehills and creek bottoms again.

In Bootlegger Slough, behind Straight Island, we saw eight white-winged scoters whistling bell-like and croaking gutturally, and an otter swimming. Then the Kokrine Hills loomed ahead, although in pushing against the current's grip, we were traveling at only twice a walker's speed. "Keep an eye on your drift," Charlie reminded Keith, because each tow, including steering home light, felt different at the wheel. Numerous creeks, twisting off the hills, built up benches that, when stabilized by self-seeded aspens, willows, and birches, became so homey a settler might set up a wall tent or cabin, trapping the box valley behind it and culling a local moose or two, then buying a gill-net to sink into the eddies, and searching the streams he could hike to for any nuggets that the frosts or spring gulley washers might have dislodged and nobody noticed before. When an old guy finally died, with the sun on his face as he lay in bed, but his dogs dying on their chains in the dooryard, too (which is why somebody passing in a boat or on a snowmobile realized), they might look under the floorboards for the jumbo aspirin bottle the geezer could have stored his nubbly findings in. *And where'd he dug?* Before notifying the troopers or distant relatives, they would walk transects of whatever terrain such an oldster's legs and lungs could still have carried him to.

Four complicated ridgelines ascended like shelving behind Charlie's diffident-looking cabin, thirty-eight miles out of Ruby, when you peered at it from mid-river through the long entrance slough or slot his Ukawutni Creek fed into. And over from there on the south shore the three fancifully named islands, Edith, Florence, and Kathaleen, shielded the considerable mouth of the Nowitna, which drained a large territory, including a national wildlife refuge, and a veritable piñata of surprises for any naturalist or beaver trapper. I thought of the poor hippie just marooned in its undulations by the malicious rich bastards with the pontoon plane who'd been chortling about him in Tanana. Rivers like this one, or the Innoke, the Koyu-kon, the Tanana, the Chandalar, the Porcupine, joined the major flow with minor fanfare because its scale and force minimized them. Yet you heard of hyped repositories of mother lode or schemes to create safari spas on different tendrils, where a Serengeti-style migration of caribou herds might amble through.

At sunset our wake cut the placid river's surface like quilted silk, till the moon rose, with a black grin spread across its face—a straight stripe of cloud. Charlie told us his brother and he had brought two trapping partners from Connecticut originally, but one went back when his girlfriend wrote to say she was pregnant, and the other, named Dan, vanished in his shirtsleeves and felt underboots—all his outer clothing left behind in the cabin, along with Charlie's husky chained outside. It was a disappearance so sudden and illogical in broad daylight that the best explanation seemed either a Bigfoot or a grizzly, and a neighbor, Frank Titus, put out Bigfoot snares and leghold traps, because one of them had been scaring children in the evening lately. Charlie was an agnostic about that, favoring instead the theory that, since Dan had just shot and gutted a black bear but not yet skinned or butchered it, a mate could have been lurking near its body and wreaked vengeance when he returned. Charlie himself had never shot one, not even the grizzly that busted in his door last summer and wrecked the house, after ripping the sod off his roof. Grizzlies were sparser, more dangerous, though trickier at conceal-ment, and came through the mountain passes to the valley at salmon season. They tasted like stringy fish—aged and processed through a bear's gut, to eat—whereas a black bear cub would be succulent. We saw one at Grant Creek, penned on the bank with a malamute for company, by a settler called Bushy Charlie.

Galena was only two hundred-twenty feet above sea level, though six hundred miles from the sea, and only thirty feet lower than Tanana. So the river's turbulences were not due to declina-tion, but its lofty sources. And the maps were studded with "Indian village," or "cem.," which turned out to be abandoned as we drew abreast of them. But at Illinois Creek, "Herman the German" had both a greenhouse and his outdoor garden, and four boats on the beach, two freezer trucks, parked, to preserve salmon till a plane came to pick them up, fields cleared so he could keep a cow, and a tall radio aerial on a mast. Every structure he'd built looked extended by afterthoughts or later addenda. At Lancaster Creek, the "Juggernaut" earthmovers we had delivered, along with two Cats and a backhoe, destined for excavations at Gold Hill, still sat at the bottom of the tractor trail. Eunice asked Lou, the engineer, why our washer-dryer wasn't working; what was wrong with it? "Nothing," he said. "It just doesn't work."

Troy, the son of an investor in the company, and along as a second mate to learn the river (and similarly under pressure, as he confessed discontentedly, to take flying lessons), was writing in a schoolboy hand on lined paper all of the crossings we'd made, like me. He told Linda he wasn't "a real people person that likes piles of people around," so he would "probably become an Alaskan eventually," but wanted to "look at the wife material Outside first, not marry here." Keith, listening, said these native women, in marrying whites, or "marrying out," were marrying their conquerors, as always happened in history, and that pilots like Charlie, who knew all the personalities of the river, flirted with them relentlessly, up and down.

I woke up Monday, July 25th, to the white dentition of the Palisades, behind Clay Island and Clayhill Slough, with the Blind River drainage opposite them. These weren't so unlike other pale bluff formations along the river except for looking extraordinarily toothy or chewed, and therefore ready to yield up more tumbly contents—spill the beans. You might see a treasure hunter quarrying for tusks, suspended halfway down the cliff in an empty fifty-five-gallon drum from a spruce tree on the top, Keith said—like a Lilliputian, I imagined, working on Gulliver's teeth. The Blind and Atutsak rivers both made inconspicuous, almost secret entrances, where we saw Canada geese too young to fly swimming in the slow water and three young sandhill cranes rehearsing the preliminaries of the courtship steps they would dance next spring. A white-haired white man carried a rifle slung across his back, and a young Indian couple strolled on another beach. Driftwood was stacked for burning beside a tin smokehouse that had rusted into many patches of brown, by canvas tenting blue and green and black, and laundry yellow and red, on a gray expanse of gravel, where mottled sled dogs barked at us, and a furry-looking rowboat was pulled up that serviced the nets. Tozitna Island, behind Circle Island, boasted a handsome spine of spruce trees, behind which lay Tozitna Slough, then Steamboat Slough, immediately adjoining the Tozitna River's actual and substantial debouchment, which was mostly concealed behind a bar across its mouth, although you could clearly see a dark cut bank curving out of sight toward the higher swells and fifty-five-hundred-foot territory it drained.

We reached the town of Tanana by early afternoon of this, our sixth day out of Nenana, and Charlie had an earache attended to by the nurse practitioner at the health clinic, while the rest of us stretched our land legs for an hour. "Tanana" means Mountain River in Gwitch'in, Keith informed Linda and me, serving as it does both the Wrangell and Alaska Ranges. He said he grossed $5,000 a month, a deckhand $1,200, mates in between. We heard about another tug man who'd just broken some ribs, coming down the Tanana, when his barge hit a mud bar and an oil drum, jarred loose, banged into him. In a shallow quick stretch like that, "Keep your nose up so you don't fall down," Charlie said, rubbing his sore ear. On the coast, Charlie had captained Navy-surplus landing craft for provisioning the Norton Sound villages—in fact, the *Pat*, on which the accident had happened, consisted of the best surviving halves of two of these welded together. He said St. Michael had a protected bay and pleasant beaches, and the Eskimos when drunk were likely to give their spare change to the kids, whereas the village of Stebbins, practically next to it, "is one of your more unsavory towns, a lot of stabbings. You could call it Stabbings."

Charlie wore new moose hide beaded moccasins trimmed with beaver fur made for him by a girlfriend. Living on his earnings, he could afford to give most of the furs he trapped to whatever femmes he favored, although in white company he sometimes referred to other Indians as "niggers." Nulato and Kalskag were also violent towns, he said. Looking at the state flag, a Big Dipper pointing at the North Star, we heard about Bushy Charlie, who lived in the low, nested cabin in the clearing at Grant Creek. Whistling Jack, another old timer, whistled for years to cover his shortness of breath. He was called that but nobody knew how sick he was, until he died alone in his chair at home. And when he was found and the undertaker came to prepare him for the grave, straightening him out, the pocket of breath that had remained trapped in his lungs whistled out. "It's all right, Jack. It's all right, Jack," his girlfriends said, as they helped.

For twelve hours on the Yukon I'd watched for kayakers and seen only one, despite the many grassy, stabilized landings to camp on, and clouds like custard topping or shaving cream, because the silty currents could be so deadly for anybody who capsized. The principle of the fish wheel is that the river runs fast and turgid down, while the salmon are swimming *up*, its catch-baskets windmilling invisibly, inexorably, and the bank gleamed with carmine as the fillets dried. But if the price of gold rose sufficiently, there would be more need for freight tugs on the river, and the hapless *Bingo*, still mired off Station Rock near Squaw Crossing, was living proof of a bet on a mining revival.

The two dejected co-owners, based downriver in the town of Russian Mission, came aboard, along with the *Rampart* and *Kantishna* captains—Yutana was being paid $10,000 a day for their help in raising the boat—and a bluntly, contemptuously incredulous insurance adjuster, twice Keith's age but a former captain himself, who couldn't stomach the foolishness of two hobbyists who must have supposed the wild, lock-less Yukon was like the harnessed and leveed Mississippi. Why didn't they buy life vests and row down from Old Crow in the Yukon in a Boston Whaler for a sensible adventure? Now instead they were over a barrel and he was supposed to bail them out? The stocky, red-bearded one, in a halibut jacket and Ketchikan sneakers, pacing sorrowfully, claimed to be a commercial fisherman but reminded me of goofily enthusiastic writer friends of mine who began biographical projects they later regretted or undertook novels they couldn't finish—whose best-laid plans likewise veered astray, except that the money lost was piddling. I couldn't tell if trust funds were involved; but no plush amounts. The second owner had a black beard, concealing a quite unsteady-looking face, comprising too much space between the eyes and nose and mouth, it seemed to me, although his Coke-bottle glasses probably magnified his bewilderment. On top of the salvage charges would be extensive dry dock repairs and contract cancellations, possibly with penalties, for loads the sixty-foot *Bingo* had been scheduled to push. He wore an Oxford shirt and office pants, having flown up pronto on the same chartered float plane as the underwriters' angry, white-haired marine salvage specialist, and a Coast Guard officer, who was specifying that the *Bingo* must be removed, as a maritime hazard, regardless of the cost. This silly moniker, painted in one fly-specked coat of white on the black stern, lay canted toward the uncompromising sky. On the pilot-house's gaping door were still posted "Instructions for 'Bladder' Usage," and among the relics visible inside, two tins of Quik chocolate milk mix bracketed the throttle; you needed only to glance at Red Beard's tummy to understand where that had gone. The pallid, slight, stoop-shouldered Coast Guardsman in blue coveralls, silently on-scene also to prevent or record oil spills, told me he didn't like Alaska, was putting in for transfer to duty in Massachusetts. But Red Beard was trying to cheer up his friend by repeating an old punch line of theirs—*"Your boat's in Montana"*—from when they'd had it trucked from New Orleans to Seattle, and a weeklong snowstorm in the Rockies converted an eight-day trip into a month's delay. He was touching precisely because, although they were in over their heads, their gambit hadn't just been about gold, but romance, and the intricacies of this great, veined river system.

The *Rampart* had a crane on its barge, pushed lengthwise close, that was straining to lift the *Bingo*'s stern, and the *Kantishna* a D-8 Cat on the deck of its barge for rudimentary winching at the bow, while the cables stretching underneath were being fiddled with by divers in red and black wet suits—these the novice deckhands from Yutana's tugs, at first nervous at submerging themselves in the Tanana's fast, murky waters, then enjoying, even exuberant at the challenge of swimming under the *Bingo*. Their equipment was of course substandard in the insurance man's estimation. With his somber, black-rimmed glasses, his mouth had set into lines such as he must have worn for decades in chewing people out for foolishness, as a captain, and at times a diver himself, he said, politely moving me out of the danger zone in case a cable snapped. He took some strategic photographs for his company's files, adding that "These are Admiralty waters." When the black-bearded owner in the Oxford shirt asked unsteadily, "How do you think this will all affect our insurability?" he answered with a straight face: "Quite substantially."

After the cabling had been refastened under the *Bingo*'s hull, she still proved too heavy for the winch and crane to lift. So two holes were drilled in her deck for hoses to pump the water out during the night, whereupon the cracks that had let it in could be caulked. The morose owners, the scornful insurance adjuster, and the silent Coast

Guardsman came aboard the *Tanana* for a lugubrious steak supper, moderated a bit by the *Kantishna*'s equable captain's presence and especially the *Rampart*'s pilot, Doug, from the Ozarks, a peppy, merry, high-strung, good-natured man who, although he wintered now in the Yucatan, used to spend the off-season working on Exxon Oil Company Mississippi River tugs, so that whenever the discussion homed in on other idiots who had holed and sunk their boats, he could expound instead upon the *Bingo*'s former haunts. The Cessna's charter pilot, who had flown everybody up from St. Michael who had come, was a hothead who'd usurped the operation of the crane himself, it was being so badly cowboyed by a neophyte, he thought, and still sputtered with frustration. He was an aggressive manager type, sandy-bearded, boiling with impatience under his bristly crewcut and not given to irony or tact, so when he flew off with his employers to beat the sunset, it was a relief.

Red Beard—reminding me again of a woolly writer-friend whose weakness was to always ebulliently plunge into a minor-figure biography whom no one else would want to read about, or else some spy novel whose settings were unfamiliar to him—launched into a disquisition on the Bureau of Indian Affairs' policy of building new prefab housing for its clients in towns like Russian Mission, Kaltag, Nulato, Koyukuk, or Anvik set back a quarter-mile from the riverfront, which might make bureaucratic sense but, to a lover of the Yukon such as him, undermined the natives' cultural compass. Out of sight of the river that was their larder, highway, and bank account, they were high and dry—uprooted—got to drinking more, aimless or fighting, like government wards. Often they'd let some white man take over their trapline during the winter, and laze around at fish camp, tending the wheel, or not show up at all for the fish runs, instead of laying gillnets out through every bychannel. When people hardly saw their river, they forgot the succulent ducks, the otter pelts out in the sloughs, and then you had this crazy suicide rate. Unlike gold, the furs on a creek regenerated after the old-timers left—the black and gray wolves and white and red foxes. A poignant man—drowning his disappointments in data and speculation.

Patrick, who had appropriated the riot gun I'd found in the brush at Campbell's Crossing, told Linda he was going to Las Vegas with a thousand dollars to splurge after freeze-up, as he'd always wanted to do. Said also that he'd recently married an alien Pakistani girl for a promised thousand dollars, only six-fifty of which she could come up with before her Immigration Service hearing, so he didn't show up, and she was deported. He assumed since it hadn't been consummated, it wouldn't count. Charlie said yes, his brother and he limited their catch to fifty marten a year, so they'd never run out. Lou, fending off Eunice's cheesecake, said he'd been dodging her calories for half of his lifetime—and she wasn't even his wife. In fact, he'd never been home—wasn't it awful?—for the birth of a child. I told Linda it was good for me not to be home for a while, where Gandhi's example was savaged by my wife's magazine colleagues, and Pinochet's torture of opponents in Chile, by contrast, condoned or approved. McCarthyism was hailed, and conservation as a cause mocked, in the ugly birth pangs of neoconservatism, and my teenage daughter, as if quarantined, met very few of my friends. So in New York, where I sometimes wrote about tugboats, I was a river person, too.

• • •

Watching the grappling operation the next morning from our Texas deck, Linda and I were reminded of an injured football player being assisted off the field with his arms draped over two comrades. Blocks and tackles squealed as the *Rampart* and *Kantishna*, after tightly clamping their barges on either side of the *Bingo*, floated the holed-in, boxy, primitive-looking craft excruciatingly slowly through the shallow turmoil of Squaw Crossing—all three Yutana pilots' launches out in front, registering soundings, Charlie included—till she sometimes seemed hardly worth saving. Then we waited several more hours while Charlie in his workboat charted our own passage, including only one of our barges at a time, with thirteen buoys placed strategically to mark the twists and turns. The problem was not really a shortage of water in the Tanana River, but a surplus that had been washing over sandbars that ordinarily steered these delta currents predictably. We needed to circle to scour a couple of passages a trifle deeper in order to pass.

"Roger on that. Fall down on the starboard a bit," Charlie instructed Keith. "Is that water telling the truth? Pretty lumpy in here. Lumping up. Am finding 4's and 5's and 6's. Do you copy? Kinda keep your swing right on down to the other buoy. Pretty skimpy up to there, but you're right on the money. Won't be long before it cuts through that bar, but it sure ain't cut through yet."

Dervishes were dancing on the river, the current spiraled so. We'd picked up the *Bingo*'s launch to deliver to Nenana, where the *Bingo* would go; and it was full of the debris of shipwreck, such as loose onions and potatoes rolling around that the crew had thrown in to live on, when they fled. Another Yutana tug, the *Pat*—its drive shaft now fixed—was backed up, waiting upstream to reach the main-stem river, en route to St. Michael on a job, but was going to hook up with the *Bingo*'s discarded barge, called the *Stoney*, to return it to Russian Mission. I would miss the splendors of the Yukon—those impromptu beaches, stiff bluffs, and currents like logs rolling, or revolving pythons. Only every dozen miles or so had a fish wheel or string of nets, near a mossy cabin or tan wall tent, appeared, plus a skiff, a smokehouse of canvas and roofing tin, with fish hung like pelts curing inside, from crimson to sienna to gray, and a laundry line, and dogs lunging from their stakes along the bank. Near Charlie's Ukawutni Creek, where Victor and Hardluck Sloughs converged, he'd pointed out his neighbor Mark Freshwater's place, with a garden, a swing, an outhouse, and other conveniences, including outdoor disembodied auto seats, where his own four dogs spent the summer—he'd tooted the *Tanana*'s horn at them. Mark was a diligent Gwitch'in who trapped the mouth of the Nowitna all winter, Charlie said, and had helped his brother and him ensure that Cora Titus, a surviving resident of Kokrines, still had moose meat and stove wood, after her husband's stroke. Pretty hills rose three thousand feet, and a defunct telegraph line from the coast to Tanana had run through there, but a priest laid a hex on the Indian community when his church was desecrated and nobody helped him discipline the vandals. People began to die or shoot one another, and they left it to the Tituses and Bigfoot. She'd run a snare line for rabbits for her stews, and nowadays was said to be still snaring rabbits in the bushes around the Pioneers Home in Fairbanks. He hoped the bear boards hadn't been ripped off his cabin windows again.

I wouldn't forget the "Boneyard," as rivermen called the Palisades, eroding into molar or bicuspid shapes, with a scraggly forest on top, where several spots had appeared just about ripe to pop more prehistoric relics into the Yukon before my eyes. The sun was tickling the

underbelly of the clouds, and a rainbow arced from the south. The dervishes conjured on the water by spouts made me remember dervishes
in Omdurman six years earlier, when I was working on a book set in
Africa, instead of the north. We are all "children of the stars," as natu-
ralists say, but there are a great many stars. Mongo, a new deckhand,
twenty-three, from Chicago, hired out of Fairbanks and one year out of
the Air Force, who gave a "Polish salute" when buying a drink, asked
if I was going to write about "how they're destroying Alaska," meaning the Lower 48 hordes, with garbage, pollution, and six-guns in their
holsters. Said he wanted a wife and children—but would go Outside for
her—to homestead with, where they'd live all year, "and anyone who
pollutes there will be full of hot lead." Said in building a cabin, just two
people can carry the plywood on poles, and one man can move house
logs with a "come-along," a crank and cable or chain. He'd registered
for acreage near the head of the Susitna, but voided it when he found
meltwater still standing on the land in the middle of June.

Charlie claimed that his brother found shacking up with live-ins
easier. You could change 'em better: no divorce, not a lot of recriminations. The family might want them back in the village anyway,
and the same went for the old boyfriend. The girl got her share of
the furs as a peace offering, and felt more conversant with, confident
about, entering the wide world beyond the river. Bush pilots frequently landed in villages to drop off a bureaucrat and head back to
Fairbanks with an empty seat. So there was nothing illegal in offering
it to a girl who begged to fly to the big city and had attained her ma-
jority: nor, then, if she had her identity papers, for a long-haul trucker
from Minneapolis to let her sit in the cab with him clear out of Alaska
altogether. And, without the intimidating hassle of having applied
to a university, etc., she could find herself living like the rest of the
world did, according to the TV sets back in the village, and then in a
dozen years maybe asking her kids, "Hey, did you guys know you're
half-Indian?" At Fort Yukon I'd met a middle-aged man in a cabin
isolated alongside the river who was wistful, not bitter, recalling his
love affair with a white woman who'd spent a year in town, teaching or nursing, whereupon, not wishing to brusquely break off with
him when she left, she invited him to accompany her home to Santa
Cruz to try another life. And with no recriminations, he said it hadn't
worked. But his time with her was the happiest of his life.

The thirty-hour upstream trip to Nenana from the turbid Yukon on the "liquid mud" of the Tanana was now underway. The *Bingo*'s launch, riding on the deck of our *Skagit* barge, was so unsettling to look at, however—the life rings, drenched blankets and mackinaws, plus loose oars thrown on the duckboards—we covered it up with a tarp. Troy, being an owner's son, clapped his hands for obedience from the deckhands. Only two years out of high school, he worked too frenetically, losing his temper too much. But Keith, at the wheel, was reading Charlton Ogburn's *Gold of the River Sea*, under our low blue smokestacks with the yellow stripes. He'd grown up with seven sisters, which may have softened him and made him a patient captain. His brother Glen, the second engineer, a more precise, aloof man, had an Alaskan's tall wallet sticking out of his hip pocket with a chain attached to it, hooked to his belt loop.

The *Bingo* owners had been graduate-school roommates in the Lower 48 and both had families to support. I suggested that, just as psychiatrists live off people's miseries, bush pilots live on their dreams, the wish for a different script, a new theater, a larger stage. But Charlie talked of miners who'd "run on poor pickin's and finally run out of ground." The old side-wheeler steamboats used to burn a cord of wood in an hour (the officers in uniform; and till 1953 passengers lounging on the deck), so chopping and stacking that at wood yards along the bank was a mundane source of income for prospectors whose ship wasn't coming in. And Lou—at fifty-nine, even older than I was—said no, he was in a terrible rut. "Been here thirty years. Shows a total lack of ambition." He was eating olives, refried beans, salmon soup, and cake, with a beer. I allowed as how one of my own Kansas relatives had vanished on a gold-rush quest into the Yukon around 1900, and his partners never would tell why.

"Or could," Charlie corrected, because his partner from back home on the Connecticut River—the one whose girlfriend hadn't written to him to hurry and marry her before their baby was born—had disappeared in his shirtsleeves without a trace. I nodded. On the Black River near Chalkyitsik, I'd heard about a young stranger simply starving to death in his cabin unbeknownst to the Indian community a two days' hike downriver, because he'd failed to lay in a winter moose before the herd left the valley for high country in the fall, or shoot ducks before they all flew south, or rabbits and spruce grouse, or net whitefish and sucker fish on their autumn runs up every creek. When he started walking for help in January, he was too weak, the snow too deep, the wind too cold. And on the Coleen, another tributary of the Porcupine, a man had starved alone only two years ago—his pathetic diary later found.

We listened to about twenty fishing boats out on saltwater give their locations to a dispatcher. Keith said he preferred river work to the ocean's swells. These snub-nosed tugs were so blunt in the bow that they might dip underwater slightly if not pushing a barge, and the *Tanana* had had to be towed north from Seattle to Bethel after its manufacture. Keith was a birdwatcher, rather than a hunter, and so called the Department of Fish & Game "the Fish & Feathers," and pointed out loons, owls, kingfishers, cranes, or snags bobbing in the current like an otter's nose. "Look for the deadman," he suggested, meaning a half-buried post on the shore with a metal eye for a cable by which backpackers used to haul themselves across. Vivid green grass grew in the beaver swales and willows in the weedy oxbows, whose leaves blew white, back-side-to, as we steamed slowly past. Reading the surface, he followed dark streaks, because flat, still water might denote a shallows, as a boiling patch also could. He looked for dark streaks crossing the river toward the least stable shoreline and steered where the river was freshly cutting.

Even as the disabled *Bingo* was being transported toward Nenana ahead of us, we encountered another beaching. A sternwheeler houseboat, the *John M. McCauley*—essentially a motorized barge with living quarters on it—had grounded on a sandbar and was churning up turgid muck, while three of its four passengers, standing knee-deep in the water in front, cranked on a come-along that they had cabled to a tree. A retired sea dog, resident in Fairbanks, had spent three years building it for pleasure—one of those Alaskans who ripens into a gentle giant, as the macho veneer rubs off—and the Tanana, a five-hundred-thirty-mile "mountain river" indeed, rustled and muscled right past Fairbanks from its distant headwaters near the Wrangell peaks. What better waterway to try it on? But a retired Yutana tug captain had told me he'd known when to quit—when he no longer felt strong enough to haul people out of the water, if they fell in. Over the rail of his tug he'd gripped 'em and wouldn't let go unless he went over, too. If a barge got away, threw over its anchor chain, and the pilot's skiff, too, flipped, he'd "seen 'em in the water, but never had a man drown."

In bed, I reminded Linda that I'd arrived in Alaska this time to join her with a baby box turtle in my breast pocket, as a sign of commitment (her best friend had warned her this was weird and to be leery of me, but she had welcomed the turtle into our mythology and games), when she rightly complained that I was more focused on the river than her. I said I was willing to leave New York for Alaska if permanence would follow. I was fifty and teaching at places like Iowa and Columbia, writing *Times* editorials, and essays elsewhere, as I had done for about fifteen years, but I no longer needed the pizzazz of the great city to goose my productivity (in fact, wound up in Bennington, Vermont, where the poor baby turtle, who had thrived meanwhile, was gobbled up by a crow). Yet I needed stability, even if it were the staff housing at a regional hospital, whereas she wanted to improve herself once again. Her first marriage, to the psychiatrist, had disabused her of any notion that being a nurse was a big deal; and I was thoroughly rooting for her, except in the sense that I wanted no more personal flux. I wanted to sit tight and write my books.

At eight fifteen next morning, when Yutana's office manager checked on the position of all its boats, we were two miles below the Kantishna's intricate mouth. I'd slept lightly so as not to miss many maneuvers during the captain's twelve-hour watch. Humble fish hung like skins by the hundreds on racks at fish camps that in the winter would double as trapping cabins, but we also saw kings appear to jump for joy as they finally encountered, recognized, and veered to enter from the muddy Tanana the exact particular clearwater tributary whose clean, direct flow they had left as small fry for the ocean three years before. After the kings and chums had run, the silver salmon would take their turn. (Pinks, or humpies, were mainly caught in southeastern Alaska, and the commercial bonanza of reds, or sockeye, in Bristol Bay.)

Johnny Campbell's Crossing, and the Scotchman's Crossing, the German's Crossing, Davis Crossing, Bruno's Neck (where Bruno hit a rock), Martha's Farm (where once you could buy vegetables), Mission Island, Hooper's Bend, Monkeyrudder Slough, Baker's Creek: We'd passed the narrative of names of old wood yards, quarrelsome codgers, slaughter spots where the caribou swam across the Tanana, or crash-ups. By three-thirty p.m. we'd reached Old Minto, an Indian hamlet of a dozen houses abandoned twenty years before, where patches of sheet metal were falling off, twenty-nine miles short of Nenana—and, nine miles closer than that, *older* Old Minto, in a more advanced condition of decrepitude. Often, on the cut banks, a white birch or dark spruce, heeling over, pointed fifty feet straight out at us, held momentarily by a few last roots but falling to the river's mastication like mown wheat. Mongo, the Chicago kid hired as a deckhand off the street, marveled but said he was impressed enough—ready to go back. Alaska, crammed with extremes, attracts new citizens with the shifty eyes of folk who may have left their previous residence in a hurry, without unduly bidding goodbye. But he was a youngster, learning lessons from the trip.

We saw fish camps where Indian families, except for the children, ignored our boat, but then a white man, tending a net, dropped his pants and mooned us. Our propellers were so noisy that at certain crossings they seemed about to shake the stern apart—which may have been why; it alarmed the fish. Salmon were hard to pocket as it was, because although the muddy water obscured their vision, the same current strong enough to turn the paddles of a fish wheel and capture them might be a current they would try to avoid breasting in their thousand-mile swim. Around seven in the evening we met the Indian-owned push boat, *Ramona,* coasting downstream and looking quite unlike us. That is, she had one two-hundred-horsepower engine, a sixth of our total power, Keith said, and needed only two feet of water to travel in, instead of four. Two lovely long-haired galley cooks in yummy sweaters waved at us, with two deckhands beside them to feel jealous of, who piled it on by mimicking our gawking at the girls through binoculars by raising their fists like goggles pressed against their eyes. No officers were visible to give orders, or protruding aerials or officious flags flapping or running lights turned on. The owner was known to be deaf, so they rarely kept in radio contact with him; and gulls were following them, as birds never followed Yutana boats, because we weren't kind-hearted enough to feed them. The *Ramona* was shoving two short flat green barges along, with trailers and barrels on top, and they glanced our way as if to mock our regimented hierarchy and radio-directed scheduling, our envy of their more leisurely or impulsive departures, or Indian rhythms on "Indian time," versus Yutana's moving more than thirty thousand tons of cargo per year on the Yukon's river system.

At nine-thirty p.m., when at last we tied up at the Nenana wharf, a loaded barge was already waiting for the *Tanana*'s next shuttle out, with Caterpillars on it and a truck and a drilling rig, to go to a mining operation at Grayling, way back southwest, as far below Galena as the Tanana's outlet was above it, and opposite Holikachuk, Hologachaket, and Shageluk on the Innoko River. The girls on the bar stools at Moocher's had combed their glossy tresses according to our radioed arrival time and were watching the door for the first man to lunge through and maybe ring the ship's bell for a round all around. Then they might well hook up for tonight—money clips were being pulled out. I wished they were on the *Ramona* instead. People were reminiscing about Clinkerdaggers Bar in Fairbanks, and the outhouse races they had here in the winter, setting the contraptions on skis.

Lou and Eunice spent the night on the boat, like Linda and me, while the swallows larked like badminton birds. The town's twinned personality as both a railroad and a riverboat hub bestowed an elan on this modest cog in Alaska's economy—a Last Place where people had departed from civilization, climbed out on a limb and maybe sawed themselves off. We placed phone calls, nibbled at each other and fitted our arms around curves that had grown a little less familiar in the brouhaha of the river. We didn't set off for Fairbanks, although it was close, having no friends or errands there. I knew it as a jumping-off city where you'd climb into a Cessna with a pilot who seldom got out except to sleep in his trailer near the airport. The university boasted pleasant crannies and the ridgeline neighborhoods splendid views of the serrated white peaks of the Alaska Range to the south. Niilo, a Finn, and Joan, his Boston Brahmin wife, would take me in when I arrived by plane or train, but I also knew the frigid loneliness of downtown in midwinter, when everybody, tightly hooded, hastened toward shelter, conserving their heat and energy by minimal contact. My friend, the poet John Haines, had a homestead cabin at Mile 68, to the east on the Alcan Highway, along the Tanana, but the state characteristically treated him worse than the winters did, at a later time of need. Marriages, too, snapped in Fairbanks; then later pairings.

We left the Tanana bailiwick to drive south clear to Talkeetna, underneath the Mount McKinley massif, and our questing friend's house for the night—he of the aborted dairy farm, the raw divorce from a school librarian, the Greenland dogs tethered amongst cottonwood trees alongside the lovely Susitna, which purled at the same time as it rushed muscularly toward Cook Inlet and the Pacific Ocean. An oversized Iowa transplant, he was whittling his dog team down to hobby numbers, having abandoned his Iditarod hopes, and his cows were gone. For five years, he said, he had given his children "museum piece skills," like birthing a calf, dressing a hog, or raising working dogs (though it turned out well for the daughter who went into Denali studies). At loose ends but no "bush rat," he was a touching, well-liked guy, growing greenhouse vegetables, and the engineers on the Anchorage-to-Fairbanks freight trains whistled a sunset salute or midnight greeting to his insomniac's light as they chugged by. Cessna 180's with retractable skis reverberated overhead as they shuttled athletic trust-funders and remittance men from all over the world to base camps at seven thousand feet up the noble peak from Talkeetna's airstrip, next to the railroad station, or back down to town again. We trouped to the rambling hotel with its Harding mementos, where such climbers congregated for drinks and recriminations after a failed assault or maybe to celebrate summiting, with toasts to their guides. We heard tables raucous with both, plus talk of Paris, Gstaad, Tokyo, the Andes, Katmandu, with well-preserved wives or the trophy kind in ski lodge garb; then headed the hundred-twenty miles south to "L" Street in the morning. At the Monkey Wharf we soon witnessed the saloon stages of progressive disillusion of a damsel from Cotton Village or Chuathbaluk too quickly in her cups and wed to a dude from Detroit, where she didn't "ever want to visit again!" He'd already assumed a frigid, loner's stare, contemplating signing up for an eight-month stint in Indonesia or the Middle East. He felt penned-up here and she rootless elsewhere. Not the most opportune byplay for us to watch, with the monkeys cowering behind glass in back of the bar.

We'd skittered back toward the pliability of Anchorage, where the matter of bare survival didn't squander so much of your marrow. Geography and shouldering the elements defines so many Alaskans' self-image that you may need to remind yourself that you're flying under the radar here anyway, intent upon Outside things, such as getting a novel out of it, in my case, or parlaying a nursing rapport with Native Americans in the North toward a career in anthropology. But inevitably in a switchback world Alaskans are divided, too, as when a celebrity governor later became so part-time she simply quit in mid-term. A random bar may look like a theatrical farce, with hangman's or highwayman's beards cheek-by-jowl with pretend sour-doughs missing only a burro, or faux-mushers lacking only their dogs, or biblical wise-men—yet you might find an absconding accountant under that impersonation of a patriarch, the bristly bush a platform for fraud. Survivability is ambiguous: which graybeard had elbowed his companions off the sled to feed the pursuing wolves? That real-life fuzzy-capped stampeder, haloed in a full beard and wolfskin hood, with caribou mitts and moose boots, a beaver-hide pack on his back, and gold pans and steel traps on his sled, who ate lynx, porcupine, and muskrat, too (as I have), fed some remnant to Indian widows' families he encountered in the wilds but let others starve, just as, ear-lier, the Indian or Eskimo bands, when they patrolled the territory, sometimes rescued starving, hallucinating sourdoughs scrabbling for food or firewood with a broken leg in a snowstorm, when they came across them, or did not, shuffling them along instead to die, flaking bark off a blown-over tree as if it were fur, and flesh must lie under-neath, then perhaps to be gnawed themselves by a winter grizzly. A stranded whaler or miner wandering in the mountains might find his fate tipped by the Pocahontas principle—some native woman lacked a man and took him on, sponsoring his survival for a while. Then, come summer, with more whites around, would he abandon her or stick with the band as catalyst and trader-middleman? Which Santa Claus beard concealed a mouth that had grinned while the guy was bushwhacking another trapper on a river they both coveted, before slipping his body under the ice for the currents to dispose of, or a guy who'd given moosemeat to orphans if they "smoked" him.

In my marriage I felt I was on a rotting ice floe, wanting to leap to another. At the end we didn't like each other's work much, and since work was central for each of us, we needed what are called in-fidelities. That mine in this case was five thousand miles away made it somewhat antiseptic, I thought, but I did feel an abundantly tender and poignant respect toward Marion during the two decades when we were raising our daughter and I was refashioning myself from a novelist into an essayist. Our lives were a work in progress but Marion's, alas, was cut short at sixty-one by cancer.

After Linda's ten-year journey through graduate schools, post-Alaska, she moved on to marriage, motherhood, and tenure as a professor, while my own foundering marriage dissolved and I entered upon a new quarter-century relationship in New England that has sustained me. I returned only briefly to the margins of Alaska on later assignments, but never anywhere that aroused wistful memories of Linda.

Approaching eighty now—a vantage point of blurry vision, when you presume that you possess more wisdom than you probably do—I can't judge what might have happened had we stayed together. Our love was powerfully real, but each of us wound up doing pretty well. Partnerships are unique, and to compare them can be haphazard or invidious—one had been twinned with adventuring, another to the gravitas of child-rearing; one to the ambitious pursuit of a career, another with achieving equanimity in old age. This journal portrays Alaska thirty years ago and gratefully recounts a love affair between two people with failed marriages already behind them. Many people come to Alaska fleeing broken marriages, although numerous other couples also break up there, from the torque of civilization colliding with an extraordinary land. As peripatetic as we were, our romance thrived in the wilds. And what a land!

America, too, is a work in progress; and, absent its oil, Alaska a kind of coccyx on the body politic, reminding us—if we dream on it—of a Lewis-and-Clark past. As with jazz, the blues, rodeos, we sample a whiff of what has elapsed, in a national dreamscape severed from the hourly news. Nature has long since been knocked to its knees elsewhere, and to "move on" has become the national mantra. Our callused eyes are inured to such realities as we "reinvent" ourselves. But what invention will equal Alaska's rodeoing salmon runs and ducks like pigeons on the Yukon?